THE
AKEDAH

THE AKEDAH

THE BINDING OF ISAAC

LOUIS A. BERMAN

JASON ARONSON INC.
Northvale, New Jersey
Jerusalem

"The Sacrifice of Isaac" by Woody Allen. Reprinted by permission of the publisher. From *Getting Even* by Woody Allen (New York: Random House, 1970).

"The Near Murder" by Jakov Lind. Reprinted by permission of the publisher. From *The Stove* by Jakov Lind (Bronx: Sheep Meadow Press, 1983).

This book was set in 11 pt. Utopia by Alabama Book Composition of Deatsville, Alabama, and printed and bound by Book-Mart Press of North Bergen, New Jersey.

Library of Congress Cataloging-in-Publication Data

Berman, Louis Arthur.
    The Akedah : the binding of Isaac / by Louis A. Berman.
        p.   cm.
    Includes bibliographical references.
    ISBN 1-56821-899-0 (alk. paper)
    1. Isaac (Biblical partriarch)—Sacrifice.   2. Bible. O.T.
Genesis XXII, 1-19—Criticism, interpretation, etc.   3. Bible.
O.T. Genesis XXII, 1-19—Criticism, interpretation, etc., Jewish—
History.   4. Abraham (Biblical patriarch) I. Title.
BS1235.2.B39   1997
222'.1106—dc21   97-5627

Manufactured in the United States of America. Jason Aronson Inc. offers books and cassettes. For information and catalog write to Jason Aronson Inc., 230 Livingston Street, Northvale, New Jersey 07647.

In Memory of
David Polish (1910–1995)
Zecher l'bracha
Rabbi, teacher, and friend

CONTENTS

NOTES ON DOCUMENTATION

Throughout this book, chapter and verse references not otherwise labelled [e.g., (12:5)] refer to Genesis.

Citations are given by page number [e.g., (p. 413)], often at the end of a paragraph, for the work of the author named throughout that paragraph. The title of the author's book or article appears in the bibliography. If the bibliography lists more than one item for that author, the citation gives the year of the item and page number [e.g., (1961, p. 44)].

Abbreviations used in this book are:

C.E. Common Era (same as A.D.)
EJ *Encyclopedia Judaica,* 1972
JE *Jewish Encyclopedia,* 1901
JPS Hebrew Bible, Jewish Publication Society 1967 Translation

Preface

Why Did Abraham Do It?

Young Abraham was clearly the Bible hero of my boyhood, not David who slew Goliath—not Joseph who interpreted Pharaoh's dreams—but Abraham who had the temerity and courage to smash his father's idols. Facing all the "Thou shalts" and "Thou shalt nots" of a Jewish upbringing, I appreciated that my religion also conveyed the story of a boy who dared to smash his father's idols.

I suppose I was always something of a doubter—an attitude encouraged by my mother's fascinating combination of religious observance and skeptical observation. When we were children, she would remind us to watch our social behavior, exhorting us with the Yiddish saying "M'darf mehr moyreh hob'n far menschen vie far Got" ("People are more to be feared than God").

What puzzled me was how young Abraham the idol smasher became Abraham the father who mutely proceeded to obey God's request that he sacrifice his only son. The question lingered in the back of my mind until retirement gave me the luxury of spending time on matters unrelated to raising a family or earning a living.

As a counseling psychologist on the staff of a university counseling center, my job largely consisted of helping young people over the rough ground between adolescence and adulthood. We took over where professors and deans threw up their hands and said, "Maybe you'd better talk to a counselor."

A recurrent problem in college student counseling is the student who can't choose a major or who keeps changing his major. (Unless you choose a major and fulfill its requirements you can't graduate, no matter how good your grades are.) Choosing a major is one step toward deciding on a career. For many young people this decision is an agonizing one, or one they would rather not think about.

Part of what makes career choice so difficult, I discovered, is facing up to parental pressures. One parent demands one thing, and the other parent wishes for something else. The young person can't please them both and—worse yet—may have to resist them both. If the parents are agreed on the young person's future, it may not be a future that their offspring wants.

Why do parents try to dictate the career paths of their sons or daughters? Is it to feel control over another person's life? Are they motivated by social prestige or financial gain? Does it give them a vicarious pleasure of some sort? Whose life is it anyway? What about the plans, dreams, and hopes of the young person himself? Gradually, I realized that my job as a vocational counselor was helping my young clients come to terms with their parents' wishes and then feel free enough to take the advice of mythologist Joseph Campbell to "follow your bliss."

Whether a psychoanalyst unravels an Oedipus complex or a vocational counselor helps a young person confront parental demands, psychological practice relates to the reality of generational conflict. Whose life is it anyway? Conflict between generations brings us back to the story of Abraham and Isaac.

Our courts are still struggling with questions concerning the manner and the extent to which children have distinct rights of their own. When do "the best interests of the child" take priority over parental rights? Here is an issue that is as old as the Bible and as new as this morning's newspaper.

The story of Abraham and Isaac dramatizes this issue. Is a child the property of his father who is free to use him to express his devotion to God; or must the child be respected as a person in his own right, with his own kinship to God? These questions led me to reread the Akedah story, consulting the commentaries of many rabbis, some psychiatrists (Erich Wellisch, Erich Fromm, Silvano Arieti, and Theodor Reik), and a diverse group of writers including Søren Kierkegaard and others.

Silvano Arieti, a man of profound scholarship, prefaced his thoughts on Abraham with the warning that he was not a professional Bible scholar, a theologian, or a philosopher.

> Must a man who is neither a professional Bible scholar nor a theologian nor a philosopher apologize for discussing the story of Abraham and for trying to show the relevance of the story to the basic issues of our time? I believe not. And because I have long and intimately related the great historical heritage with the experiences of my own life and with the fields in which I have acquired some particular competence, I feel entitled to set out on this journey. (p. vii)

If such a warning was appropriate for Arieti to make, it is more fitting for me to issue the same caveat. I too am neither a theologian nor a Bible scholar, though having earned a Ph.D., I feel at home among books and journals. A library may seem like a stuffy place, but it is also a treasure house of ideas. In the quiet of the library, I listen to voices—transposed into print—teaching, arguing, explaining. Libraries have been my major research tools for this project: the Asher Library of the Spertus Institute of Jewish Studies, the Northwestern University library, the University of Chicago library, the Jesuit-Krause-McCormick Theological Library, the Garret Theological Seminary library, the University of Illinois at Chicago library, the Bruce Gordon Library of Beth Emet synagogue in Evanston, the public libraries of Evanston and Wilmette, Illinois, and—through interlibrary loan services—libraries all over the country! Librarians are wonderful people, eager to help everyone share in the knowledge of others. Through this book I hope to share the benefits of their assistance. Speaking of books, these remarks would be incomplete without acknowledging that my project benefitted greatly by access to the Judaica library of the late Prof. Robert Kauf.

Arieti undertook to study Abraham the man, not just the Abraham of the Akedah experience. One cannot understand the Akedah without learning about Abraham and his world and about the biblical context in which the Akedah narrative appears. Many years ago, Rabbi David Polish emphasized the importance of context in understanding the Akedah.

> By reading the twenty-second chapter of Genesis alone, the real clue to its meaning will elude us. . . . Standing alone . . . the Akedah story [is] a fragment whose secret cannot be found. . . . [Kierkegaard and many others commit the same] error of beginning with chapter 22 in Genesis. (1957, p. 17)

The simple biblical narrative in chapter 22 of Genesis has stirred the imagination of many thoughtful persons. I have had the privilege of examining many of these commentaries and relating them, in a more or less systematic way, to the biblical text and the midrashim. Reading this book will lead, I hope, not only to a sharper focus on the spirit of the text, but also to a richer appreciation of the story's manifold implications.

As convener of this imaginary symposium, I have enjoyed a generous amount of help and the moral support of my publisher, Arthur Kurzweil. My wife, Helga Kauf-Berman, served as proofreader, sounding board, and translator of French and German documents. My son Daniel gave me valuable editorial assistance. At the Asher Library, Dan Sharon, Richard Tennes, and director Michael Terry were always supportive and helpful.

Among the friends whose help and critical comments were extremely useful, I would like to especially thank Rabbi Peter Knobel, Professors Laurette Kirstein, Bernard Kogan, David Zesmer, Cantor Jeffrey Klepper, Sidney Black, and Dr. Kalman Kaplan. Yivo Institute music archivist Chana Mlotek uncovered Yiddish source material for me, and Adele Miller assisted in its translation. I am thankful to Prof. G. H. Aasi, Chairman of Islamic Studies at the American Islamic College for acquainting me with the Akedah in the Islamic tradition. I am particularly grateful that the late Rabbi David Polish, of blessed memory, read an early draft of this book and offered supportive and constructive critical comments.

Any shortcomings here are, of course, my responsibility. For whatever merits this book contains, I am grateful to all who have helped me in all sorts of ways.

Louis A. Berman
May, 1996
Wilmette, IL

Introduction

Not Everybody's Favorite Story

Helen, a friend and colleague, doesn't mince words. When I told her I was writing a book on the Sacrifice of Isaac, she commented, "That's a horrible story. Ever since I was a kid I thought it was ugly. Why are you spending your time on it?" There are many signs here and there that Helen is not alone. Many books of Bible stories, particularly those written for children, omit the Sacrifice of Isaac, or the Akedah (the Binding), as it is known in the Jewish world.

The fact that Genesis 22 is known in the Jewish world as the Akedah, not the Sacrifice or the Averted Sacrifice, also suggests its subject matter is hard to handle. There was a time when Reform rabbis liked to shock the public with proof of how liberated they were from the tradition. On November 6, 1960, the *New York Times* (p. 33) reported on a sermon given at Central Synagogue by the Reverend Dr. David Seligson. The rabbi confessed that he had found the Akedah unintelligible as a child, incredible as an adult, "and, as a father, I must regard [it] as impossible." The rabbi deplored "the unquestioning acceptance of what had been handed down and the readiness to countenance any kind of barbarism or inhumanity in its name." He encouraged his congregants to likewise show "the inquiring spirit prepared to question and to change, to challenge that which no longer commands our intelligent consent."[1]

Times have changed. The iconoclasts of our times are not Reform rabbis, in all likelihood, but the comics and satirists of our day. Let us look at what Woody Allen and Jakov Lind have done with the Akedah. The fact that both their satires have been reprinted in anthologies of Jewish wit and Jewish fiction, suggests that their stories have widespread appeal.

Here is a sample of what Woody Allen does with the Akedah. Abraham hears the voice of the Lord and after some silly banter with Isaac and Sarah, he takes Isaac to the mountain top and is prepared to sacrifice him

> . . . but at the last minute the Lord stayed Abraham's hand and said, "How could thou doest such a thing?"
> And Abraham said, "But thou said—"
> "Never mind what I said," the Lord spake. "Doest thou listen to every crazy idea that comes thy way?" And Abraham grew ashamed. "Er—not really . . . no."
> "I jokingly suggest thou sacrifice Isaac and thou immediately runs out to do it."
> And Abraham fell to his knees. "See, I never know when you're kidding."
> And the Lord thundered. "No sense of humor. I can't believe it."
> "But doth this not prove I love thee, that I was willing to donate mine only son on thy whim?"
> And the Lord said, "It proves that some men will follow any order no matter how asinine as long as it comes from a resonant, well-modulated voice."
> And with that, the Lord bid Abraham get some rest and check with him tomorrow. (Novak and Waldoks, p. 220)

---

1. According to the 1901 *Jewish Encyclopedia*, "Many American Reform rituals have abolished the Akedah prayers." Dr. Seligson may therefore be regarded as expressing a time-honored point of view in the Reform Judaism of his time.

Jakov Lind has been compared with Günther Grass, but he is even more grotesque, more cruel. His version of the Akedah is a short story entitled "The Near Murder." A rich, old couple had everything—"horses, cattle, and dogs, plantations, fishing grounds and large woods"—but children, "and for this they were very sad." The woman told her husband a stranger informed her she would have a child, and she laughed because "an old woman cannot have a child." But bear a child she did and "their happiness was now complete."

One day the man "heard a voice behind him: 'Take your son and kill him.'" Accordingly, one morning he took his son hunting.

> When they reached the wood, the man said to his son, "I must listen to an inner voice and this voice has told me to kill you."
>
> As the son saw no way out from the forest . . . and saw men with guns ready all over the place, he knew that this was his end. "All right," he said to his father. "Shoot."
>
> The father tied his son to a tree, lifted his gun, and was about to pull his trigger when a voice at his back said: "Don't be insane. I just wanted to know whether you were ready to kill him. As I see you are, let him go, and kill a goat instead." . . . The father aimed his gun at [a] goat and killed it. He untied his son, said not a word, and they both walked silently back to their home. The woman was happy to see her son alive. She had given up hope.
>
> Later at night, she asked her husband: "Why did you behave so strangely? Why did you want to kill him?"
>
> "It's not him I wanted to kill. It's your doubt, your laughter, I wanted to destroy." (Schwartz, p. 148)[2]

---

2. The reader who is offended by irreverent satire of the Akedah should know that even more cruel satires of this Bible story are presented on the Israeli stage, according to Glenda Abramson (pp. 111–112). She offers the following two examples: playwright Avraham Raz has Isaac, in revenge, binding Abraham to the altar (*Leil ha'atzmaut shel Yisrael Shefi*, 1969). The *enfant terrible* of the Israeli stage, Hanoch Levin, wrote a scandalous satire in which a zealous Abraham cannot understand his son's reluctance to cooperate with the fulfillment of a divine command. "Very nice, Isaac," Abraham

Genesis 22 has been described as a masterpiece of storytelling. The comments of Erich Auerbach have become classic; he noted that the simplicity of the Akedah was not a sign of naïveté but a sophisticated literary strategy that allows the reader to "fill in the details," to structure the story according to his own imagination. Many dozens of midrashim have not only filled in the details, but have revised—and even reversed![3]— the original story. This too, it may be argued, indicates an underlying discomfort with the original story.

At the same time, the Akedah continues to stimulate an enormous number of midrashim and commentaries. Says Elie Wiesel, "We can find the entire corpus of the Jewish history in the Akedah. . . . Some Hasidim call the Jewish people the Akedah people. . . . To me, the event on Moriah is more important than the revelation on Sinai" (1995 Lecture).

Artists of all times have felt challenged to recreate the story in graphic form. The results have varied from the hypnotized and dumbstruck figures characteristic of most paintings, to the savage interpretation of Caravaggio, to the sheltering, loving figures of Rembrandt's famous etching.

The range of responses the Akedah evokes is part of its fascination. Most of us regard the story with a mixture of revulsion, awe, and what Einstein has called "holy curiosity." With these feelings and more, let us embark on our exploration together.

---

says sarcastically to his uncooperative son. "Make it difficult for your unfortunate father; put him in a bad mood, as if he hasn't already got enough on his plate. . . . I know it's easy to accuse me." (*Queen of the Bathtub*, 1969)

3. For example, a number of midrashim minimize the command of the angel, "Do not raise your hand against the boy" and insist that Isaac was nicked, killed, or burnt to ashes, rose to heaven, and was resurrected. These midrashim are discussed in more detail in chapter 13, "The Martyrdom Interpretation."

PART I

THE AKEDAH
AND ITS CONTEXT

1

ABRAHAM AND HIS WORLD

We cannot understand the Akedah narrative until we familiarize ourselves with the entire Abraham story leading up to the Akedah.*

Legend tells us of Abraham the angry young man who smashed his father's idols,[1] a rebel against the Mesopotamian establishment of his time, perhaps three thousand years ago. However, the biblical story of Abraham introduces us to an older herdsman, married but childless. Abraham had grown up and

---

*In this summary the names Abraham and Sarah are used consistently except for direct quotations from the Bible, JPS translation, in which the names Abram or Sarai are used.

1. A midrash describes young Abraham as an assistant to his father, a dealer in idols. Convinced that there is only one true God, he was not a very good salesman for his father's merchandise. One day he asked a customer his age and then exclaimed: "Woe to him who at fifty would worship a one-day-old idol." The customer departed in shame.

Another midrash tells about a young Abraham smashing the idols and facing the wrath of his father. "Who smashed the idols?" asked Terah. "The chief god there," said Abraham. "You know perfectly well that clay idols don't move," said the father. "Then why worship them?" asked Abraham (Plaut, p. 94).

spent much of his adulthood in Mesopotamia. According to archaeological evidence, Abraham's native land had a civilization that knew science and law and was a society with a well-developed religious, social, cultural, and political life.

With his aged father, wife, and orphaned nephew Lot, Abraham left this civilized homeland and set out for the less urbanized, more agricultural land of Canaan.[2] Together they settled at an intermediate point, Haran. When his father died, the seventy-five-year-old Abraham, his wife, and nephew Lot, left Haran for God had commanded him[3] "go forth . . . [and] I will make your name great."

> Go forth from your native land and from your father's house to the land that I will show you. I will make of you a great nation. And *I will bless you; I will make your name great, and you shall be a blessing.[I]*[4] I will bless those who bless you and curse him that curses you; and all the families of the earth shall bless themselves by you." (Genesis 12:1–3)

Together with Sarah, Lot, his flocks, herdsmen, servants, "and all the wealth that they had amassed" (12:5),[5] Abraham travelled toward Canaan, and when they arrived, the Lord appeared to Abraham and repeated his promise: "*I will give this land to your offspring*" *[II]* (12:7).

Abraham's first years in Canaan were troubled. "There was a famine in the land" (12:10), and Abraham sojourned in Egypt.

---

2. Why did Abraham leave his homeland? Philo conjectures that Abraham's opposition to the Babylonian astrologers was the reason for his emigration. (Philo [c. 20 B.C.E.–50 C.E.] was a noble Alexandrian Jew who wrote in Greek on philosophy, history, and the Bible.)

3. Plaut asks: "Did God in fact speak to Abraham . . . ? To biblical man and to believers today the matter was and is clear; God did speak. . . . Many interpreters would understand God's challenge as something Abraham believed he had heard and consequently he acted in accordance with this belief" (Plaut, p. 93).

4. Italic phrases and bracketed numerals emphasize God's repeated promises to Abraham of progeny. (Emphasis added.)

5. Where chapter and verse number are given without specification of the book, the book is Genesis.

Sarah's beauty caught the eyes of Pharaoh's courtiers, and they took her to the palace. Fearing that Pharaoh's men would kill him if he was her husband, Abraham pretended that Sarah was his sister.[6] God "afflicted Pharaoh and his household with mighty plagues" (12:17), and Pharaoh reunited Abraham and Sarah. With Lot, they returned to Canaan, now "very rich with cattle, silver, and gold" (13:1).

Now Abraham separated from Lot because their herds had become very great. There was quarreling between their herdsmen over grazing and watering areas, no doubt. Together, they had probably become too big a target. Abraham allowed his nephew to choose lands to claim for himself. Lot chose a land that was well watered, but he fatefully overlooked the fact the people of that area "were wicked and sinners before the Lord exceedingly" (13:13). Zvi Adar underscores the ethical message of the story: "He who chooses land to live on would be well advised to study its population, and not only the quality of the land" (pp. 55–56).

God once more reassured Abraham still childless and now separated from his only kin, that he would be rich in progeny.

> Raise your eyes and look out from where you are, to the north and south, to the east and west, for I give all the land that you see to you and your offspring forever. *I will make your offspring as the dust of the earth, so that if one can count the dust of the earth, then your offspring too can be counted. [III]* (13:14–16)

According to W. Gunther Plaut, the chapter that follows, Genesis 14, is quite enigmatic "despite enormous research" (p.

---

6. A midrash asks: Did not Abraham by his deception expose Sarah to adultery? Yes, but his plan was executed under duress and was therefore justified. Still, had adultery occurred, Abraham would have been held guilty (Plaut, p. 101).

The moral of this story, says Zvi Adar, is that Abraham acted dishonorably and Pharaoh acted laudably. "The father of a nation can act dishonorably and the heathen king can act honorably and with justice." The Bible does not excuse the weaknesses of its heroes or ignore "the humane and good in people of other nations" (Adar, p. 52).

102). Lot and his household are taken captive in an invasion of
Sodom and Gomorrah; Abraham mustered three hundred and
eighteen men and freed his kinsmen. The king of Sodom
offered Abraham all the riches he had amassed, but Abraham,
who wanted only to free his kinsmen, said, "I will not take so
much as a thread or a sandal strap of what is yours" (14:23).[7]

As before, "the word of the Lord came to Abraham in a
vision," and again Abraham was reassured he would have a son
of his very own and countless descendants. His offspring
would be enslaved for four hundred years, but "in the end they
shall go free with great wealth" (16:14).

> [God said:] "Fear not, Abram, I am a shield to you; your reward
> shall be very great." Abraham reminded God that he was still
> childless. God assured him that *none but your very own issue
> shall be your heir. . . . Look toward heaven and count the stars,
> if you are able to count them . . . so shall your offspring be."
> [IV]* (15:1, 4–5)

Still childless, Sarah offered Hagar, her Egyptian maid servant to Abraham. "Consort with my maid: perhaps I shall have
a son through her," said Sarah (16:2). When Hagar became
pregnant, Sarah and Hagar fought. Hagar ran away, but an
angel of the Lord persuaded her to go back, "Submit to
[Sarah's] harsh treatment . . . [and] I will greatly increase
your offspring" (16:9–10). "Hagar bore a son to Abram, and
Abram gave the son that Hagar bore him the name Ishmael.
Abram was eighty-six years old when Hagar bore Ishmael to
Abram" (16:15–16).

When he was ninety-nine, Abraham again heard God's
promise: "I will establish My covenant between Me and you,
and I will make you exceedingly numerous" (17:2).

> This is my covenant with you: You shall be the father of a
> multitude of nations. . . . *I will make you exceedingly fertile,*

---

7. In chapter 14 says Adar, "we see Abraham the courageous and
fearless in contrast with Abraham the cautious and fearful" of
chapter 13 (p. 57).

and make nations of you; and kings shall come forth from you.
[V] I will maintain My covenant between Me and you, and your
offspring to come, as an everlasting covenant throughout the
ages. . . . I give the land you sojourn in to you and your
offspring to come, all the land of Canaan, as an everlasting
possession. I will be their God. (17:4–8)

As a sign of the covenant, "every male among you shall be
circumcised . . . at the age of eight days," sons and slaves
alike (17:10, 13). Finally, God promised Sarah that she would
give Abraham a son, ". . . nations; rulers of peoples shall issue
from her" (17:16). Abraham circumcised "all his household":
himself, thirteen-year-old Ishmael, his homeborn slaves, and
those bought from outsiders (17:24–27).[8] Chapter 18 displays
another aspect of Abraham's character—his hospitality. Three
mysterious visitors (angels) are invited to relax and dine with
Abraham. One of them predicts that their host's wife "shall
have a son!" (18:10).[9]

Again, God says that *"Abraham is to become a great and
populous nation [VI]* and all the nations of the earth are to
bless themselves by him" (18:18). Just as God promises to
create a Holy People, He vows to destroy the very wicked cities
of Sodom and Gomorrah. Abraham protests, "Here I venture to
speak to my Lord, I who am but dust and ashes." They argue
back and forth about how many innocent people would make
a wicked city worth saving. "Let not the Lord be angry if I speak
the last time: what if ten should be found there?" (18:32).[10]

---

8. Plaut discusses various aspects of circumcision, the practice of
many peoples besides the Jews (Egyptians, Moabites, Ammonites),
on pages 118–119 of *The Torah: A Modern Commentary.*

9. Plaut concedes this is an "annunciation" by angels, but it will
not lead to a divine birth (p. 124).

10. If Abraham argued with God so boldly about saving Sodom
and Gomorrah from destruction, why did he not question the
command to sacrifice Isaac? Because, answered the sages, it is more
fitting to argue in the interests of others than to argue in one's own
interests. Rabbi Akibah, however, insisted that Abraham should have
protested: "Yesterday you promised me. . . ." The divine order

The angels journeyed on to Sodom where Lot invited them into his household. The wicked Sodomites wanted Lot to hand over the strangers so they could abuse them (sexually?), but Lot protected them. In return, the angels miraculously shielded Lot and his household and ushered them out of the city as it was being destroyed by a "sulfurous fire from the Lord out of heaven. . . . Lot's wife looked back and . . . turned into a pillar of salt" (19:24–26). Lot and his daughters survived, and incestuous episodes created the ancestors of the Moabites and the Ammonites (19:31–38).

Again, Abraham journeyed into a strange kingdom and feared for his life should the king want Sarah. As before, Abraham posed as Sarah's brother and let Abimelech, king of Gerar, take her. "But God came to Abimelech in a dream by night and said to him, 'You are to die because of the woman that you have taken, for she is a married woman.'" A frightened Abimelech returned Sarah to Abraham and chastised him for misleading him. To correct any offense he may have committed, Abimelech gave Abraham "sheep and oxen, and male and female slaves . . . [and] a thousand pieces of silver" (20:14–18).

"Sarah conceived and bore a son to Abraham in his old age. . . . And when his son Isaac was eight days old, Abraham circumcised him, as the Lord had commanded him. . . . The child grew up and was weaned, and Abraham held a great feast on the day that Isaac was weaned" (20:2–8).

---

should not have gone unchallenged. Even the Holy One might have backed down (Milgrom, p. 145, quoting the classic rabbinic text, Semahot, 88).

Indeed, there is a midrash that does depict Abraham arguing with God: "Is it with you . . . as with men talking, who say one thing one day and another the next? Yesterday you said 'But my covenant I will retain with Isaac,' and now you tell me to slaughter him! Where is the covenant?" (Midrash Tehillim 29:1).

Wiesel adds his voice to the midrashim that insist that Abraham should have argued with God on behalf of Isaac. "If Abraham spoke up on behalf of a corrupt and wicked city, logically he should have spoken up for his one innocent son" (1995 Lecture).

Now Sarah asked Abraham,

'Cast out that slavewoman and her son, for the son of that slave
shall not share in the inheritance with my son Isaac.' The matter
distressed Abraham greatly, for it concerned a son of his. . . .
[God reassured Abraham, and bid him to acquiesce] *'for it is
through Isaac that offspring shall be continued to you. [VII]* The
son of the slave-woman, I will make a nation of him too, for he is
your seed.' (20:10–12)

Abraham did as he was told; miraculously Hagar and Ishmael survived their expulsion.[11]

Abimelech recognized that "God is with you in everything
that you do," and offered Abraham a mutual nonaggression
pact (21:22–34). Now the aged patriarch, at peace with his
neighbors, head of a large and thriving household including a
son of his own, and *seven times* promised[12] that he would
father a mighty people, faced a truly extraordinary test of his
trust in God's word.

---

11. Writes Plaut: "The Bible attempts no justification of Abraham
or Sarah, nor certainly of God. In the story, His ultimate designs
prevail; He directs the actions of men in His own mysterious way.
What on a human plane appears as Sarah's harsh and overprotective
behavior is on the divine level part of God's plan. Sarah's desires
coincide with the idea of destiny; hence her actions find God's
approval while Abraham's do not" (Plaut, p. 142).

12. As noted in italic phrases and bracketed roman numerals;
emphasis added (see n. 4).

2

GENESIS 22:
THE AKEDAH WITH COMMENTARY

Now we open up the Bible and read (or reread) Genesis 22. We have adopted the Soncino translation because the opening phrase is particularly faithful to the original Hebrew. At the end of this chapter is a commentary on various phrases and sentences that occur in the text. These phrases raise many of the issues that are dealt with throughout this study.

1] And it came to pass after these things, that God (E)[1] did prove Abraham, and said unto him: 'Abraham': and he said: 'Here am I.' 2] And He said; 'Take now thy son, thine only son, whom thou lovest, even Isaac, and get thee into the land of Moriah; and offer him there for a burnt offering upon one of the mountains which I will tell thee of.' 3] And Abraham rose early in the morning, and saddled his ass, and took two of his young men with him, and Isaac his son; and he cleaved the wood for the burnt offering, and rose up, and went unto the place of which God (E) had told him. 4] On the third day Abraham lifted up his eyes, and saw the place afar off. 5] And Abraham said unto his young men: 'Abide ye here with the ass, and I and the lad will go yonder; and we will worship, and come back to you.'

6] And Abraham took the wood of the burnt offering, and laid it upon Isaac his son; and he took in his hand the fire and

---

1. Throughout Genesis 22, references to God are followed by (E) or (A), to designate that the original text reads either Elohim or Adonai (YHVH).

11

the knife; and they went both of them together. 7] And Isaac spoke unto Abraham his father, and said: 'My father.' And he said, 'Here am I, my son.' And he said: 'Behold the fire and the wood; but where is the lamb for a burnt offering?' 8] And Abraham said: 'God (E) will provide himself the sheep for a burnt offering, my son.' So they went both of them together.

9] And they arrived at the place which God (E) had told him of; and Abraham built the altar there, and laid the wood in order, and bound Isaac his son, and laid him on the altar, upon the wood. 10] And Abraham stretched forth his hand, and took the knife to slay his son. 11] And the angel of the Lord called unto him out of heaven, and said: 'Abraham, Abraham.' And he said: 'Here am I.' 12] And he said: 'Lay not thy hand upon the lad, neither do thou any thing unto him; for now I know that thou art a God(E)-fearing man, seeing thou hast not withheld thine son, thine only son, from Me.' 13] And Abraham lifted up his eyes, and looked, and behold behind him a ram caught in the thicket by his horns. And Abraham went and took the ram and offered him up for a burnt offering in the stead of his son. 14] And Abraham called the name of that place Adonaijireh; as it is said to this day: 'In the mount where the Lord is seen.'

15] And the angel of the Lord (A) called unto Abraham a second time out of heaven, 16] and said: 'By Myself have I sworn, said the Lord, (Y) because thou hast done this thing, and hast not withheld thy son, thine only son, 17] that in blessing I will bless thee and in multiplying I will multiply thy seed as the stars of the heaven, and as the sand which is upon the seashore; and thy seed shall possess the gates of his enemies. 18] And in thy seed shall all the nations of the earth be blessed because thou hast harkened to my voice.' 19] So Abraham returned unto his young men, and they rose up and went together to Beer-sheba; and Abraham dwelt in Beer-sheba.

COMMENTARY

Verse 1. "After these things" The story opens with a statement so ambiguous, some translations delete this phrase altogether.

For example, JPS begins Genesis 22, "Some time afterwards . . ."

Verse 1. "After these things" Writes Rabbi Yaacov Culi: "This
is redundant because it obviously happened after the preced-
ing events" (p. 313). But after *what* events?

Verse 1. "God did prove Abraham" It has been suggested that
this phrase (sometimes translated as "God put Abraham to the
test") is intended to reassure the reader that God did not want
Abraham to actually sacrifice Isaac; He wanted only to test
Abraham. E. A. Speiser agrees that this phrase seems intended
to allay the reader's anxiety by assuring him at the very outset
this is only a test (p. 164).

Why did God test Abraham? Not to see if Abraham was a
man of great moral strength, but because, in the words of
Saadia Gaon, "God wished to demonstrate Abraham's righteousness to mankind" (Nehama Liebowitz, p. 189). The rabbis
of *Targum Jonathan*[2] argue similarly:

> Said Rabbi Yonatan: A potter doesn't test defective jars, for no
> sooner would he strike them once, they would break. . . . He
> tests the sound ones. No matter how many times he strikes
> them, he cannot break them. [Said] Rabbi Yossi ben Hanina: The
> flax grower knows when his flax is beautiful, the more he beats
> it, the better it gets, the more it glistens. But if it is defective
> he has hardly to touch it and it splits. So the Lord does not test
> the evil ones, only the just. . . . Said Rabbi Elazar: Concerning
> the master of the house who has two cows, one strong and one
> weak. Which gets the yoke? Naturally, the strong one!

Verse 1: "Here am I" An omniscient God knows, of course,
where Abraham happens to be located, and the response "Here
I am" in its literal meaning would therefore have been point-

---

2. *Targum Jonathan* is a sixth century C.E. translation of the
Pentateuch into the Aramaic vernacular of Babylonian Jews and was
used to teach the Bible to those for whom ancient Hebrew was
already a foreign language. In the *Targum,* literal translation is
interwoven with popular rabbinic interpretations. This makes the
Targum of enduring interest to students of the rabbinical tradition.

less. The words translated as "Here I am" actually mean "I am at your service," "What is your pleasure?" or simply "Yes, Sir."

Verse 2: "Take now thy son" The Hebrew phrase *Kach-nah et-bincha* is **not** a direct command; it has more of the connotation of a request. ("I wish you would . . .")

Verse 2: "Take now thy son" This request is answered by a silent acquiescence. Is this the same Abraham who quarreled with God and who bargained with God over sparing the inhabitants of Sodom and Gomorrah? How do we interpret Abraham's mute acquiescence? (a) he was living in a world in which child sacrifice had been practiced (usually under rare circumstances) many years before the Mosaic Law explicitly banned it; (b) Abraham knew this was an extraordinary demand and, in fact, contrary to God's law, but he understood it was a test of his obedience; (c) extraordinary circumstances seemed to justify this command. This is the thesis of chapter 16, "The Disaster Interpretation;" (d) his mute reaction indicated that he was dumbstruck at this singular perhaps unthinkable demand.

Unthinkable, even in the time of Abraham? This is suggested by the fact that Abraham seemed forced to be less than candid with his servants, and to be evasive to his son's questions. There is no indication that he told his wife, Sarah, about the extraordinary act God asked him to perform.

Verse 2. "Offer him there" Was Abraham commanded to offer Isaac *as* a burnt offering or *for* a burnt offering? Various commentators have noted that Abraham was never actually commanded to **sacrifice** Isaac. Some insist God commanded Isaac be brought up to the mountain and laid out as if for a sacrifice.

Verse 3. "Early in the morning" Starting out early in the morning symbolized Abraham's eagerness to carry out God's command. Another interpretation of this phrase is the command came to Abraham during the night in a dream. (In the Koranic Akeda, it is explicit that God came to Abraham in a dream.)

Verse 3: "Took two of his young men with him" Why did Abraham need the company of two servants? Answers Rashi:

"No person of nobility goes out on a journey without two servants" (p. 248).

Verse 3: "He cleaved the wood" Why did Abraham split the wood himself when he had two servants at his side? Three commentators offer three different answers. Rashi says it was to show Abraham's readiness to carry out God's command (p. 247). Lippman Bodoff has more recently argued, on the contrary, that by busying himself with a task his servants might have done for him, Abraham was delaying his fateful journey, giving himself (and God?) a chance to alter the course of events (p. 78). Benno Jacob makes the psychological interpretation that Abraham needed to work off his emotional state (pp. 494–95).

Verse 4. "On the third day" This would indicate a journey of thirty to forty miles. This fact casts doubt on the tradition that the Temple was later built on the site of the Akedah, since the journey from Beer-sheba to Jerusalem would take less than twenty-four hours.

Why a three-day journey? Maimonides suggests God chose to give Abraham time for deliberation and introspection, and to insure that Abraham's act of obedience was performed intentionally, not in a state of shock.

Verse 4. "And saw the place afar off" Abraham not only saw where the offering would take place, he also understood the importance of this experience for the future history of Israel.

Verse 5. "We will worship, and come back to you" Was Abraham dishonest with his servants as to his actual intentions on the mountain top, or did he sense somehow he would "pass the test" and Isaac's life would be spared? Rashi supposes that Abraham "foresaw that they would return" (p. 249).

Verse 6. "Laid it upon Isaac, his son" This phrase comes closest to answering the question, How old was Isaac? At least he was old enough and strong enough to carry a load of wood sufficient to consume the intended sacrifice. The Jewish historian, Josephus (d. 100 c.e.) portrays Isaac as twenty-five years old. Talmudic commentators see him as thirty-three years old, which pleases Christian advocates of the prefiguration theory for Jesus was also thirty-three at the time of the crucifixion (see chapter 21).

Verse 6. Rabbi Yaacov Culi asks: Why did Abraham load the wood on Isaac? "Why did he not use the donkey?" (p. 314)

Verse 6. "The knife" Speiser uses the word *cleaver*, noting that Abraham was carrying an implement used for slaughtering animals.

Verse 7. "Here I am, my son" is perhaps too formal a translation. Abraham's reply might have been more in the spirit of: "Well, boy, what is it?"

Verse 7. "Where is the lamb?" "The father's answer is tender but evasive, and the boy must have sensed the truth by now" (Speiser, p. 165).

Verse 8. Here is perhaps the most poignant and eloquent silence in all literature (Speiser, p. 165). The strained and inhibited interchange between Abraham and Isaac stands in marked contrast with the tender and candid conversation of Ibrahim and his son in Sura 37 of the Koran (see chapter 22).

Verse 9. "And bound Isaac, his son" According to a midrash, "Isaac begged Abraham to bind his hands and feet firmly, because . . . he was a strong youth and Abraham was an old man and [Isaac] was terrified lest he would instinctively react against the sight of the open blade" (Wellisch, p. 76). If Isaac reflexively injured himself, he would become unfit for sacrifice.

Verse 9. *"And laid him on the altar, upon the wood"* Not upon the *fire*, though according to the laws of sacrifice, writes Rabbi Yaacov Culi, "one must first kindle the fire, and only then can one slaughter the sacrifice" (p. 315).

Verse 10. "And took the knife" Many artists portray a menacing dagger or sword. An exception is the small, round-edged knife (suggesting a *hallaf*, a *shechita* knife?) pictured by Rembrandt. In Akedah artwork by Jewish artists, one sometimes sees a *hallaf*.

Verse 10. "To slay his son" The original Hebrew is *li'shchot et-b'no*. Might this be better translated "to sacrifice his son"? The translation issue is discussed in chapter 3, "The Medium is the Message."

Verse 11: "The angel of the Lord called unto him" God himself commanded Abraham to sacrifice Isaac, but an angel of the Lord stopped him. Rabbis have speculated why God gave the command himself, but sent an angel to cancel it. Elie

Wiesel, in a pardonable moment of anthropomorphism, suggests God was "too embarrassed" to admit He had changed his mind! (p. 91).

Wiesel also recalls a midrash in which Abraham refused to accept the angel's order, but insisted God himself rescind the order to sacrifice Isaac. "The Akedah was a double test: not only did God test Abraham, Abraham also tested God" (1995 Lecture).

Verse 12. "And Abraham lifted up his eyes, and looked, and behold behind him a ram" As in verse 4, "Abraham lifted up his eyes." Seeing is a key concept in the Akedah. The Akedah experience opened Abraham's eyes to the nature of God and to the nature of human experience.

Verse 12. "Lay not thy hand upon the lad" According to the Zohar, when Abraham was told to stop, he feared God had found him unfit to carry out the sacrifice. Abraham reflected, "Could it be perhaps that he [Abraham? Isaac?] was found unfit and therefore my sacrifice was not accepted?" A heavenly voice reassured him: "Go eat your bread in joy . . . for God has already accepted your deeds" (Vayikra Rabba 20:2).

According to Rashi, Abraham, who had not questioned God beforehand, now asks God, "Why did you ask me to bring Isaac here as a sacrifice?" God answers, "I will not break my covenant. . . . I did not tell thee to slaughter him, but to bring him up and lay him on the altar. Thou hast brought him up, now take him down" (p. 250).

Verse 12. "Now I know that thou art a God-fearing man" Would not an omniscient God have known in advance what Abraham's response would be? Or does the gift of free will give each person a flexibility even God cannot predict? The omniscience paradox is solved by the statement that God put Abraham to the test to show the world what God knew in advance, that Abraham was truly a God-fearing person (Rashi, p. 246, 251).

Maimonides regarded Abraham as greater than Moses (Wiesel, 1995 Lecture).

Verse 13. "And Abraham went and took the ram, and offered him up . . . in the stead of his son" This passage clearly describes animal sacrifice as a substitute for human sacrifice.

Rashi notes that not only at Moriah but "at every service Abraham [thereafter] performed with the ram, he prayed and said, "May this be acceptable to Thee as it had been done on my son . . . as if his blood had been spilled, as if his skin had been torn off, as if he had been burnt and become ashes" (p. 251).

Verse 14. This phrase has been translated in a variety of ways: "In the mount where the Lord is seen" (Soncino);[3] "On the mountain of the Lord there is vision" (JPS) "In the mountain of the Lord it was provided" (New English Bible) However translated, this phrase repeats the theme of seeing expressed in verses 4 and 12. The Akedah opened Abraham's eyes.

Verses 15–18. Is this portion an insertion? Nahum Sarna agrees with many Bible scholars that these verses were inserted into the Akedah story at a later date; that they are in the style of a sermon rather than a narrative like the rest of Genesis 22. He also asserts that "possessing the gate of his enemies" reflects the concern of Jews during a later period of history, the time of the Jewish kingdoms, not the age of Abraham.

Moberly presents a recent survey of scholarly opinion on the secondary nature of verses 15–18, and concludes the consensus view is as stated above (pp. 302–311). Rendsburg, however, argues these verses are structurally necessary to Genesis 22 (pp. 33–34).

Verse 18. "And in thy seed shall all the nations of the earth be blessed; because thou hast harkened to My voice" Here is an origin of the doctrine of inherited merit, so prominent in Jewish liturgy and discussed in further detail in chapter 18. Rashi promotes this doctrine with the words, "Abraham thought the Almighty will remember this binding and in memory of it pardon Israel every year, and save them from punishment. . . . God will forgive the sins of His people when He looks upon the mountain and remembers" (p. 252).

Does not each generation benefit from the achievements of

3. This translation anticipates that Moriah would become the site of the future Temple. Rashi expands this phrase to mean, "On this mountain the Almighty will appear to his people" (p. 252).

earlier days: philanthropists, inventors, poets, artists, scholars, medical and scientific researchers long dead? The Christian doctrine, "Christ died for our sins" has a Jewish counterpart: "Abraham offered Isaac for our blessing." It must of course be added that liturgical pleas for *Zekhut Avos,* or "inherited merit," had its halachic challengers (see chapter 18, fn 4). Inherited merit and vicarious atonement may be well-established in Jewish prayer, but they are not so firmly established in Jewish theology. With a rare touch of humor, Jo Milgrom refers to *Zekhut Avos* as "the credit card that never expires" (p. 100).

Verse 19. "Abraham then returned" Why is Isaac not specifically named as returning with Abraham? If a mere lad is on a trip with his father, some have argued, it must be assumed the son goes wherever the father goes. But when father and son separated from the servants, Abraham told them, "I and the lad will go yonder, and we will worship."

The ambiguity of this passage invites the midrashim that Isaac had indeed been sacrificed, his body reduced to ashes. His spirit rose to heaven where he was resurrected and returned to earth. (More on this in chapter 13). This ambiguous passage suggests that after Moriah, Abraham and Isaac did not return together; "their relationship had changed" (Wiesel, Lecture, 1995).

3

THE MEDIUM IS THE MESSAGE

Genesis 22 in Yiddish and in Kierkegaard's Danish

If you are truly fluent in Hebrew, you are probably not reading this book. It was not written for Bible scholars but for readers who share one layman's curiosity about the Akedah. More likely, you know some Yiddish, and through its similarity to English and German, you can also make out a sentence in Danish.

Why Danish? Danish is the language through which the Akedah came into the thoughts of Søren Kierkegaard. He wrote what is doubtlessly the most known commentary on the Akedah, *Fear and Trembling.* The title describes Kierkegaard's feelings of shock and distress over this Bible story, which led him to suppose that obedience to God's request required Abraham to abandon every principle of morality. How did Kierkegaard arrive at this conclusion? A good answer would probably touch on his up-bringing which was most unusual and severe. In turn, we would have to study the theological point of view fostered by this background. Additionally, Kierkegaard's response to the Akedah may have depended, in part, on the language in which he read the story of Isaac's averted sacrifice.

The thesis of this chapter is, in the words of Marshall

MacLuhan, "The medium is the message;" a reader's response to the Akedah depends in part on the language in which he or she reads it. We will return to Kierkegaard and the Danish Bible. Let us turn to a more familiar translation for most readers: The Akedah in Yiddish.

Of all modern translations of the Bible, only the Yiddish translation actually retains the Hebrew words for some sacred concepts. For example, in the Yiddish translation of the Akedah, altar is *mizbe-ach*, to sacrifice is *shechten,* and angel is *malach.* Therefore, it may be argued, a Yiddish translation retains more connotations of the Hebrew original than other translations.

Still, translation cannot be an easy job. An Italian proverb warns: *Tradotto, tradutto,* "a translator traduces." From the Talmud comes the warning: "He who translates a verse verbatim is a liar, and he who alters it is a villain and a heretic" (Kiddushin 49a).

A systematic translation of the entire Hebrew Bible was the lifework of well-known Jewish poet, linguist, and lexicographer, Yehoash Solomon Bloomgarden (1872–1927).[1] As his work progressed, it appeared in installments during the 1920s in the newspaper *Der Tag.*

In producing his translation of the Bible, Yehoash (as he signed his work) was guided by the fact that, for many generations, teachers of Yiddish-speaking children would translate *(fartaytchen)* the Bible into their vernacular. There was a strong oral tradition for Yehoash to follow when he produced his monumental translation. Here is how Yehoash translated Genesis 22:

---

1. Yehoash was a remarkable person—a poet and writer of ballads and fables in both Hebrew and Yiddish. He also mastered classical Arabic and translated portions of the Qur'an into Yiddish. He coproduced a Yiddish-Hebrew dictionary and translated the *Rubáiyát* and *Hiawatha* into Yiddish. Born and raised in Lithuania, he emigrated to the United States, travelled to Palestine, returned to the States, and wrote a book on his travels. He began his Yiddish translation of the Bible in 1905 and it occupied him, on and off, for the rest of his life.

Un es is geven noch di-dozike geshe-enishn hot Got gepruved Avrahamn un hot tsu im gezogt: Avraham! Ot er ge-entfert: Do bin ich. Hot er gezogt: Nem dayn zun, dayn eyn-un-eynzikn vos du host lib, Its-chokn, un gey dir keyn land Moraiah un bring im oyf dorten far a brand-opfer[2] oyf eynem fun di berg vos ich vel dir zogn.

Hot Avraham zich gefedert in der fri un er hot ongezotelt zayn eyzl un genumen mit zich zayne tsvey yungen un zayn zun Its-chokn; un er hot tse-hakt dos holts farn brand-opfer un er is oyf-geshtanen un iz gegangen tsu dem ort vos Got hot im gezogt.

Oyfn dritn tog hot Avraham oyf-gehoyln zayne oygen un hot derzen dem ort fun vayten. Un Avraham hot gezogt tsu zayne yungen: Blaybt aych do mitn eyzl, un ich un der yingl veln geyn biz ahin un mir veln zich buken un zich umkern zu aych.

Un Avraham hot genumen dos holts farn brand-opfer un aroyf-geton oyf zeyn zun Its-chok un er hot genumen in zayn hand dos fayer un dem shlacht-messer, un zey zeynen beyde gegangen banand. Hot Its-chok zich opgerufn tsu zayn foter Avrahamn un hot gezogt: Meyn fater! Hot er ge-entfert: Do bin ich, meyn zun! Hot er gezogt: Ot is dos fayer un dos holts, un vu iz does lam far a brand-opfer? Hot Avraham gezogt: Got vet zich shoyn zen a lam far a brand-opfer, mayn zun. Un zey zeynen beyde gegangen banand.

Un zey zeynen gekumen tsu dem ort vos Got hot im gezogt, un Avraham hot dort geboyt a mizbe-ach, un hot oysgelegt dos holts, un er hot gebunden zeyn zun Ist-chokn un im aroyfgeton oyfn mizbe-ach ibern holts. *Un Avraham hot oys-geshtrekt zayn hand un hot genumen dem shlacht-messer tsu shechten zayn zun.*

Hot a malach fun Got gerufen tsu im fun himmel un hot gezogt: Avraham, Avraham! Hot er ge-entfert: Do bin ich! Hot er gezogt: Zolst nisht oys-shtreken dayn hand ofyn yingl un zolst im gornisht ton, vorum atsind veys ich az du bist Gots-forchtik az du host nit farmitn dayn zun dayn eyn-un-eynsiger fun mir.

Hot Avraham oyfge-oybn zayne oygen un hot derzen erst

---

2. Apparently, the oral tradition specified a clearly Germanic term, *brand-opfer*, rather than the Hebrew *olah*, even though children traditionally studied Leviticus before Genesis, and therefore were already familiar with the terminology of animal sacrifice.

hinten hot a vider zich ayngedreyt in a tsvayg mit zayne herner.
Is Avraham gegangen un hot genumen dem vider un hot im
oyfgebracht far a brand-opfer onshtot zayn zun. Un Avraham
hot gerufen dem nomen fun yenem ort "Adonoy-yirah," azoy vi
es vert noch haynt gezogt: Oyf dem barg fun Yehuda vert gezen.
   Un der malach fun Got hot gerufn tsu Avrahamn a tsvayt mol
fun himmel un hot gezogt: Ich shver bay zich, zogt Got, as vayl
du host getan di-dozike zach un host nit farmiten dayn zun,
dayn eyn-un-eynzigen, iz bentchen vel ich dich bentchen, un
mern dayn nomen azoy vi di shtern in himmel, un azoy vi di
zamd oyfn breg fun yam. Un dayn nomen vet arben dem toyer
fun zayne feint. Un bentchen veln zich mit dayn zomen alle
felker fun der erd derfar vos du host tsu-gehert tsu mayne kol.
   Un Avraham hot zich umgekert tsu zayne yungen, un zey
zeynen oyfgeshtanen un zeynen gegangen banand kayn Bar-
sheva. Un Avraham iz gebliben in Bar-sheva.

A critical verse (22:10) has been rendered above in italic: *"Un
Avraham hot oysgeshtrekt zeyn hand, un hot genumen dem
shlacht-messer tsu shechten zayn zun."* In Yiddish translation,
this sentence uses a cognate of the Hebrew *li-sh'hot,* to
perform a ritual slaughter or to make a sacrifice. The reader of
the Hebrew (or Yiddish) is reminded Abraham is not simply
slaying or killing his son; he is performing a religious ritual.
   However, most translations do not convey the connotation
of *li-sh'hot et beh-no* (to make an offering, or a sacrifice of his
son). Instead, they describe Abraham as simply poised to *slay*
or *kill* his son. For example, the King James translation uses
*". . . and took the knife to slay his son." The JPS translation
states similarly, "Abraham picked up his knife to slay his son."
The New English Bible translates ". . . to kill his son."* The word
translated as knife also has different connotations in both the
original Hebrew and in Yiddish. The Hebrew word *ma'akelet*
stems from the root *akhal,* and is therefore described euphe-
mistically as a "food maker."
   Kierkegaard no doubt read the standard Danish translation
of the Bible: *"Og Abraham rakte sin Haand ud og greb kniven for
ad slagte sin Son."* The reader will recognize *slagte* as a cognate
of *slaughter.* A Danish-English dictionary translates *slagte* as
"kill, slaughter, butcher, massacre." Perhaps this helps explain,

in part at least, why a reading of the story in Danish reduced Kierkegaard (and many others) to fear and trembling. One may contrast Kierkegaard's response of "fear and trembling" with the mood of Abraham described in *MeAm Lo'ez*: "He was as happy as if he were escorting Isaac to his wedding. . . . Isaac did not know what would be done to him, and therefore felt no sadness" (p. 326).

Why JPS uses the phrase "to slay his son" rather than "to sacrifice his son"[3] is a puzzle. It is easier to understand why a Christian translator might translate "to slay" or "to kill;" it is a traditional Christian thesis that the Old Testament describes the primitive moral level of a world waiting to be redeemed by the Messiah. The Christian tradition shows an ambivalent attitude toward the Akedah. On the one hand, the story suggests that the ancient Hebrews lived at a primitive level of morality (chapter 14, "The Deglorification Interpretation"). On the other hand, Genesis 22 glorifies Father Abraham as the Knight of Faith (chapter 21, "The Akedah and the Christian Tradition").

"The medium is the message" and the connotations of the Akedah depend, in part at least, on how the story is translated.

---

3 The author did find the phrase, Abraham "took his sword to *sacrifice* his son" (emphasis added) in *A Children's Bible*, published in England, translated from German.

4

THE FEAR OF GOD

*For now I know that you fear God, since you have not withheld
your son, your favored one, from me.*
                    —Jewish Publication Society Bible

Now I know that thou art a God-fearing man.
                                        —Soncino Bible

Now I know that you are a God-fearing man.
                                    —New English Bible

Now I know how dedicated you are to God.
                                        —Anchor Bible[1]

Does the word *fear* help us or complicate our understanding
of Abraham's attitude toward God? Here we will examine the
thought of a Reform Jewish scholar of a generation ago,
Bernard J. Bamberger, and a leading Hasidic scholar of our
own day, Adin Steinsaltz.

In his 1929 paper "Fear and Love of God in the Old
Testament," Bamberger argued that in the Bible the fear of God
usually refers to a kind of *conduct*, not to a kind of *emotion*. For
example, in II Kings 17:28, the Samaritans ask for a Hebrew
priest to teach them "how to fear the Lord." The psalmist offers
to teach his disciples "the fear of the Lord" (Psalm 34:12). In

---

1. Speiser acknowledges a literal translation would say "that you
fear God," but adds "the manifest stress is not so much on fear, or
even awe, as on absolute dedication" (p. 163).

Exodus 20:16–17, the concept of fear is used in the same sentence to describe both an emotion and also to describe ethical conduct. After the giving of the Ten Commandments,

> the people said to Moses 'You speak to us . . . and we will obey; but let not God speak to us, lest we die.' Moses answered the people, 'Be not afraid; for God has come only in order to test you, and in order that the fear of Him may be ever with you, so that you do not go astray.'

Did Moses contradict himself or was he using the word *fear* in two distinctly different ways?

Bamberger cites several biblical passages in which fear is used in a context that clearly describes inner terror (p.41). Whether *yirah* means terror or right conduct can be discovered from the context. In the following lines from the Psalms, fear of the Lord clearly refers to the worship of the Lord:

> "Ye that fear the Lord, trust in the Lord; he is their help and their shield" (Psalm 115:11).

> "He will bless those who fear the Lord, both small and great" (Psalm 115:13).

> "Let them now who fear the Lord say that his mercy endureth forever" (Psalm 118:4).

> "Ye who fear the Lord, bless the Lord" (Psalm 135:20).

In the following Psalm, "fear of the Lord" refers to ethical conduct:

> Come, ye children, hearken unto me; I will teach you the fear of the Lord. . . . Keep thy tongue from evil, and thy lips from speaking guile. Depart from evil, and do good; seek peace, and pursue it. (Psalm 34:11–14)

There are occasions in the Bible which speak literally of the fear of God. In all such instances, the word used is not *yirah*, but *pachad*:

In I Samuel 11:7, Israel responds to Saul's summons because "the fear of the Lord fell on the people."

Asa's army "smote all the cities round about Gerar; for the fear of the Lord came upon" Asa's enemies (II Chronicles 14:14).

"And the fear of the Lord fell upon all the kingdoms of the land that were round about Judah, so that they made no war against Jehoshaphat" (II Chronicles 17:10).

Pachad is the Hebrew word that most often refers to terror in a literal sense. More poetic references to terror use the words *hul, gur, gevurah, hatat, eim, bet*.

Bamberger shows in several instances the love of the Lord, and fear of the Lord mean about the same thing: to worship him faithfully, and to obey his laws.

"Therefore, thou shalt love the Lord thy God, and keep his charge, and his statutes, and his ordinances, and his commandments, always" (Deuteronomy 11:1).

"I command thee this day to love the Lord thy God, to walk in his ways, and to keep his commandments and statutes and his ordinances" (Deuteronomy 30:16).

"I, the Lord thy God, am a jealous God, visiting the iniquity of the fathers upon the children . . . of them that hate me, and showing mercy unto thousands of them that love me, and keep my commandments" (Deuteronomy 20:5–6).

"To love the name of the Lord, to be his servants, everyone that . . . taketh hold of my covenant . . . them will I bring to my holy mountain, and make them joyful in my house of prayer" (Isaiah 56:6–7).

Like fear, love is defined not as a spontaneous emotional expression, but as a moral obligation that leads to worship and keeping of the commandments: "Take good heed of yourselves, that ye love the Lord your God" (Joshua 23:11).

In the following line, Israel is commanded both to fear God

and to love him. In the biblical context, "the two terms are practically synonymous and interchangeable," says Bamberger— a concept that is hard to grasp by one who has always regarded fear as the antithesis of love.

> And now, Israel, what doth the Lord thy God require of thee, but to fear the Lord thy God, to walk in all his ways, and to love him, and to serve the Lord thy God with all thy heart and with all thy soul. (Deuteronomy 10:12)

To summarize Bamberger's thought, in the Bible *yirah* which is translated as fear may designate either of two things. The word may simply designate terror, or *yirah* may be shorthand for *yirat-Adonai*, fear of God, which designates not an emotion but a practice: the worship of God, obedience to God's commandments, and ethical conduct. Similarly, biblical use of the term *love-of-God* usually designates a moral obligation leading to worship and keeping of the commandments, rather than a primarily emotional expression. According to Bamberger, this leads us to note that in the Bible love of the Lord and fear of the Lord mean about the same thing: to worship him faithfully and to obey his laws.

Using the language of psychology and literary analysis, we note that the differences between ordinary fear and fear-of-God and between ordinary love and love-of-God are those of a relatively simple emotion versus a **sentiment**. A sentiment is a complex of several emotions, intertwined with various feelings, attitudes, habits, and predispositions; some perhaps in conflict with each other. Fear-of-God and love-of-God both are sentiments, not emotions. Both include the emotions of fear[2] and love.

---

2. Fear, and the **suffering** that accompanies fear, is no doubt a component of the biblical concept of fear of God, and of the Hasidic concept of *Gevurah*. David Baumgardt rejects the "easy bravura" of those midrashim in which Abraham and Isaac express an eagerness to do God's bidding. The **suffering** Abraham and Isaac stressed by Christian interpreters suggest "deeper layers of meaning of the Akedah." The silence of Abraham and Isaac's journey is far more than a literary device, it expresses a wordless agony. "Abraham silently,

Keep in mind that Biblical Hebrew is a poetic language, and in poetic language a part may represent a whole object or idea. (The ancient Greeks named this figure of speech the synecdoche.) This poetic convention allows one to call an old man "the beard" and to call a home "the hearth." The same poetic practice permits one to refer to fear-of-God as fear, or love-of-God as love. Whether a biblical reference to fear refers literally to the emotion or figuratively to the sentiment depends, of course, on context. Context is all.

Now we turn to Adin Steinsaltz. In Hasidic thought, fear and love are also closely intertwined. There are many levels of both love and fear, *chesed* and *gevurah*, according to Steinsaltz. The highest level of fear is the towering fear of God, and at this level, release from fear enables one to experience the love of God, the feeling that one is truly the object of God's love, in a rapturous and ecstatic way.

Hasidic thought contributes this understanding of the Akedah: God commanded Abraham to sacrifice his son in order to raise both Abraham and Isaac to this ultimate level of fear, the fear of God. This, according to Steinsaltz, "is the highest level of Fear that can be reached, where it is no longer fear but a matter of facing the magnificence of His Glory" (p. 149). When the voice of the angel commanded, "Do not raise your hand against the boy, or do anything to him," Abraham and Isaac were then prepared to experience the love of God in a most rapturous and ecstatic way.

Thus, in the Akedah the highest level of fear, a terrible awe, *gevurah*, leads to the expression of that supreme love, *chesed*,

---

and under pain hardly grasped to its full extent . . . goes ahead silently . . . without knowing where the journey to Moriah would lead, with a heavy heart and even with a gnashing of teeth" (pp. 289–297).

Happiness (Baumgardt prefers the term *joy*) is a higher moral aim than suffering. "But Judaism also teaches that there are highest joys that, in the nature of things and according to the unfathomable will of God, are linked up with suffering. These joys can be bought only at the price of pain; and the only comfort religion can give is to establish that they are worth that price" (p. 298).

which is the love that passes between man and God. In the Hasidic mind, there is a mystical connection between terror and love, and the Akedah dramatizes this connection. Says Steinsaltz: "Terrible awe may, and sometimes must, precede and provoke the supreme love" (p. 150).

5

THE TEN TRIALS

The Abraham story describes the very beginnings of God's efforts to bring into being a holy people, which might grow and thrive and eventually lead to "a future community of all men" (1968 Buber, p. 29). This universalistic goal becomes clear in God's blessing of Abraham when he passes that most agonizing test of obedience: "*All the nations of the earth shall bless themselves by your descendants,* because you have obeyed my command" (verse 18, emphasis added).

However, before Abraham could be made the father of a chosen people, he was tested (subjected to trials or revelations) for his spiritual endurance, for his **obedience** to God's command, for all the qualities of heart and mind that would qualify him to father a holy people. Abraham passed some of these tests better than others. The Akedah represented the final test of Abraham's obedience to God.

To place the Akedah in its context, first retrace all the tests that preceded the Akedah. The rabbinical tradition holds that Abraham faced ten tests. Martin Buber lists only seven revelations. The following list of ten tests[1] is based mainly (though

---

1. The tradition of Abraham's ten tests goes back to Chapter 5 of *Pirke Aboth.* (See Mishnah 4 of Chapter 5 in *Pirke Aboth.* Over the

not entirely) on Buber's discussion. The seven revelations listed
by Buber are marked by asterisks(*).

> *1. **God sends Abram out** of his native land—"to the land
>   I will let you **see**" (12:1). Abraham, a prosperous seventy-
>   five-year-old herdsman, is asked to leave the country of
>   his kinsmen. Go "to a land that I will show you,"
>   commands the voice of an unknown God. This is also a
>   test of **separation**—Abraham, are you willing to leave
>   the land you grew up in, leave your kinsmen and
>   friends, leave the gods of your ancestors, leave your
>   homeland forever, for a destination and a destiny that
>   you do not know, for a God who is hidden and whose
>   ways are mysterious?
>
> *2. **God reveals himself** to Abraham; lets Abraham 'see

---

years, different writers have assembled different lists of ten. Here is
Maimonides's list of Abraham's ten trials. An asterisk (*) precedes
each item which is **not** included in this chapter's list of ten trials.)

1. Abraham's exile from his home in response to God's command (Genesis 12:1).
*2. The famine in the land of Canaan, which seemed to belie
   God's promise, "I will make you into a great nation, and I will
   bless you" (Genesis 12:2).
3. The violence done to Abraham in the taking of Sarah into
   Pharaoh's house (Genesis 12:10–20).
*4. Abraham's battle with the four kings (Genesis 14).
*5. Abraham's need to take Hagar as a wife after his despair over
   not having children with Sarah (Genesis 16:1ff.).
6. The command to circumcise himself although he was an old
   man (Genesis 17:11).
7. The violence of having his wife taken into the house of the
   king of Gerar (Genesis 20:1–18).
8. Abraham's compulsion to send away Hagar although she had
   borne him a son (Genesis 21:9–21).
9. The difficulty of sending away his son Ishmael (Genesis
   21:12).
10. The binding of Isaac. (Genesis 22) This was Abraham's Last
    Trial from which Segal derives the title of his book.

Him' when Abraham arrived in the land of Canaan. God says, "I will give this land to your offspring" (verse 7). Abram **sees** the land, and also **sees** God.

3. **Abraham's flight to Egypt,** and his disguise as Sarah's brother. Buber does not mention this verse (12) in his enumeration of Abraham's seven revelations. Maimonides, on the other hand, derives two of Abraham's ten trials from this episode: (1) the famine in Canaan, which seemed to cast doubt on God's promise; and (2) Abraham's separation from Sarah when she "was taken into Pharaoh's household" (12:15). Speiser notes that "interpreters through the ages have found the material both puzzling and disturbing" (p. 91). If Abraham so feared for his life that he was willing to let Sarah be taken "into Pharaoh's household," was Abraham expressing doubt of God's power to protect him and Sarah? [Abraham will repeat this feint in Gerar, allowing Sarah to be "taken" by Abimelech, king of Gerar. (Genesis, chapter 20)] In any case, Abraham continued to be a candidate for the role as father of a Holy People. Abraham's repeated adoption of this feint is discussed in chapter 7, as an example of "Sinning for the Sake of God."

*4. **Abraham parts with Lot.** This separation is phrased as a practical move. Since there had been quarreling between their herdsmen, and their possessions were so great, the land could not support them staying together" (13:6). Nonetheless, this was also a final separation of the aging Abraham from his kinsmen. He had "burned another bridge behind him," and thus strengthened his link with God.

God promises the land to Abraham's offspring. "And the Lord said to Abraham . . . (**Raise your eyes and look out** from where you are . . . for I give all the land that you **see** to you and your offspring forever)" (13:14–15).

*5. **Abraham expresses doubt,** saying that he is already old and has no offspring: "O Lord God, what can you give me, seeing that I shall die childless" (18:1). God promises Abraham an heir from his "very own issue. . . . 'Look toward heaven and count the stars. . . . So shall your offspring be.' And because he put his trust in the Lord, He reckoned it to his merit" (15:4–6).

*6. **Again, God reveals himself.** When Abraham was ninety-nine years old, again, "God allows himself **to be seen** by Abram," and says to him, "I will establish my covenant between Me and you, and I will make you exceedingly numerous" (17:1–2).

7. **Abraham, at ninety-nine, is commanded to circumcise himself** (17:11). This episode, says Speiser, helps "bring out the numinous (i.e., mysterious) character of Adonai's partnership with Abraham" (Speiser, p. 126). The divine command tests Abraham's obedience and spiritual strength, but it would not seem odd to Abraham, who must have known of circumcision, since it was in his time "an old and widely diffused practice . . . observed by many of Israel's neighbors" (Speiser, pp. 126–127).

8. **Abraham expels Hagar and Ishmael.** Abraham is reluctant to send the boy away. He does it because Sarah insists, and God supports this action, "for the sake of Israel's mission"—another separation story (Buber, p. 40).

*9. **Abraham tests God.** Abraham's intercession on behalf of Sodom, exhibits Abraham's temerity, his readiness to argue with God: "Will you sweep away the innocent along with the guilty? . . . Shall not the Judge of all the earth deal justly?" Abraham asks God's pardon for his boldness: "Here I venture to speak to my Lord, I who am but dust and ashes" (18:20–27). Perhaps God is not altogether pleased with Abraham's hubris.

According to Buber, "Abraham utters *the boldest speech of man in all Scripture,* [bolder] than anything said by Job in his dispute with God, greater than any, because it is the word of . . . [an intercessor who has lost] even the awe of God" (Buber, p. 40, emphasis added).

*10. **God tests Abraham.** According to Rashi, God tests Abraham for somewhat the same reason God tested Job—because Satan raised doubts about their loyalty.

"At none of the banquets which Abraham made, did he
sacrifice before Thee a bull or a ram," . . . [said Satan
to God. God replied:] "Abraham did nothing except in
the interest of his son. If I said to him, Bring him before
Me as a sacrifice, he would not have hesitated." (Rashi,
p. 245).[2]

The Akedah was Abraham's "greatest ordeal . . . [and led to]
his greatest blessing" (1968, Buber, p. 41).

Buber notes the command "Get thee" occurs in only two
places in the entire Bible, in verses 12:1 and in 22:2 of Genesis.
Both demand Abraham **separate** himself; first, from his past;
second, from his future. "Despite the promises given him by
that same God . . . both times God does not tell the man
where He is sending him" (Buber, p. 41).

Common to both episodes is the fact that, "God sends man
into an uncertainty." Abraham must perform an "inhuman
act . . . at the Lord's bidding." This time, Abraham does not
argue, answers not in words, "but by deed. . . . 'And he
went' " (1968, Buber, p. 41).

The theme words *to see* which mark the Abraham story as a
whole, dominate chapter 22 as they do no other chapter of the
Abraham story. Here, **to see** describes "the way of God and
man . . . in all its depth and meaningfulness. . . . Abraham
sees the place where the act must be accomplished." He
answers Isaac that God will **see to** (provide) the lamb for the
burnt offering. "In the saving moment he lifts up his eyes and
sees the ram." Abraham names the altar God Will See (1968
Buber, pp. 41–42).

Did Abraham name the mountain "God Will See," "God Will
Provide," or "God Lets Himself Be Seen"? The King James
translation provides, "In the mount of the Lord it shall be
seen." The Revised Standard Version translates, "On the mount
of the Lord it shall be provided." The New English Bible offers

---

2. See chapter 11 on Satan's midrashic role in the Akedah story.
According to the Zohar, Satan came to the banquet disguised as a
beggar, and even to this day, continues to visit every banquet to
which the poor are not invited.

the translation, "In the mountain of the Lord it was provided." This last one may be the translation of choice because it recognizes that *yireh*, the Hebrew word for *see*, which also means *see to*, or *provide*. This translation also answers Isaac's question, "Where is the sheep for the burnt offering?"

Also, it may be noted that *to see* and *to fear* (*yir'e* and *yer'e*) have similar sounds in Hebrew. If *to fear* is short for *to fear God*, then to *see, to provide*, and *to fear God*, or *to worship God* are near-homonyms, suggesting such word play as "worship God, and see God; if you worship God, you will see God; man worships and God provides." The Bible is full of near-homonyms and is suggestive of such word play, which means reading the Bible in translation cannot match the experience of reading it in Hebrew.

To Buber, seeing is the keyword of the Abraham story and is crucial to each of the revelations that mark the life of Abraham. Through seeing, Abraham discovers God, and God discovers Abraham. Other commentators suggest separation is the key concept in the Abraham cycle. Is Abraham willing to separate himself from his past and from all human ties for the sake of his loyalty to God?

What is the meaning of separation and seeing in the Akedah story? Perhaps it means one must be separated from the past before seeing the world in a new light; through worship comes seeing; through the Akedah, Abraham was able to see what God is like—a God of justice and mercy whose ways are nonetheless hidden and mysterious. If the Akedah was demanded, as Buber suggests, as an atonement for Abraham's questioning of God's justice, perhaps its message is that God's ways are a mystery to human understanding. Here is a God who asks for an unthinkable sacrifice, only in the end to reverse himself, and to reveal himself (to be seen) not only as a commanding Elohim, but as a compassionate Adonai, a God of mercy and loving kindness.

6

THE BIBLICAL CONTEXT
OF THE AKEDAH

Commentaries on the Akedah are too often limited by a neglect of the *context* in which this story appears. Instead of studying the Akedah narrative in its biblical context and as one episode in the Abraham cycle of Genesis, the commentator elaborates on the Akedah narrative somewhat in isolation from its original context. Without quite realizing it, the commentator views the Akedah as a personal experience, and sees the event in light of the author's *own* background of attitudes and beliefs.[1] Kierkegaard dwells at length on how a nineteenth-

---

1. Historians label this the error of *presentism*—of regarding a remote historical event as if it were happening in the present.

Fear and Trembling is the title of Søren Kierkegaard's commentary on the Akedah story. It conveys the author's conviction that Abraham must have had a truly dreadful experience. "When I have to think of Abraham, I am as though annihilated . . . I am paralyzed" (p. 44).

Rabbi Joseph Gumbiner has asserted that Kierkegaard used the Akedah story to portray the essence of Christian faith as rising above logic and reason and perhaps calling for the suspension of the ethical. "*Fear and Trembling* is beautifully written, salted with great

century Protestant might react to the unlikely event of an
Akedah experience, which tells us more about Kierkegaard and

---

wit, provocative of much philosophical meditation" but has no link
with Jewish thought (p. 148).

Response to the Akedah story with "fear and trembling" is not a
uniquely Christian tendency. Elie Wiesel describes the episode as
"terrifying in content" (p. 69). Similarly, David Polish describes
Abraham after he has heard God's command that he offer up his son:
"He is a shattered man, going almost trancelike toward a deadly act
that he must carry out but with less than perfect faith. God commands, Abraham submits. There is no conversation, only the sentence of doom and the silent response" (1988, p. 162).

Similarly, Sheldon Zimmerman seems to be comparing Isaac to a
youngster of our time when he says, "Isaac acquiesed much too
silently. 'Hey, this is crazy! I am not going any farther. Tell me why'
would have been a much more fitting response. . . . Isaac had the
right to yell and scream. . . . I think Isaac fails in his silence" (Miller,
p. 15).

Similarly, Robert Milch describes Abraham's situation as it would
be felt by a person of our time. God's command is backed by "no
clearly stated reason—not that any reason conceivable to human
minds would be satisfactory" (p. 397). Abraham's obedience must
have been accompanied by great anguish, adds Milch; his journey to
Mount Moriah must have been agonizing, for he had been called
upon to do an "unspeakable thing . . . a thing beyond all ken, an act
in violation of everything humanity has been given to understand of
morality and decency."

Milch continues: "In ordinary human terms [the act of sacrificing
one's son is] insane and sadistic." Today, such an attempt would label
the father "a raving maniac and . . . [would arouse] all the powers of
society and of the state to prevent him from destroying himself and
an innocent child." The act of child sacrifice "contravenes all which
common sense, human judgment, and conventional religion reckon
to be man's proper mode of behavior." But, as Milch himself admits,
his words express the standards of *our* day, not Abraham's.

Norman Gottwald begs the reader of the Akedah story not to feel
"repulsed by the crudity of the concept of human sacrifice." It is
important to recognize that in ancient "Canaanitic practice . . . it
was not a rare occurrence for children to be sacrificed. Any devout
soul in that time could have understood the divine will as requiring

nineteenth-century Protestantism than it does about Abraham and the God of Genesis.

According to Robert Alter, the habit of analyzing a biblical story in isolation from its context can also flaw traditional Jewish scholarship. Too often an exegesis is made from a specific phrase or "small pieces of the text" and becomes the basis of "elaborate homiletical structures that have only an intermittent relation to the integral story told by the text" (1981, p. 11).

As a biblical story, the Akedah is unique. Yet is would be hard

---

of him the sacrifice of his dearest possession. The outcome of the story gives a most emphatic rejection of child sacrifice while it respects and retains the *intention* of sacrifice: the giving of everything to God. Elohim accepts the intention in place of the act" (pp. 253–54).

Likewise, Robert Gordis emphasizes "the sacrifice of a child was an all-but-universal practice in ancient Semitic religion and beyond. . . . Abraham, living . . . in a world permeated by pagan religion, did not feel himself confronted by a moral crisis when he was commanded by God to sacrifice Isaac, and he proceeded to obey" (p. 108).

> In the patriarchal age, this horror of child sacrifice, an attitude in which Judaism was unique in the ancient world, still lay in the distant future. Abraham, living nearly a thousand years before Micah in a world permeated by pagan religion, did not see himself confronted by a moral crisis when he was commanded by God to sacrifice Isaac, and he proceeded to obey. His faith was being subjected to the most painful test possible, but he was not being asked to violate the moral law as he understood it (Gordis, p. 108).

> [Even in the time of the prophets, Micah asks, if only rhetorically, whether God wants the sacrifice of one's first-born.] With what shall I come before the Lord, and bow myself before the High God? Shall I come before him with burnt offerings, with calves of a year old? . . . Shall I give my first-born for my transgression, the fruit of my body for the sin of my soul? [Micah answers:] He hath shown thee, O man, what is good; and what doth the Lord require of thee, but to do justly, and to love mercy, and to walk humbly with thy God. (Micah 6:6–8)

The error of presentism flaws any attempt to evaluate the event from another era as if it were occurring in our time. When you attempt to put yourself in Abraham's shoes, first ask yourself, "Did he wear shoes?"

to find an aspect, an element, or a theme in the Akedah that does not appear elsewhere in the Bible. Here is a list of themes found in Genesis 22 and appearing in other parts of the Bible as well.[2]

God asks Abraham to travel to an unspecified destination. In 12:1, God says to Abraham, "Get thee out of thy country . . . unto a land that I will show thee." In 22:2, God now says, "Take now they son . . . and get thee into the land of Moriah . . . upon one of the mountains which I will tell thee of."

Revelation on a mountain top. Abraham's rendezvous with God on Mount Moriah foreshadows Moses' revelation on Mount Sinai. Abraham was sent to Mount Moriah to learn a testing God was also a merciful God; Moses was called to Mount Sinai to receive the Law. Both occasions are closed by God's blessing: "In blessing I will bless thee and in multiplying I will multiply thy seed as the stars of the heaven" (verse 17). "Thou shalt be blessed above all people; there shall not be male or female barren among you, or among your cattle" (Deuteronomy 7:14).[3]

God asks Abraham to put the knife to the body. In 17:11 God commands, "Circumcise the flesh of your foreskin," making the Akedah not the first time that God asks for the shedding of human blood.[4]

Testing. In the Akedah, God tested Abraham. In itself, this is no surprise since God tested Abraham's obedience[5] again and

---

2. In *The Art of Biblical Narratative*, Robert Alter points to the significance of recurrent themes in the Bible.

3. Jo Milgrom observes that despite the striking similarity between these two events, this similarity does not seem to be noted in rabbinical literature (p. 28, fn. 1).

4. Perhaps Abraham used the same knife he later brought to Moriah to circumcise himself, Ishmael, and Isaac. Circumcision may be regarded as an abbreviated, symbolic expression of the impulse toward infant sacrifice, Rabbis Miller and Riskin agree (Miller, p. 28). Today, the *mohel* is the agent of the father, and the *brit milah* ceremony expresses both a "tension between the generations," and the impulse to return to God his most precious gift.

5. Christian writers see the Akedah as a test of Abraham's faith.

again, commanding Abraham to leave his native city, Ur, and travel "to a place that I shall show you."

The Bible describes a testing God. The psalmist sings, "Examine me, O Lord, and prove me; test my heart and my mind" (Psalm 26:2). Throughout the Bible, God warns that he is testing Israel. In Judges 2:22, God declares he will not drive out all the nations from the Promised Land, "that through them I may test Israel, whether they will keep the way of the Lord to walk therein, as their fathers did keep it, or not."

Solomon tests two women who claim the same infant as their own. God's testing of Job is a particularly close parallel to the Akedah, and the comparison is analyzed in detail by Bruce Zuckerman in *Job the Silent*.

Human sacrifice. There are numerous examples such as the sacrifice of Jeptha's daughter (Judges 11:34–39) or King Moab's sacrifice of his son when his capital was under seige (Kings II 3:27). Manasseh, the flagrantly idolatrous king of Judah, "made his son pass through the fire" (Kings II 21:6). The psalmists lamented the sins of those who sacrificed "their own sons and daughters . . . shed innocent blood . . . to the idols of Canaan" (Psalm 106:37–38). The prophets, Isaiah, Jeremiah, Ezekiel, Hosea, and Micah all inveighed against those who built altars "to burn their sons and daughters in the fire" (Jeremiah 7:31).[6]

The rivalry between brothers, one of whom is stronger, older, and more physical. Cain and Abel, Jacob and Esau, Joseph and his brothers—all repeat the theme that marks the troubled relationship between Isaac and Ishmael which leads to Ishmael's expulsion and sets the stage for Genesis 22, where Isaac can be described as "thine only son."

Jewish writers are more likely to see the story as a test of Abraham's obedience, fear of God, or love. According to rabbinical tradition, Abraham was tested ten times; this is the theme of chapter 5.

6. The Talmud offers two interpretations of the expression "passing infants through fire." Dedication to Molech was expressed by either (a) forcing children to walk between two fires, or (b) tossing children back and forth over a fire till they were burned (Sanhedrin 64b). Nineteen biblical references to infant sacrifice are listed at the end of these Notes.*

Rivalry between wives. The rivalry between Hagar and Sarah, which sets the stage for Genesis 22, foreshadows the rivalry between Rachel and Leah. Typically, the favored wife is barren, while the other wife bears children.

God tells Abraham he will be the father of many nations. The pledge was made to Abraham in Genesis 17:4, amplifying the promise made in 13:16, that God will make Abraham's seed "as the dust of the earth." Again in 15:5, God says to Abraham, "Look now toward heaven, and count the stars. . . . So shall thy seed be." In Genesis 21 God promises to make of Hagar a nation. (He is believed to be the ancestor of the Ishmaelites.) In Genesis 25, Esau, son of Isaac, is named father of the Edomites. In Genesis 22, after Abraham passes the supreme test of obedience, God promises, through the voice of an angel, "In thy seed shall all the nations of the earth be blessed, because thou hast obeyed my voice."

The ancestor of a tribe endangered. Ishmael, whose survival was threatened, was saved as if by a miracle; similar to what happens to Isaac.

The plight of a barren woman, and God's promise that she will conceive, is another repeated biblical theme (e.g., Sarah, Hannah, the wife of Manoah, the Shunammite woman).

Abraham is separated. In the Akedah, God tests Abraham's willingness to separate himself—painfully and irreversibly—from his son Isaac, as he had commanded Abram to separate himself from his country, his kindred, and his father's house. Later he separated himself from Lot. At Sarah's insistence and with God's support, Abraham had separated himself from his son Ishmael. Separation is a recurrent theme of the Abraham cycle, and the Akedah narrative is only one of many instances in which Abraham confronts the questions: "Can I give up every human connection—social and blood ties—and survive? Is my connection with God really strong enough to sustain me?"[7]

The surprise ending. The Akedah narrative builds to what seems like an inevitable conclusion, but there is a sudden reversal of events. The narrative twist, "the surprise ending,"

---

7. Erich Fromm suggests this line of thought on pp. 89–90 fn.

characterizes many other Bible stories. For example, blind old Isaac wants to give the birthright blessing to his eldest son, but Rachel contrives for Isaac to bless Jacob instead. Jacob works seven years for Rachel and is given Leah instead.

These plot reversals label human affairs as unpredictable. In the words of Alter, "The repeated point of the biblical writers is that we cannot make sense of God in human terms" (1992, pp. 22–23). If man was made in the image of God, and man's ways are unpredictable, God is also unpredictable.

> There is, in the view of Hebrew writers, something elusive, unpredictable, unresolvable about human nature. Man, made in God's image, shares a measure of God's transcendence of categories, images, defining labels. (Alter 1992, p. 67)

Restated, the Bible offers a view of reality that is ambiguous not because it is "out of focus," but because it is believed that reality is inherently multivocal, that reality challenges and may even defy human understanding. The Bible presents a point of view that God cannot be understood, that God is unknowable, a mystery. This view of reality is well-conveyed by the story-telling style of the Akedah: spare, terse, ambiguous.[8]

---

8. The literary power of the Akedah's ambiguity is the subject of Auerbach's classic commentary.

*Nineteen biblical references to infant sacrifice:

1. "Any man among the Israelites . . . who gives any of his offspring to Molech, shall be put to death; the people of the land shall pelt him with stones" (Leviticus 20:2. This prohibition is repeated in Leviticus 20:3 and 4).
2. "When the Lord thy God shall cut off the nations from before thee . . . and thou succeedest them, and dwellest in their land, take heed to thyself that thou be not snared by following them . . . [in their ways of serving their gods, for their ways are an] abomination to the Lord. . . . Even their sons and daughters they have burned in the fire to their gods" (Deuteronomy 12:29–31).
3. "Let no one be found among you who consigns his son or

The masters of ancient Hebrew narrative were clearly writers
who delighted in the art of indirection, in the possibilities of

---

    daughter to the fire" (Deuteronomy 18:10). This prohibition is
directed against Molech worship, "an abhorrent Canaanite
cultic practice," comments Plaut (p. 1456). Plaut's note says
See Sanhedrin 64b, Sifre Deuteronomy 171.

4. "For it came to pass, when Solomon was old, that his wives
turned away his heart after other gods. . . . Then did Solomon build a high place for . . . Molech . . . and likewise
did he for all his foreign wives, who burned incense and
sacrificed unto their gods" (I Kings 11:4, 7, 8).

5. "At the price of his last-born" (I Kings 16:34).

6. Achaz "made his son pass through the fire" during the
Syro–Ephraimite War (II Kings 16:3).

7. "And the children of Israel did secretly those things that were
not right against the Lord their God . . . and wrought wicked
things to provoke the Lord to anger" (II Kings 17:9–11). Another
allusion to Molech worship?

8. "And they left all the commandments of the Lord their
God . . . and served Baal . . . and they caused their sons
and daughters to pass through the fire" (II Kings 17:16–17).

9. [King Josiah ordered the destruction of idols and pagan altars
in Judah] "that no man might make his son or his daughter to
pass through the fire to Molech" (II Kings 23:10).

10. "We have sinned with our fathers, we have committed
iniquity, we have done wickedly. . . . Our fathers . . .
mingled among the nations, and learned their works, and
they served their idols. . . . Yea, they sacrificed their sons
and their daughters, . . . shed innocent blood . . . unto
the idols of Canaan; and the land was polluted with blood"
(Psalms 106:6, 7, 35–38).

11. "Are ye not children of transgression, a seed of falsehood,
inflaming yourselves with idols under every green tree [refers
perhaps to a fertility rite which involved sexual arousal],
slaying children in the valleys under the clefts of the rocks?"
(Isaiah 57:4–6).

12. "Go forth unto the valley of Hinnom . . . and proclaim there
the words that I shall tell thee, and say, Hear the word of the
Lord. . . . Thus saith the Lord of hosts, the God of Israel,
Behold, I will bring evil upon this place, concerning which

intimating depths through the mere hint of a surface feature, or
through a few words of dialogue fraught with implication. The

---

whosoever heareth, his ears shall tingle. Because they have
forsaken me, and have desecrated this place, and have
burned incense in it unto other gods, whom neither they nor
their fathers have known . . . and have filled this place with
the blood of innocents. They have built also the high places of
Baal, to burn their sons with fire for burnt offerings unto Baal,
which I commanded not, nor spoke of it, neither came it into
my mind. Therefore, behold, the days come, saith the Lord,
that this place shall no more be called Topheth, nor The Valley
of the Son of Hinnom, but The Valley of Slaughter" (Jeremiah
19:2–6).

13. "Thus saith the Lord of hosts, the God of Israel, Amend your
ways and your doings. . . . Will ye steal, murder, and commit adultery, and swear falsely, and burn incense unto Baal,
and walk after other gods whom ye know not? . . . But this
thing I commanded them, saying, Obey my voice, and I will
be your God. . . . But they hearkened not, nor inclined their
ear, but walked in the counsels and in the imagination of
their evil heart, and went backward and not forward. . . .
And they have built the high places of Topheth . . . to burn
their sons and their daughters in the fire, which I commanded them not" (Jeremiah 7:3, 9, 23, 24, 31).

14. "For the children of Israel and the children of Judah have only
done evil before me . . . saith the Lord. . . . They built the
high places of Baal . . . to cause their sons and their daughters
to pass through the fire unto Molech . . . this abomination . . . [this] sin" (Jeremiah 32:30, 35).

15. "Thou hast taken thy sons and thy daughters . . . and these
hast thou sacrificed unto them to be devoured. . . . Thou
hast slain my children, and delivered them to cause them to
pass through the fire for them" (Ezckicl 16:20–21).

16. "The children rebelled against me; they walked not in my
statutes. . . . Their eyes were after their fathers' idols. . . .
They caused to pass through the fire all their first-born"
(Ezekiel, 20:21, 24, 26).

17. "For thus saith the Lord God: 'Behold, I will deliver thee into
the hand of those whom thou hatest . . . because thou art
polluted with . . . idols . . . and have also caused their

attraction to narrative minimalism was reinforced by their sense that stories should be told in a way that would move directly to the heart of the matter" (1992 Alter, pp. 65–66)

According to Alter, content, style, and the underlying message of the Bible, all account for the enduring fascination of this body of literature. What he writes of biblical literature in general is especially true of the Akedah.

The Bible has invited endless exegesis not only because of the drastic economy of its means of expression but also because it conceives of the world as a place full of things to understand in which the things of ultimate importance defy human understanding. (1992 Alter, p. 22)

Although we can never grasp the whole truth of the Akedah, a valid approach to understanding the story requires we consider the context in which the narrative appears. The Akedah is only one episode of the story of Abraham's preparation to become the father of a Holy People. It is a narrative of a time when animal sacrifice was already the norm and human sacrifice was certainly not unknown, especially in times of crisis. Virtually every theme, aspect, and element of the Akedah appear elsewhere in the Bible. It is in this context that the Akedah story can begin to make sense.

---

sons, whom they bore unto me, to pass for them through the fire, to devour them. . . . When they had slain their children to their idols, then they came the same day into my sanctuary to profane it' " (Ezekiel 23:28, 30, 37, 39).

18. "O Israel, thou hast sinned. . . . And now they sin more and more, and have made them molten images of their silver. . . . Let them that sacrifice men kiss the [molten images of] calves" (Hosea 10:9, 13:2).

19. "Shall I give my first-born for my transgression?" (Micah 6:7).

7

Situation Ethics in the Bible

Sinning for the Sake of God

The Akedah stands on the monumental paradox that God ordered Abraham to commit the gravest of sins, the sacrificial slaughter of a human being. The narrative opens with the words "God tested Abraham" as if to reassure the reader in advance: it was never intended that Isaac actually be slaughtered; this was only a test. Still, it is a paradox that God should ask for the sacrifice of Isaac, and that Abraham—who had argued with God over the destruction of Sodom and Gomorrah—should carry it out without a word of protest.

For centuries, Jews and Christians have agonized over this paradox, and Kierkegaard gave this otherwise nameless predicament an auspicious name: the teleological suspension of the ethical. Jews comforted themselves with the belief that Abraham thus rose to such an exquisite height of obedience to God's will (What other father would slaughter his only beloved son?) so Jews for all generations would inherit a share of Abraham's merit. All of this does not quite dispel the contradiction that God would ask Abraham to perform an act violating so fundamental a law of human civilization.

Yet, what Abraham was ready to do on Mount Moriah was, in essence, no different from what happens in the pages of the

Bible time and time again: sinning for the sake of God. This is a concept, translated from the Hebrew *averah lishmah*, made explicit in the Talmud. There it is written: "A sin for the sake of Heaven is greater than a commandment done not for the sake of Heaven."

Just as secular lore includes the contradictory proverbs "The end justifies the means" and "The end does not justify the means," rabbinical lore includes a rule that says just the opposite of "one may sin for the sake of God." The rule, *mitzvah ha-baa b-avera* means "it is forbidden to commit a sin in order to perform a mitzvah."[1] An example given by Maimonides is that one may not steal a *lulav* in order to properly celebrate Succoth. That is to say, the sin cannot be greater than (or even as great as) the mitzvah it permits.

The Talmud offers one example of sinning for the sake of God, the biblical story of Yael who enticed Sisera into her tent, had sex relations with him, got him drunk, and then drove a tent stake through his head. When Yael seduced the enemy, Sisera, she did so to save the people of Israel. This was a sin for the sake of God, "an act deserving of approval, even though a transgression of the Law of God" (Jerome I. Gellman, p. 35, citing Nazir, 23b; the story of Yael occurs in Judges 4). Following are more biblical examples of sinning for the sake of God, acting contrary to the Law under exceptional circumstances:

> For his own safety, Abraham represented Sarah as his sister and allowed her to live in Pharaoh's household (as Pharaoh's wife?).

> Phineas killed the Simeonite chieftain Zimri and his Midianite mistress. Phineas's action turned away the wrath of God and ended a plague which God had let loose upon Israel because of the Israelites' whoring and idol worship (EJ Zimri).

> Esther had sexual relations with the Persian King, Ahasuerus.

---

1. Thanks to Rabbi David Polish for calling my attention to this principle. It is discussed in Philip Birnbaum's *A Book of Jewish Concepts*, p. 390.

Samson committed suicide when he caused the Philistine Temple to collapse, undermining an adversary of the Israelites and destroying many of Israel's enemies.

God commanded Moses to convey the Tablets of the Law to the people, but Moses smashed them when he saw the people worshipping the golden calf.

When Elijah prepared a sacrifice on Mt. Carmel, it violated a prohibition against sacrifices outside the Temple.

King David worshipped idols when he feared he would be murdered, so the Israelites would not lose their faith if they learned that their king had been murdered. "Better they see a sinful king murdered than a righteous one" (Jerome I. Gellman, p. 64).

The Hasidim broadened the concept of sinning for the sake of God to include forbidden acts committed when immediate circumstances did not excuse it, but when the person had an intuition the ordinarily sinful act was indeed the will of God. This rule would include such biblical acts as the following:

Tamar disguised herself as a prostitute and became pregnant by her newly-widowed father-in-law Judah because he had refused to let her marry Shelah, the younger brother of her late husband. Judah had twin boys, one of whom was the ancestor of King David. According to tradition, Tamar had the gift of prophecy and knew she was destined to be the ancestress of King David (and therefore of the Messiah) and was determined to fulfill her destiny (EJ, Tamar).

King David had an illicit relationship with Bathsheba which produced their son Solomon, who would build the Temple in Jerusalem.

The Hasidic master, Rabbi Mordecai Joseph Leiner of Izbica, (1802–1854), taught "where God wills that we go against the Law, our acts are no longer sinful, even in the eyes of God"

(Jerome I. Gellman, p. 59). It is true Hasidim had a special interest in pardoning certain kinds of sinful behavior.[2]

Sinning for the sake of God is not a concept known only to students of the Talmud or Hasidism; it is an everyday rule of Jewish life. Rabbis have always been willing to relax or even suspend mitzvoth under special circumstances. The preservation of life, for example, justifies all sorts of otherwise forbidden acts: working on the Sabbath, eating forbidden foods, or violating a fast day. Traditionally, when a woman brings a chicken to her rabbi and asks him if it may be eaten or must be discarded, the rabbi first asks himself: "Will a family go hungry if the chicken is ruled *trefe*?" If the answer is Yes, the rabbi is unlikely to demand that the chicken be thrown away.

In 1966, Joseph Fletcher, professor of Social Ethics, Episcopal Theological School, Cambridge, Massachusetts, wrote *Situation Ethics*, which put in writing a rule that had always guided the folk-wisdom: "Circumstances alter cases." Partly because his discussion was couched in Christian rhetoric, Reverend Fletcher's book got a most unsympathetic reception from Jewish thinkers.[3] But a religion that gives rise to the idea one may sin for the sake of God surely recognizes that "circumstances alter cases."

---

2. In the history of Hasidism, sinful acts have been permitted or even encouraged at certain times for certain reasons; for example, to hasten the coming of the Messiah. Rabbi Jacob Joseph Leiner set down a rule "for discerning whether one is indeed acting for the sake of Heaven or acting only in one's self-interest: 'If he does not gain pleasure from the sin itself, which is evil in his eyes, and he is ashamed from the sin, and suffers on account of it, [realizing] that he must do it . . . for the sake of Heaven, then it is permissible'" (Jerome I. Gellman, p. 50).

Commenting on the biblical story of Judah and Tamar, Rabbi Leiner asserts that "God put into them a lustful desire so strong that they were not able to resist it. As it has been said: the angel in charge of lustfulness forced Judah to act." Gellman paraphrases Rabbi Leiner's rule: "an overbearing desire to act in sinfulness is a sign that the act is in accordance with the Divine Will, even if not in accordance with standing Divine commands" (J. Gellman, p. 38).

3. Berkovits denounces *Situation Ethics* as "a desperate attempt to

Have we strayed too far from the issue we addressed at the outset? Does the fact that a poor family may eat a chicken of questionable *kashrut* have anything to do with whether a father might sacrifice his son? Yes, much depends on the circumstances. What kind of circumstances would justify the ritual slaughter of a human being?—very extraordinary circumstances. Chapter 16, "The Disaster Interpretation," includes some speculations about such extreme circumstances that have justified sinning for the sake of God.

---

give some respectability to the everyone-doing-his-own-thing type of life style of a bankrupt civilization" (p. 33).

Gordis is likewise rather unfriendly toward *Situation Ethics* which he describes as "intellectually respectable," but feels it would compound "all ethical problems" rather than solve them (p. 48).

> As each person is confronted by a moral problem, he becomes a battleground for opposing pressures, but there are no principles nor precedents to guide his decisions. Moreover, each man's neighbor is free to come to a different conclusion, since no two situations are completely identical. Finally, in the absence of objective standards, there would be no justification for rewarding one course of action and punishing another, or for establishing various degrees of one or the other—a condition approximating the state of affairs prevailing in our judicial system today. In other words, is our present confusion to be our permanent condition?

By his comments, Gordis reveals he does not understand *Situation Ethics* as Fletcher presented it. Fletcher uses Christian rhetoric, and perhaps that is why neither Berkovits nor Gordis gave him a very close reading. Fletcher writes that the overarching value by which all situations may be judged is Christian love.

Jews should not be frightened by the concept of Christian love and should bear in mind this concept comes right from the Bible— *rahamim, ahava.* "Love thy neighbor; I am the Lord" is inscribed in Leviticus and is part of that chapter's prescription for the behavior appropriate to a Holy People.

The rabbi who is more reluctant to label a chicken as *trefe* if an adverse ruling would make a family go hungry, is taking into consideration his compassion for a poor family; he 'tempers justice with mercy.' *Hesed v'rahamim*—Fletcher could have phrased *Situation Ethics* purely in the language of the Hebrew Bible were he not addressing a Christian constituency.

8

THE POETIC IDIOM OF BIBLICAL HEBREW

Did God Command Abraham to Sacrifice Isaac?

Exhausted, their supply of water gone, Hagar lay a famished and weeping Ishmael under a bush to die. She sat down a short distance away and burst into tears. "An angel of God called to Hagar from heaven and said to her, 'What troubles you, Hagar? Fear not, for God has heeded the cry of the boy. . . .' Then God opened her eyes and she saw a well of water" (Genesis 21:17–19).

Maimonides explained that "God opened her eyes" is only a figurative way of saying Hagar now saw what she had not noticed before (Guide I 44). If that is how Maimonides wants us to interpret "God opened Hagar's eyes," how does he want us to interpret "God spoke to Abraham"? Did it happen as Cecil B. DeMille would film the event—with Abraham standing trance-like, his chin raised, his eyes half-shut, his mouth open, his arms stretched out, while, between thunder claps, a rich baritone voice booms out from behind the clouds? Or is it more likely "God talked to Abraham" in exactly the same way "God opened Hagar's eyes"?

If we take the phrase "God spoke to Abraham" as poetic, figurative language, its literal equivalent would be something

55

like this: Abraham had a problem—a vexing, agonizing problem—and his mind dwelled on it for a long time. Suddenly, he was seized by the thought, "I know exactly what I should do. I am so deeply convinced this is the right thing to do, it is as if I heard God tell me to go ahead and do it." (One might say to Abraham—speaking across the centuries—"You mean your conscience spoke to you." Abraham might answer: "What's the difference?")[1]

Author of "Exposition of Genesis" in *The Interpreter's Bible*, Walter Russell Bowie seems to agree with the above presentation. When we read, "God spoke to Abraham," we are told of something that went on in the mind of Abraham: "an inward voice . . . seemed to press upon his conscience . . . [and] he thought it was the voice of God" (p. 643).

Buttrick likewise appeals to the Bible reader to accept the figurative, poetic nature of biblical language. A literal reading of the Bible, on the other hand, results in "an impossible simplicity," and its characters become not human beings but "blind and helpless instruments of God." The literal-minded reader, says Buttrick, shows "not reverence, but a mild blasphemy, when [it is assumed] that God turns a man into a typewriter [or a robot?]; and certainly [a literal reading] is a disparagement also of human nature. But it seems simple and safe. It lifts from the mind the burden of painful study" (p. 167).

Figurative speech is not peculiar to Genesis; it is the idiom of the Hebrew Bible. To tell us Hanna could not conceive, the Bible says "God had closed Hanna's womb." The Jewish Publication Society translation: "You are most kind to your handmaiden" could more literally be worded: "May your handmaiden find favor in your eyes."

The New English Bible translates Job 7:17–18 as "What is man that thou makest much of him and turnest thy thoughts

---

1. Vauter puts it in these words: "That God said to Abraham that he should take his son and offer him up as a holocaust means that to a man of proven religious sensitivity it once came as an inner conviction that his highest duty required of him to destroy his only heir in service of some greater good" (p. 256).

towards him, only to *punish him* morning by morning or to test him every hour of the day?" (Emphasis added) A more literal translation of the actual Hebrew text would ask, "Why do you *set your heart against him*?"

If the words "God spoke to Abraham" are to be taken figuratively, likewise may we regard the statement "Abraham picked up the knife to slay his son. . . . An angel of the Lord called to Abraham from heaven, telling him, 'Do not raise your hand against the boy, or do anything to him.'" Translated into more literal language, it may be taken to mean "Abraham picked up the knife to slay his son. Suddenly the thought rushed into his mind that God did not want him to raise his hand against the boy, or do anything to him. The thought came to him so forcefully and clearly, it was as if an angel of the Lord called down to him from heaven."[2]

So, Father Abraham, does this mean you were wrong to believe that God wanted you to sacrifice your son on Mount Moriah? "Yes," he might admit; "I was certainly wrong. But obeying my inward voice as I had heard it led me to an experience (my Christian friends would call it an epiphany) that finally revealed to me the true nature of my God. He is not a God who wants this ultimate act of homage; he is a God of love, a God of mercy, to whom each life is precious."

The thesis of this chapter is the phrase "God spoke to Abraham" may be taken to mean "Abraham felt with all his heart that this is what God wanted him to do." This thesis is suggested by a comment made by Maimonides, but is more systematically supported by three Christian biblical scholars: Bowie, Buttrick, and Vauter. This point of view has also been advanced, it should be noted, by Martin Buber in his 1952 analysis of Kierkegaard, published in a French-language journal, *Dieu Vivant*.

---

2. Vauter summarizes and rewords verses 11 and 12: "The Lord's messenger called him from heaven and told him that no such thing was desired of him means that this same man arrived at a new conception of what is pleasing to God, or even, if you will, a new conception of God himself" (p. 256).

If the phrase "God spoke to Abraham" means Abraham felt with all his heart this is what God wanted him to do, Buber argues, this introduces an important ambiguity: Was this indeed God's wish or not? We must always remember that "Molech imitates the voice of God" (1952, p. 73). We must also remember God speaks in "a still, small voice" (I Kings 19:12), and fundamentally God "asks nothing but justice and mercy" (1952, p. 73).

Here, Buber's analysis of the Akedah comes as a response to Kierkegaard's implied question, Dare we, who call ourselves believers, obey what comes to us as the word of God, even though the command may violate our sense of morality? Buber's caution is that a command to sacrifice is always ambiguous. Molech often imitates the voice of God. However, there is no ambiguity about the principle that God asks nothing but justice and mercy.[3]

In the light of what Bowie, Buttrick, Vauter, and Buber have said about the voice of God, a thoughtful reading of the Akedah can lead to the conclusion that perhaps it was *not* the voice of God that asked Abraham to sacrifice his son in the first place. "It was not the will of God that Abraham should sacrifice Isaac," argues Professor Bowie,

> . . . *the nature of God was revealed in the moment when he* [or the angel of God] *stayed Abraham's hand and prevented the sacrifice.* Abraham was not blessed for correctness in his conception of God's will; he was blessed because *when he thought he knew God's will, he was willing to obey it to the limit.*" (p. 645, emphasis added)

---

3. Buber's discussion makes it clear that he is not advising Abraham or passing judgment on Abraham's response to God's command, but is advising young people who say they must sacrifice their own true interests for one reason or another. Buber seems to be saying, "Remember that Molech shouts but God speaks with a still, small voice. Fundamentally, God asks not for sacrifice, but for justice and mercy."

9

Two Portraits of Isaac

To Isaac, the Akedah must have been a most traumatic experience. One midrash states he actually died of fright when Abraham lifted up his knife and was revived by the heavenly voice admonishing Abraham not to slaughter his son (Pirkei de-Rabbi Eliezer 31). According to another midrash, when Isaac was at the altar, he looked directly at the Shekhinah and was blinded (Genesis Rabbah 65:10, Talmud).

Why should the Akedah experience have been more traumatizing to Isaac than to Abraham? First, Abraham was already an old man with a well-established character, and Isaac was only a boy, still in his formative years, psychologically as well as physically. Second, Abraham was playing an active role that was not a threat to his own life; the role of Isaac was both life-threatening and helpless. If the Bible narrative was true-to-life, Isaac would show that his personality had suffered from the Akedah experience. Perhaps this is why the Bible offers only a sketchy and less-than-flattering picture of Isaac. Over the years, various midrashim have generated a clear-cut and heroic figure of an Isaac who looked exactly like his father to silence gossipers who might question Abraham's paternity (Bava Mezia 87a).

THE BIBLICAL ISAAC

The Akedah narrative does not give the reader a vivid picture of Isaac. How old was he at the time? (We know he was old enough to carry a load of wood.) What did he look like? Was he small and boyish, or tall and strong? Auerbach's classical analysis assures us that the absence of descriptive detail is no flaw but serves this important literary effect: to make the spiritual dimension of the event so powerful that physical details become unimportant. Jo Milgrom suggests the Akedah narrative has a mythic nature that distinguishes it from other portions of the Bible[1] (pp. 18–19). The very absence of descriptive detail enables Isaac to stand for all children of whatever age and characteristics, however they get along with their fathers.

The entire life story of Isaac as told in the Bible, in Speiser's words, is "disconnected and meager . . . inconspicuous. . . . Isaac could not have been a memorable personality" (Speiser, lviii). In the Book of Genesis, nothing is said of Isaac's childhood except that he was circumcised (21:4) and that his weaning was celebrated (21:8). In the death and burial of Sarah, Isaac is not even mentioned (23).

W. Gunther Plaut asks, What does the Akedah narrative tell us about the personality of Isaac? "Only once does Isaac speak and ask the fateful question; thereafter he is a mere object of the drama. Abraham, the prince and patriarch, the honored and aged friend of God, overawes his timid son, whose will to independence may well have been crippled by doting and protective parents. He has no personality apart from his father. As one they walk together to the sacrifice, and silently Isaac submits to the dreadful act" (pp. 150–151).

---

1. Auerbach's description of the literary style of the Akedah, Milgrom reminds us, does not characterize the Bible as a whole. Many Bible passages, she assures us, "abound with expansive development" (p. 18).

At the age of forty, Isaac is still unmarried, and Abraham sends a servant to Haran to bring him back a suitable wife (24:4). Until the birth of Esau and Jacob, Isaac's wife, Rebekah, was barren through twenty years of marriage, and Isaac had no concubines (25:20,21,26). When he faced a famine, he wanted to go to Egypt, but "the Lord had appeared to him and said, 'Do not go down to Egypt; stay in the land which I point out to you'" (26:2). Isaac went to Gerar and there, like Abraham, he felt impelled to pass off his wife as his sister, fearing the men of Gerar would murder him in order to possess his wife (26:6–11).

Isaac was a successful herdsman—he possessed many flocks and herds—and was also a success at farming. "Isaac sowed . . . and reaped a hundredfold the same year" (26:12). He must have been a wealthy man with a large retinue. He clashed with the Philistines over water rights, and Abimelech, king of the Philistines in Gerar, visited Isaac in Beersheba where they concluded a pact of mutual nonaggression (26:13–31).

As a father, "Isaac favored Esau because he [Isaac] had a taste for game" (25:28), though Esau's marriage to a Canaanite "was a source of bitterness to Isaac and Rebekah" (26:35). Old Isaac asked Esau to "hunt me some game. Then prepare a dish for me such as I like, and bring it to me to eat, so that I may give you my innermost blessing before I die" (27:1–4). But just as Sarah had favored Isaac, Rebekah now favored Jacob and conspired to substitute a dish of domesticated lamb for a dish of wild game and to obtain Esau's blessing for Jacob. Isaac was "seized with very violent trembling" (27:33) when he learned that he had been deceived, and Esau "wept aloud" (27:38).

It apparently took Rebekah's complaint (27:46) for Isaac to persuade Jacob not to marry a Canaanite woman, and to send Jacob to his brother-in-law, Laban, to find a wife.

Writes Morris Adler: "Nothing spectacular happened to Isaac. He made no particular contribution, no addition to the tradition he received from Abraham; he injected no idea, no startling insight. The tradition arising out of a great intellectual ferment seems, in the life of Isaac, to have reached a plateau . . . He remained loyal, and in all of his actions a tradition was preserved" (Adler, p. 105).

THE MIDRASHIC ISAAC

In Genesis 22 Isaac is a rather passive figure but the rabbinical literature gives him a more positive and even glamorous role. In the Bible story, he is described as a lad and old enough to carry a load of wood. Various midrashim raise his age to twenty-five or thirty-seven. As a mature adult, Isaac would have a mind of his own and would not acquiesce simply because he was his father's son.

Josephus calculated that between the birth of Isaac and the Akedah, Abraham spent twenty-six years in Hebron. The conjecture that Isaac was thirty-seven at the time of the Akedah is based on the midrash that Sarah died in anguish when Satan told her Isaac had actually been sacrificed (Seder Olam Rabbah c.1.). Since it is known that Sarah was ninety when Isaac was born, and said to have died at 127, this makes Isaac 37 at the time of the Akedah.

The Akedah episode was an agonizing experience for Isaac as well as for Abraham. What had Isaac done to deserve this treatment? The sages raised the possibility that Isaac was being punished for an overweening boastfulness about his devotion to God.[2]

Ishmael . . . boasted before Isaac, that he [Ishmael] was circumcised when he was thirteen years old and did not object, whereupon Isaac said to Ishmael, "Thou thinkest to lower my merit on account of what happened to only one member of thy body. If the Almighty had said to me, sacrifice thy whole self unto Me, I would not have hesitated." (Rashi, p. 246)

On their fateful three-day journey, Isaac's only utterance comes as they separate from their servants to climb the

---

2. Wiesel objects that if God were punishing Isaac, He would have spoken to him, which He did not (1995 Lecture).

mountain with wood, firestone, and knife: "Father . . . Here are the firestone and the wood; but where is the sheep for the burnt offering?" (22:7). After Abraham's somewhat evasive answer, there is no further conversation between Abraham and Isaac. Speiser describes this passage as "the most poignant and eloquent silence in all literature" (Speiser, p. 165).

Midrashic retellers of the Akedah were dissatisfied with this silence and have Abraham and Isaac deliver eloquent speeches to each other. Abraham explains what he is doing, and Isaac joyfully agrees to be sacrificed. He asks his father to tie him well so the sacrifice will not be spoiled by an involuntary flinch. In Pseudo-Philo, a Jewish historian of the Hellenistic period, Isaac tells his father he feels honored to serve as a sacrifice to God: "About me generations will be instructed and through me peoples will come to see that the Lord has made the soul of a man worthy to be a sacrifice."[3]

Another midrash describes a very different interaction between father and son: Abraham tells Isaac that *he* is the sheep. Isaac begins to weep and accuses Abraham of lying. "Father, father, so this is the Torah you talked about to my mother Sarah when you said, 'I am going to take him to the schoolmasters.'" At this point Abraham cannot contain himself and breaks down, weeping bitterly and tearing the hairs out of his head and beard. Now Isaac tries to comfort Abraham: "Father, do not be distressed. Come now and carry out the will of your Father in heaven: may it be His will that a quarter of my blood serve as an atonement for Israel" (Spiegel, p. 49).

Three days of journeying gave Isaac ample time to reflect on what was about to happen to him; to resist or escape. (According to legend, Satan warned Isaac he was to be sacrificed.) Since Isaac went willingly to the sacrificial altar, Isaac was not

---

3. Swetnam suggests that these interpolations serve to recast the Akedah into a rallying cry for Jewish youth to go willingly to fight for their faith and risk martyrdom. This is the same motive, Swetnam argues, for advancing Isaac's age from that of a young boy, which the Akedah suggests, to that of a man of fighting age; to inspire young men to risk martyrdom and join the fight against their pagan oppressors.

merely a victim, Jacob Neusner argues, Isaac was a martyr (p. 108). To Neusner, a comparison of Isaac with Jesus is altogether apt. Like Jesus, Isaac was "a willing victim, a weak man, someone who was 'done to' but who did nothing: done in by his times, by his friends, by his father. And he went willingly" (p. 104).

Isaac is the hero of the Akedah, more than Abraham, Neusner argues. Abraham, a man of power and courage, led, and "Isaac went willingly, as Israel through all ages walked willingly with God; through fire and water, through torture and gas, [and] God's will was done to us" (p. 106). "We Jews identify with Isaac, because we see ourselves as the ever-dying people, always on the verge of extinction. So to us life is a gift '*Lehaim* [to life],' is what we say when we drink. Not (merely) to health, but to life" (p. 104).

Midrashim ennoble Isaac to truly glorious heights: the angel of death had no power over him, the evil inclination had no influence on him, and his body was never devoured by worms (Bava Batra 17a). According to *Encyclopedia Judaica*, the midrashic Isaac becomes "the patriarch possessing the deepest feelings and compassion for his descendants . . . [and] he pleads for them even when they are sinful."

10

WHAT ABOUT SARAH?

The stark simplicity of Genesis 22 omits many aspects of the event, including whatever might be noted about Sarah's role in the Akedah story. Is it possible that Sarah, who so fiercely defended Isaac's patrimony as to demand the banishment of Hagar and Ishmael, knew nothing about the momentous command Abraham had received from God?

Indeed, there does not seem to be a single known midrash that suggests Abraham consulted with her or had advised her of his momentous journey. An anonymous thirteenth century Jewish writer describes the following dialogue between Abraham and Sarah. Before taking Isaac to Moriah, Abraham says to Sarah, "My son Isaac is grown up, and he has not yet studied the service of God. Now, tomorrow, I will bring him to Shem and Eber his son, and there he will learn the ways of the Lord."

Sarah replies: "You have spoken well; go, my lord, and do with him as you have said, but do not take him far from me, or let him remain there too long, for my soul is bound up with his soul. . . . If the child is hungry, give him bread, and if he is thirsty give him some water; don't let him go on foot, or allow him to sit in the sun."[1]

However, the rabbis were sure the news of the Akedah, when it reached her after the fact, killed her. So sure were the rabbis that Sarah's death immediately followed the Akedah, they used this "fact" to calculate the age of Isaac at the time of the Akedah. Since Isaac was born when Sarah was believed to be 90, and she died at the age of 127, the rabbis calculated that Isaac was 37 years old (127 minus 90) at the time of the Akedah. Rabbis regarded this conjecture as a fact, despite repeated references to Isaac in the Akedah story as a boy or lad.

The absence of Sarah from the Akedah story has been duly observed by Christian scholars, consistent with their predeliction for finding moral flaws in the Old Testament. Visotzky popularized the recent discovery of a sixth century Greek liturgical poet, Romanos, who gave voice to the unrecorded words of Sarah. If she had known of Abraham's planned sacrifice of Isaac, this is what she might have said:

> If He who first gave the child takes it back, why did He offer him at all? Do you, old man, leave what is mine with me, and when He who called you wants him, He will reveal it to me. He who first of all indicated his birth by means of an angel will again reveal to me his death. I will not entrust the child to you. I will not give him to you. (Visotzky, p. 83)

Romanos's story continues with Abraham's warning to Sarah that God "has the power to slay him even in your arms. Therefore show your willingness and send him off" (Visotzky, p. 83). Now Sarah, in the Greek poet's imagination, expresses hope in Isaac's resurrection if he is slain, as she addresses Isaac:

> If He desires you for life, He will give orders that you live; He who is immortal will not kill you. . . . Go, then, my child, and be a sacrifice to God, go with you father—or rather your slayer.

---

1. This imaginary dialogue is from *Sefer Ha-Yashar*, an anonymous thirteenth century book "on Jewish ethics; love and fear of God, repentance, prayer, and good deeds" (EJ).

But I have faith that your father will not become your slayer, for the savior of our souls alone is good. As you leave your mother, you will find your true father, God the Lord of all. He will reveal to me that you are alive, after you have been slain; even if it is not in the present, He will reveal it in the future. (Visotzky, p. 84)

Finally, in Romanos's retelling of the Akedah story, when Sarah sees Isaac return unharmed, she swoons with joy and dies, saying: "May He who has shown you to me once more now receive my spirit" (Visotzky, p. 84).

Visotzky draws upon two fifth-century Syriac homilies to reconstruct the following Akedah story, also told from Sarah's point of view (perhaps one or both were authored by women):

[When she saw Abraham set off on a journey with Isaac] . . . terror seized her, and she spoke as follows: "Where are you taking my only begotten? Where is the child of my vows off to? Reveal to me the secret of your intention and show me the journey on which you are both going. Never has there been a time when I held you back from the performance of what is good. . . . But now when you have in mind a journey, why is the child going with you, and why are you not revealing your secret to Sarah your faithful wife who in all the hardships of exile has borne trials along with you?" (Ibid, pp. 85–86)

[Abraham says he and Isaac are going to slaughter a lamb. Sarah replies:] "If it is a sheep you are wanting to see to, be off . . . [but] leave the child behind lest something happen and untimely death meet him, for I am being unjustly deprived of the single son to whom I have given birth. Let not the eye of his mother be darkened, seeing that after one hundred years light has shone out for me. You are drunk with the love of God—who is your God and my God—and if He so bids you concerning the child you would kill him without hesitation." (Ibid, p. 86)

[She intuits that Abraham, "drunk with the love of God," does indeed intend to sacrifice Isaac, and she begs:] "Let me go up with you to the burnt offering and let me see my only child being sacrificed; if you are going to bury him in the ground, I will dig the hole with my own hands, and if you are going to build up stones, I will carry them on my shoulders; the lock of my white hairs in old age will provide for his bonds. But if I cannot go up to see my only child being sacrificed I will remain at the foot of the mountain until you have sacrificed him and come back." (Ibid, pp. 86–87)

Sarah took her only child and began to speak with him as follows, words full of wonder and with a groan: "When you go with your father, listen and do all that he tells you, and if he should actually bind you, stretch out your hands to the bonds, and if he should actually sacrifice you, stretch out your neck before his knife, stretch out your neck like a lamb, like a kid before the shearer. See, my son, that you do not [upset] your father . . . lest . . . there be a blemish in his offering. And listen, my son, to the words of your mother, and let your reputation go forth unto generations to come." (Ibid, p. 87)

[Abraham and Isaac return home together, but father asks son to wait outside while he enters the house alone. Believing that her son has been sacrificed, Sarah prays:] "May the soul of my child be accepted, for he hearkened to the words of his mother. I was wishing I was an eagle or had the speed of a turtledove, so that I might go and behold that place where my only child, my beloved, was sacrificed, that I might see the place of his ashes and see the place of his binding, and might bring back a little of his blood to be comforted by its smell. I had some of his hair to place somewhere inside my clothes, and when grief overcame me I placed it over my eyes. I had some of his clothes so that I might imagine him, putting them in front of my eyes, and when suffering sorrow overcame me I gained relief through gazing upon them. I wish I could see his pyre and the place where his bones were burnt and could bring a little of his ashes and gaze on them always and be comforted." (Ibid, pp. 87–88)

[When Isaac, safe and sound, enters the house, Sarah utters these words of thanksgiving:] "I give thanks to God who has given you to me a second time; I do obeisance to that voice which deliverd you, my son, from the knife. I praise Him who saved you from the knife. I praise Him who saved you from burning on the pyre. Henceforth, my son, it will not be 'Sarah's son' that people will call you, but . . . [the] 'offering which died and was resurrected.' And to You be glory, O God, for all passes away, but you endure." (Ibid, p. 88)

As Visotzky notes, when Sarah calls Isaac the "offering which died and was resurrected," she defines the Akedah as a prefiguration of the crucifixion and resurrection (Vizotzky, pp. 85–88). Do these Christian retellings also point a finger of criticism at the Akedah story for neglecting to recognize Sarah's role in the event? Could Genesis 22 have been so written as to involve Isaac's mother as well as his father?

The present-day Christian feminist movement has justified a fresh and vigorous wave of criticism of the Old Testament, lambasting the patriarchs for deviating from late twentieth century standards of sexual equality![2] Professor Trevor Dennis, vice-principal at Salisbury and Wells Theological College, is equally vigorous in his attack on Abraham and in his defense of Sarah.

> Abraham was turned into a saint by the Jewish theologians of the period between the Old and New Testaments. . . . In Genesis itself they [Abraham and Sarah] are fully rounded characters, subtly drawn, with their strengths matched—one is tempted to say *more* than matched by their weaknesses. (p. 35)

Dennis has little use for the Abraham who says Sarah is his sister and permits her to be taken into Pharaoh's household. The biblical narrative (12:10–20) puts Abraham "on a high pedestal of obedience and faith . . . [but] knocks him onto the floor and puts a pharaoh's boot on his back for good measure" (p. 37).

> There is something of a rags to riches story about this, and there is also a somewhat coarse and very male humor at work. Look what this 'simple nomad' has got from the pharaoh! . . . We have been taught over the years not to expect humor in the Bible. In fact, there is plenty of it, at least in the Old Testament, and I feel sure it is intended here. Yet, if we persist in looking at this story from Sarai's angle, we will not find it funny at all. (p. 39)

Dennis tips his hand in his choice of words when he rephrases the opening line of Genesis 22:

---

2. See the discussion on presentism, Chapter 6, note 1.

God has now commanded Abraham to take the child who is *her* son also and slit his throat. . . . Sarah is not even mentioned once from beginning to end. Neither God's previous record of communicating with Sarah, nor Abraham's, would lead us to think she knows anything at all. . . . [Sarah] does not share in her husband's glory. She has no chance here or anywhere else in her story to prove herself a woman of conspicuous faith and obedience. God has made no demands of *her*. . . . In these ancestral narratives she is an abused woman, and in the end, after all too brief a moment of joy, a wholly tragic character. (pp. 60–61)

Another feminist voice is that of Colleen Ivey Hartsoe. In her "Christian midrash" on the Akedah, Hartsoe shows Sarah reacting with horror, screaming and weeping, when Abraham tells her of God's command that he offer up Isaac. Sarah "said words [she] dared not utter before."

You told me it was God's will I should leave my home and my family. You told me it was God's will I should go to the bed of Pharaoh. You told me it was God's will that you have a son and I humiliated myself and a young slave-girl that Ishmael might be conceived. And now you tell me it is God's will our son must die? Abraham, Abraham, it is your own guilt speaking to you. Because you sent Ishmael into the wilderness you think giving up Isaac will atone for your sin.[3] I do not know the God that speaks to you, Abraham. I know a God who rescued me from Pharaoh's harem, a God who gave me a son in my old age, a God who kept Hagar and Ishmael safe even as you and I sinned against them. That is the God whom I worship. (pp. 13–14)

In the Hartsoe retelling, Abraham silently leaves the tent and takes Isaac on their journey. When her husband and son finally return, Sarah holds her child in her arms and thanks God for staying the hand of Abraham. Now God speaks to Sarah, telling

---

3. Note that Hartsoe gives verisimilitude to the arguments of Polish and Marc Gellman, that the Akedah was a punishment to Abraham for the expulsion of Ishmael. See Chapter 12, "The Atonement Interpretation."

her that she understands the will of God better than Abraham. (Hartsoe doesn't call herself a feminist for nothing!)[4]

> Sarah, I did speak to Abraham today, but not there on the hill. It was through you I spoke. You knew I could not want a small boy as a burnt offering. It is you that have understood sin, forgiveness, and love. (Hartsoe, pp. 13–14)

The Jewish feminist Alicia Suskin Ostriker likewise finds the absence of Sarah from the Akedah story extremely significant. In the chapters of Genesis that precede the Akedah, Ostriker accurately notes, Sarah emerges as "aggressive, wilful, protective of her perogatives, a lively and formidable personality" (p. 40). All the more reason that Sarah's absence from the Akedah story must mean something important.

It's as simple as this, according to Ostriker: the main object of the Akedah was to demonstrate that Abraham could do exactly what he pleased with Isaac, regardless of what Sarah might have said, regardless of the fact that "Isaac is her son" as well as Abraham's (p. 41).

Ostriker argues that the Akedah documents a struggle to demolish the primordial Mother-Goddess figure and replace it with a Father-God, sponsored and defended by a patriarchal society. Ostriker argues there was no need for an Akedah story "to end human sacrifice" since there was no human sacrifice problem at the time of Abraham (p. 39). The purpose of the Akedah story was to demonstrate Father Abraham could do what he wished with Isaac, and Sarah had no power to influence these events. Biblical patriarchy was bent upon "the silencing of women," according to Ostriker, and the Akedah was fashioned to serve that purpose (p. 31).

There is a significance, to Ostriker, in Abraham's twice-repeated comments to the Hittite land-sellers; he was looking for a burial site where he could "bury my dead out of my sight"

---

4. Do Dennis and Hartsoe typify the Christian feminist thrust? If so, their analysis is seriously flawed by the error of presentism and gives an impression of thinly-disguised Old Testament bashing.

(23:4,8). According to Ostriker Sarah's influence had to be disposed of; that is the meaning of the Akedah.[5]

Delivering a moral message (whether it was remotely connected to the feminist hypotheses or not) was indeed the primary intent of the Bible. However, the writers of the Bible were also master storytellers, as Alter takes pains to point out. Therefore, the stark simplicity of the Akedah story, with aspects untold or veiled (including the Sarah story), enables the reader or listener to fill in details and complete the story with the imagination. Hence, there is an omission of detail including, what to Ostriker and others, is important detail and the presence of an air of mystery, including Isaac's ignorance about what would happen next.

If Sarah knew about Abraham's momentous decision as the feminists insist she should have, how could her response to this truly terrible news, whether it took the form of support or protest, keep the goal of Abraham's journey a secret from Isaac? Perhaps Sarah's innocence of Abraham's intent, as well as Isaac's innocence until the last moment, adds to the suspense and mystery and are therefore necessary ingredients of the story as a suspenseful, compelling story. (In the Koranic retelling of the Akedah, Abraham does take Isaac into his confidence. Does this weaken the Akedah as a story?) Perhaps the secrecy is also theologically necessary since God was testing Abraham, after all, not Isaac and not Sarah.

---

5. Ostriker's analysis of the Akedah is consistent with her general view that "the biblical story of monotheism and covenant is, to use the language of politics, a cover-up . . . [to neutralize] female power. Biblical patriarchy . . . [commits] repeated acts of literal murder and oppression . . . for its triumph. . . . [T]he canonization process throughout history has rested, not accidentally but essentially, on the silencing of women" (pp. 30–31). Ostriker labels "'the Judeo-Christian tradition' . . . *a pathological culture*" and sets as her goal its "radical transformation" (p. 39, emphasis added). Given this rather paranoid attitude toward the ancient Hebrews and the Bible as a whole, the tone of her analysis of the Akedah is altogether predictable.

11

ENTER SATAN

If Genesis 22 is such an artistic masterpiece, why has the narrative been supplemented with so many legends and rabbinical midrashim, which fill in all the gaps and thus undo the artistic ambiguity critics find so enchanting? Educated tastes are different from popular tastes, and the literary standards of one generation are different from those of another.

It is safe to say, in the main, the midrashim did not spring from rabbinical seminars. They did not originate from rabbinical efforts to make explicit the implicit truths in the Bible. Rather, the midrashim seem to have been, to a large extent, a product of popular education—rabbis talking to common folks whose knowledge of Hebrew was nonexistent or limited, and who needed to have the Bible stories retold to them in the vernacular. "Retelling" began as translation, and translation led to interpolations of all sorts. New characters were introduced. New dialogue was added to make motivations plain and to lighten the demand on the listener's imagination—to fit the story into the listener's conceptual world.

Genesis Rabbah, meaning an enlarged Genesis, is a treasury of legends surrounding the Book of Genesis, chapter by chapter, verse by verse. It was probably edited in the fifth and sixth centuries in Palestine and brought together exegeses (explanations), stories, parables, and sermons, drawn from both written and oral sources. The first printed edition of Genesis Rabbath was published in Constantinople in 1512, and various scholarly, critical editions have been published over the centuries. (This chapter makes use of Ginzberg's classic *Legends of the Jews*. Except as noted, all Ginzberg citations are from Midrash Genesis Rabbah.)

Now, what does all of this have to do with Satan? The fact is Satan is totally absent from Genesis 22, but he emerges as an extremely popular character in Genesis Rabbah. Why? Satan fills in the gaps, he puts doubts and misgivings into the minds of mortals and even into the mind of God. Satan is a busybody who runs back and forth—from heaven to earth, from Isaac, to Abraham, to Sarah—doing his best to expose the characters' weaknesses and unravel the story.

In a sixteenth century Yiddish sixty-four-verse retelling of the Akedah, Abraham Hökscher of Hamburg gave Satan an even more mischievous role than he is given in Genesis Rabbah. Hökscher's elaborations are footnoted throughout this chapter.[1]

Although Satan has no place in Genesis 22 (or in the entire book of Genesis), it is easy for a biblical storyteller to lift Satan from the Book of Job and give him a similar role in the Akedah. In Job, Satan is made responsible for taunting God to put to the test a man of righteousness. In the retelling of the Akedah, the testing of Abraham is similarly the result of Satan's taunting God. This midrash gave rabbis a ready-made answer to the perennial questions, "Why did God *want* to test Abraham?" "Why did God *need* to test Abraham?"

[When Abraham and Sarah celebrated the birth of Isaac with a great banquet, a beggar appeared at their door and they failed

---

1. Hökscher's "Akedass Yitschak" appears in transliterated Yiddish on pages 107–138 of Wulf-Otto Dreessen's *Akedass Jizhak* (Leibniz-Verlag, 1971). According to Dreessen, Hökscher drew upon *va-Yosha*, a medieval midrash, and the work of an unknown poet of the early fifteenth century.

to notice him. It was Satan in one of his favorite guises. He then came before God and accused Abraham of ingratitude. God disagreed.] And the Lord said to Satan: "As I live, were I to say unto him, Bring up Isaac thy son before Me, he would not withhold him from Me, much less if I told him to bring up a burnt offering before Me from his flocks of herds." And Satan answered the Lord, and said, "Speak now unto Abraham as Thou hast said, and Thou wilt see whether he will not transgress and cast aside Thy words this day." (Ginzberg, I, 273)

Bin-Gorion relates the midrash that as soon as Abraham was asked to sacrifice Isaac, he hid his boy so Satan could not find him and somehow injure him, which would render Isaac unfit for use as a sacrifice (p. 123).

When Abraham took Isaac to Mount Moriah, obeying God's command, Satan met Abraham along the road.[2] Again, Satan was disguised as an old man and he begged Abraham to spare Isaac, for an order to slaughter him was so evil, Satan argued, it could never be the will of God. Abraham knew this was Satan, and Abraham rebuked him.

[Said Satan to Abraham:] "Art thou silly or foolish, that thou goest to do this thing to thine only son? God gave thee a son in thy latter days, in thine old age, and wilt thou go and slaughter him, who did not commit any violence, and wilt thou cause the soul of thy only son to perish from the earth? Dost thou not know and understand that this thing cannot be from the Lord?" (Ginzberg, I, 276–77)

Not easily discouraged, Satan returned as a handsome young man and whispered to Isaac that his father was a silly old man who was about to slaughter him.[3] Isaac told his father,

---

2. Hökscher's Satan asks Abraham where he is going, and Abraham answers: "To do my prayers." Satan replies: "In no country is it a custom [that] / When someone wants to pray to Ha Kadosh, Boruch Hu, / That he takes along wood, fire, and a slaughtering knife."

3. Hökscher's Satan warns Isaac: "Your young blood will be spilled and spoilt! / Turn around, go back to your mother, / Who in her old age, and with pain, bore you!"

who warned Isaac that this was Satan "endeavoring to lead us astray from the commands of God."

> [Said Satan to Isaac:] "Dost thou not know that thy silly old father bringeth thee to slaughter this day for naught? . . . Let not thy precious soul and beautiful figure be lost from the earth." And Isaac told these words to his father, but Abraham said to him, "Take heed of him and do not listen to his words, for he is Satan endeavoring to lead us astray from the commands of our God." (Ginzberg, I, 277)

Ingenious fellow, Satan now "transformed himself into a large brook of water in the road" to induce Abraham to turn back. As Abraham and his party walked through the water, it became deeper and deeper. Abraham knew this land and the brook must be the doing of Satan. Abraham sternly rebuked Satan, and the water vanished.[4]

> [Said Abraham:] "I know this place, on which there was no brook nor water. Now, surely, it is Satan who doeth all this to us, to draw us aside this day from the commands of God." And Abraham rebuked Satan, saying unto him, "The Lord rebuke thee, O Satan. Begone from us, for we go by the command of God." And Satan was terrified at the voice of Abraham . . . and the place became dry land again as it was at first. And Abraham went with Isaac toward the place that God had told him. (Ginzberg, I, pp. 277–78)

If Satan could not alter the course of events, he could at least be a troublemaker. So Satan went to Sarah and told her that her only son was about to be sacrificed. Sarah trembled,[5] but expressed her faith that if this was God's command to Abraham, "may he do it unto life and unto peace."

---

4. In Hökscher's ballad, "God punished Satan most horribly, / By forcing him to drink all the water. / He drank until his belly . . . was huge and full."

5. In Hökscher's ballad, Sarah does more than tremble; "She was terrified and fainted, / And her body collapsed."

[Satan asked Sarah:] "Where did thine husband go?" She said, "To his work." "And where did thy son Isaac go?" . . . "He went with his father to a place of study of the Torah." Satan said: "O thou poor old woman, thy teeth will be set on edge on account of thy son, as thou knowest not that Abraham took his son with him on the road to sacrifice him." In this hour Sarah's loins trembled, and all her limbs shook. She was no more of this world. Nevertheless she aroused herself, and said, "All that God hath told Abraham, may he do it unto life and unto peace." (Ginzberg, I, p. 278, from Midrash va-Yosha, 36)

Paradoxically, one could conclude Satan was more of an influence on God than on Abraham and Isaac. Just what was the role of Satan? He was an angel-prosecutor who challenged and tested. Satan was no Power of Darkness. He had no power to do evil; he liked to make it difficult (but he could not make it impossible) to do the will of God. When Abraham Goldfaden based a popular Yiddish opera on the Akedah narrative (see chapter 23), the performance was enlivened by the impish words and doings of Satan. If the Akedah were ever made into an animated cartoon, Satan would be an important and lively character: meddling into everything and symbolizing the doubts, the misgivings that haunt every ordinary human being. The baser side of human nature is Satan, and the rabbis apparently believed Abraham, Isaac, and Sarah (like the rabbis themselves?) had a baser, as well as a nobler side.

PART II

SIX INTERPRETATIONS OF THE AKEDAH

12

THE ATONEMENT INTERPRETATION

To the reader, the Akedah is a story, a wonder, a mystery; to Abraham, the Akedah was an agonizing experience. Was Abraham (or Isaac?) being punished? For what were they being punished? In his eleventh-century commentary, Rashi raises this question not as an original thought, but as one that the sages were well familiar with. Was Isaac being punished for boasting about his devotion to God (a midrash recounted in Chapter 9)? Was Abraham being punished for acquiescing too readily to Sarah's demand to expel Hagar and Ishmael? In recent years two American writers, David Polish and Marc Gellman, have revived this midrash.

"After these things" according to Polish, implies that God commanded Abraham to sacrifice Isaac **because of something that happened**. What happened? Had Abraham done something terribly wrong, something he deserved to be punished for? Let's look at his expulsion of Hagar and Ishmael, says Polish—not a pretty story.

Sarah demanded that Abraham banish Hagar and Ishmael to protect Isaac's patrimony. Abraham was troubled by Sarah's request. "And the thing was very grievous to Abraham on account of his son" [Ishmael]" (verse 11). However, Abraham says nothing; he does not speak his mind. Abraham, who spoke up for the sinners of Sodom and Gomorrah, says nothing about banishing his own son and his mother, putting them in mortal danger! True, God counseled Abraham not to be troubled and to do Sarah's bidding, but "the brutality of this deed [must have preyed] endlessly on his conscience" (1957, p. 19).

In Genesis Rabbah 54:2, Polish notes, the rabbis acknowledge "the tragedy of Abraham's act" and ask, "How does it look to outsiders?" "The nations of the world said, 'If he were truly righteous, he would not heed his wife by expelling his son. . . . If he were truly righteous, he would not expel his eldest son'" (1957, p. 19).

Abraham committed a great wrong, a betrayal, an unspeakable deed. "Abraham cannot get Ishmael out of his mind. *He is answering with Isaac because of Ishmael,*" writes Polish (emphasis added). To Abraham, God's summons means "Take [Isaac] as you once took Ishmael whom you still love" (1957, p. 20).

Continues Polish, Isaac shares the burden of guilt. As they walk together to Moriah, Isaac "is silent because he was silent when his brother had been taken away. . . . He was old enough to realize that because of him, his brother was being disinherited and driven forth" (1957, p. 21).

From this standpoint, the Akedah is a test "not so much of Abraham's loyalty to God but of his capacity . . . to push back the black tide of evil which he had once allowed to engulf him." The Akedah is an act of atonement—Abraham sheds the burden of his guilt and discovers "a new and more compassionate God," a God of mercy and forgiveness (1957, p. 21).

Nineteen years after the publication of Polish's article, Marc Gellman expanded on the same midrash, writing in more emotionally-charged language. Gellman describes Sarah's request as a "vicious demand for usurpation and murder [sic]," which Abraham answers "not with outrage, not a screaming denunciation, not even a simple 'no,'; but rather displeasure. . . . From what God saw, the progenitor of the Jewish people was nothing more than a weak-willed accomplice in murder" (p. 40).

What of God's reassuring words to Abraham to let Sarah have her way?

> God said to Abraham, "Do not be distressed about the boy, or about your slave woman. Do whatever Sarah tells you, for it is through Isaac that your line shall be continued. And as for the maid's son, I will make of him also a great nation, for he too is your offspring. (21:13)

Oh, *that?* Don't you recognize sarcasm when you see it? Gellman seems to say. "God's response drips with irony and sarcasm." It is as if God were saying, "Listen to that jealous conniving person, not to the one true God!" (Gellman's interpretation of Genesis 21:13 is a distinctly minority view.)

Gellman arrives at the obvious conclusion that the Akedah "was compelled by Abraham's vacillation at the murder of his wife Hagar and his son Ishmael."

> The willingness to kill Ishmael, however slight and momentary, created the necessity for the commanded murder [*sic*] of Isaac. The sacrifice of the least loved led inexorably to the testing of the willingness to sacrifice the best loved. (p. 41)

Finally, Martin Buber also touches on the atonement motif in his discussion of Genesis 22. Buber suggests the command to sacrifice Isaac was given "as if to actively atone for that moment of doubt" which is recorded in Genesis 15 (1968 Buber, p. 41).

> The Lord came to Abram in a vision, saying, "Fear not, Abram. . . . Your reward shall be very great." But Abram said, "O Lord God, what can You give me, seeing that I shall die childless. . . ." [God promises that] "your very own issue shall be your heir," [your offspring shall be as numberless as the stars, and this land shall be your possession. Abraham asks,] *"How shall I know that I am to possess it?"* (15:1-8, emphasis added.)

It seems God is saying to Abraham, "You, who doubted My word when I promised that 'your very own issue shall be your heir,' now you must relive this doubt with greater intensity, and then I will show you what your God promises, you can believe." Thus, through the Akedah Abraham atoned for his moment of doubt about God's power to fulfill His promises.

The liturgy of the Rosh Hashana, which ushers in the Day of Atonement, includes a reading of the Akedah, suggesting Abraham's act might have been an act of atonement. The blowing of the *shofar* symbolizes the horn of the ram that was sacrificed in place of Isaac. The prayers of the Day of Atonement plead that the merit which Abraham earned (for atonement or for obedience?) redound to the benefit of all generations of Israel. More on the Akedah in prayer, and the merits of the fathers in Chapter 18.

13

THE MARTYRDOM INTERPRETATION

Referring to the Nazi slaughter of six million Jews during World War II, Richard L. Rubenstein writes, "For those of us who have lived through the terrible years, whether in safety or as victims, the *Shoah* conditions the way we encounter all things sacred and profane" (1992, p. 200). Like Martin Buber who wrote of the eclipse of God, many Jewish thinkers confess they cannot see any clear message in this horrifying event about the ways of God or the nature of God.

Emil Fackenheim offers an explanation which may seem plausible only because we know it did in fact happen, but we must "confront its ultimate inexplicability" (1978b, p. 233). Struggling for an explanation, Irving Howe confesses he can only stare helplessly at this "mystery of mass extermination."

> Our subject resists the usual capacities of mind. We may read the Holocaust as the central event of this century; we may register the pain of its unhealed wounds; but finally we must acknowledge that it leaves us intellectually disarmed, staring helplessly at the reality or, if you prefer, the mystery of mass extermination. . . . Neither encompassing theory nor religious

faith enables us to reach a firm conviction that now, at last, we understand what happened during the "Final Solution." (Lang, p. 175)

What is a profound mystery to some seems to be perfectly clear to others, including Jacob Neusner. His interpretation of the Holocaust is particularly relevant because he relates this event directly to the Akedah. In fact, says Neusner, "No passage of Scripture so demands a reading in the light of the Holocaust as does [the Akedah]. For Abraham had to be ready to give one, but mothers and fathers in our own times gave all. And Abraham was commanded by God, but Israel in our own time was compelled by Satan" (p. 108).

Neusner quotes from Genesis 22:2 "Take your son . . . and offer him . . . as a burnt offering." By these words, God describes himself as a "demanding, incomprehensible God, one who gives and takes away." Neusner describes a God who demands the renunciation of one's most natural wishes, a God who is totally incomprehensible in terms of everyday logic (p. 105).

Describing "a God who gives and takes away," Neusner seems to be leading up to his observation that out of the Holocaust was reborn the state of Israel.

In this rebirth of the Jewish state we see . . . the resurrection of Israel, the ever-dying people, out of the gas chambers of Europe.[1] The binding of Isaac today stands for the renewal of Israel in its life as a state and in its life, throughout the world, as

---

1. Here Neusner suggests that the Holocaust was God's mysterious way of bringing into being the state of Israel. Fackenheim denounces any such interpretation as blasphemy:

A good Jewish secularist will connect the Holocaust with the rise of the State of Israel, but while to see a causal connection here is possible and necessary, *to see a purpose is intolerable.* A total and uncompromising sweep must be made of these and other explanations, all designed to give purpose to Auschwitz. No purpose, religious or non religious, will ever be found in Auschwitz. *The very attempt to find one is blasphemous.* (1987(b), page 163, emphasis added)

a people. It is as though we have died and been reborn, for if truth be told, we have died and we have been reborn. Our renewal is just as miraculous to us as the resurrection of the dead. . . . No wonder then, that we find in the details of the binding of Isaac, as our sages read it, an account of what has happened to us and what is happening to us, in the here and now." (p. 114)

"We have died and have been reborn." With these words, Neusner comes close to saying the Akedah and the Holocaust are both events of martyrdom, and these events also have something in common with the crucifixion of Jesus. Neusner notes the sages transparently compared Isaac to Jesus—"like one who carries his own cross on his shoulder." The sages also compared Isaac "to one who rose from the dead on the third day" (p. 107). To Neusner, Jesus was a "new Isaac."[2]

To Neusner, *martyrdom* is the one word that describes the Holocaust. His description of the Holocaust tends both to sanctify the Jews and demonize the Germans and their allies.[3]

The Germans sent the mothers and the children from the freight car to the gas chamber, and the mother had to choose which of her children she would hold in her arms, as she and the child suffocate in the gas. . . . No wonder, then, that after

---

2. Neusner elaborates on the Isaac-Jesus parallel: "In the same story of the binding of Isaac on the altar Israel finds itself, in that same story the church finds Jesus Christ. Isaac arose from the altar and lived, and Jesus Christ arose from the cross and lived" (p. 104). In fairness to Neusner, it should be added that the context of these comments was a book Neusner co-authored with Andrew Greeley, and addressed to both a Christian and a Jewish readership.

3. [Of the perpetrators of the Holocaust, Neusner writes:] "It was intentional, it was planned, it was deliberate, and *forgive them not, O God, for they knew exactly what they were doing*. The German Nazis and their many allies, large numbers of them faithful Christians, also read the Torah, which they call the Old Testament of the Bible, and they turned it against Israel in Europe; in very cruel ways. Many of their acts of massacre, which they called actions, took place on Jewish holy days, for instance (p. 114, emphasis added).

the war we found scraps of paper, prayers to God: "Abraham chose one and was ready to offer him but didn't, and I chose them all and they all died." (p. 102)[4]

In all the stories of the dignity of the victim of the Holocaust, the ones I find most moving are the memories of families, with the men selected for killing labor, the women and children for immediate killing. "I remember them, as they walked off hand in hand." "The last sight I had of my wife and my daughter was their walking toward the gas chambers, hand in hand." "I remember his little red coat, as he ran after his mother." These are not victims alone, they are martyrs: "God will provide himself the lamb for a burnt offering." (p. 109)

Neusner's thesis that the Akedah provides the key to under-standing the Holocaust rests on his conviction that the Akedah conveys the theme of martyrdom. There is, of course, a good deal of disagreement on this interpretation of the Akedah. Many would insist a classic interpretation is that God does *not* want human sacrifice. Among contemporary Jewish scholars, Elie Wisel[5] is particularly strong in insisting the Akedah does not convey the theme of martyrdom.

Had he killed his son, Abraham would have become the forefather of a people—but not the Jewish people (p. 76).

In the Jewish tradition man cannot use death as a means of glorifying God (p. 76).

---

4. The dean of Holocaust historians, Professor Raul Hilberg writes, "I am not aware of any such scraps of paper having been found anywhere" (Personal communication).

5. Ironically, Elie Wiesel is credited with popularizing the term *the Holocaust* to describe the genocide of Europe's Jews, suggesting the concept of martyrdom. He first used the term in a book review in October 1963. Wiesel lived in Paris for some years after World War II, and the term *l'holocauste"* was used in France to describe the carnage of World Wars I and II. Wiesel probably picked up the term in his Paris years. In 1980, he told an interviewer, "If I had known [*the Holocaust*] would become the word that would envelope all others, I am not so sure I would have chosen it" (Garber, p. 1884).

For the Jew, all truth must spring from life, never from death" (p. 76).

The idea that suffering is good for Jews is one that owes its popularity to our enemies (p. 79).

The Akedah conveys the theme of martyrdom most clearly not in Genesis 22, but in those midrashim that modify the narrative to say Isaac did in fact die and was resurrected—he died and was resurrected immediately; he died and rose to heaven and after some time returned to earth. Midrashic variants differ in exactly how the Akedah is reinterpreted to become an ode to martyrdom.

Our search for the source of this reinterpretation of the Akedah takes us to the story of Hannah and her seven sons. This story first appears in Chapter 7 of Maccabees II and is elaborated in Maccabees IV, books which are thoroughly Greek both in style and in sentiment, written by and for Jews of the Greek world around 40 C.E.

Jews of the Greek world were thoroughly immersed in Greek culture[6] and understood its emphasis on the social value of martyrdom, which was celebrated in the tragic dramas, poems, and funeral orations of ancient Greece. Maccabees II and IV are excellent examples of how thoroughly Jews of the Greek world understood the Greek way of life and were masters of Greek eloquence and richness of detail.[7]

---

6. The first translation of the Bible was made for the sake of the Jews in the Greek world. The Septuagint was the name given to the Greek translation of the Hebrew Bible, completed in the 3rd century B.C.E. by a team of about seventy Hebrew scholars. (Hence the name Septuagint.) The fact that this massive project was undertaken and completed implies two things: (a) the population of Hellenized Jews was considerable; and (b) their knowledge of Hebrew was poor or nonexistent. The influence of the Septuagint is felt by the persistence of Greek names for the books of the Bible: Genesis, Deuteronomy, Leviticus, etc.

7. The following excerpt conveys the style of Maccabees IV. As he was flogged and "racked until his limbs were out of joint," the eldest

Maccabees II and IV record in agonizing detail the death by excruciating torture suffered by each of Hanna's sons, from the oldest to the youngest, for refusing the command of Antiochus Epiphanes to perform a pagan ritual (pp. 129–33).[8]

Maccabees II and IV are panegyrics to martyrdom and recall other instances of "witnessing God unto death." For example, Eleazar is tortured and slain for his refusal to merely pretend to taste swine's flesh. "He raised his eyes to God, and said: . . . Be merciful to Thy people, and let my punishment be sufficient for their sake. Make my blood an expiation for them, and take my life as a ransom for theirs" (Hadas, 6:28–29).

According to classics scholar Moses Hadas who translated Macabees IV into English, the book is thoroughly Hellenic in spirit and "has no analogue in contemporary Hebrew literature. . . . Not only the words but the imagery also is Greek, and the artistic and systematic structure is unlike

---

son cried out, "Your wheel is not so strong . . . as to strangle my reason. Slice my members, burn my flesh, twist my joints: through all these torments I will convince you that the children of the Hebrews alone are invincible in virtue's cause." When live coals were placed under his tortured body, "that great-spirited youth, a true son of Abraham, uttered no groan. As though transformed into incorruption by the fire, he nobly endured the torments, and he said: 'Imitate me, my brothers; do not . . . abjure our brotherhood in nobility. Fight the sacred and noble fight for religion's sake. Through it may the just Providence which watched over our fathers also become merciful to our people. . . .' Uttering these words, the saintly young man broke off his life" (Maccabees IV, 9:23–25).

To convey the style of Maccabees II, the entire story of the Seven Brothers from that book appears in Appendix 2.

8. The historical context of this story is thus: In 169 B.C.E. the Syrians under Antiochus Epiphanes invaded Israel and demanded the population acknowledge their defeat by bowing down to the conqueror's gods and eating a piece of sacramental pork as a symbol of renouncing the Jewish faith. The Maccabees led a revolt against their oppressors, and just as they undoubtedly put to use Greek military technology and the Greek language, they also adopted the Greek concept of martyrdom, which Fackenheim describes as "the witnessing to God unto death" (p. 67).

anything in rabbinic literature" (p. 100). Hadas describes the author as "at home in the Jewish tradition . . . but the philosophic structure of his thought is Greek" (pp. 115–16). In both its form and vocabulary, Maccabees IV shows the influence of Greek tragedy (p. 101).

In the rabbinic literature[9] the story of Hannah and her seven sons reappears as Miriam and her seven sons. A rabbinic retelling relates the mother's famous cry: "My son, go to the patriarch Abraham and tell him, 'Thus said my mother, "Do not preen yourself [on your righteousness], saying I built an altar and offered up my son, Isaac." Behold, our mother built seven altars and offered up seven sons in one day.' Yours was only a test, but mine was in earnest" (Hadas, pp. 129–33).

It is probably significant that the martyrdom of the Seven Maccabees brothers was very soon embraced by the church. The physical remains of the Holy Seven Brothers were enshrined in the sarcophogi of a Christian church, and they were given a place on the Christian Calendar of Saints, to be commemorated on every August 1.[10]

But it took about one thousand years for the Books of the Maccabees as a whole to be translated into Hebrew. Perhaps the rabbis regarded the books as too Greek in its celebration of martyrdom to include in the literature of the Jews.[11] In the

---

9. Lamentations Rabbah 1:16, no. 50; Gittin 57b; Pesikta Rabbati 43:80; Seder Eliyahu Rabbah 30:151.

10. When the Books of the Maccabees appeared, martyrdom was an important tactic in the Christian community, which was then being persecuted by Rome, hence their embrace of the Seven Maccabees Brothers. August 1 was dedicated to The Holy Maccabees on the Roman Catholic Calendar of Saints. According to Delaney's *Dictionary of Saints*, relicts of "all seven [Maccabees brothers] and their mother . . . are believed to be enshrined in the Church of St. Peter in Chains in Rome. These are the only persons in the Old Testament liturgically venerated in the Western Church and are honored on August 1" (p. 371).

11. Were the books of the Maccabees kept out of the biblical canon because of their eulogy of martyrdom or for other reasons? Zimmerman argues that the emphasis on military rebellion was too

tenth century, the Books of the Maccabees finally reached a Hebrew readership through *Sefer Jossipon,* a Hebrew history written in southern Italy.

This panegyric of martyrdom reached the Jews of the Rhineland in time to guide their response to the unexpected and terrible pogroms of 1096.

> In that year Christian crusaders, an army of French knights led by a few great lords, after papal inducement on the way to the Holy Land . . . came upon the Jewish quarters in the Rhineland cities [of Mainz, Worms, and Cologne]. As preparation for killing Muslims in the Near East, the French crusaders inflicted terrible pogroms upon the Rhenish Jews, who were totally unprepared for the catastrophe. (Cantor, p. 167)[12]

Unlike the Nazi pogroms of recent times, the Jews caught in the Crusader pogroms were offered a choice of torture or conversion. The Jews of medieval Germany held Christianity in contempt.[13] They were swept up in the religious fanaticism of their times, and the story of Hanna and her seven sons

---

strong for elevating the Books of the Maccabees (Miller, p. 30). Open rebellion is not the only strategy for survival, and perhaps the rabbis at Yavneh (who in 93 B.C.E. decided on what to include in the sacred texts) believed Jewish survival would be favored by quieter tactics. Perhaps both open rebellion and witness martyrdom were regarded as too Hellenistic in spirit.

12. The Crusades brought to a sudden end several centuries of peace, prosperity, and privilege for Jews of the Rhineland. During early medieval times, the Jews were an active and prosperous middle class, occupying a special niche in a world of peasants and nobles. However, their world was changing economically, politically, legally, and religiously (Cantor, p. 167).

13. According to Mintz, the Jews of medieval Germany held Christianity in contempt. They "reviled Christianity for what in their perception were its idolatrous images, its blasphemous belief in a son of God, and what was regarded as the cannibalism of its central ritual" (p. 86). Master David, the Gabbai, shouted to a Crusader mob: "Alas, you are children of whoredom; believing as you do in one born of whoredom . . . your diety—the son of promiscuity, the crucified

convinced many that martyrdom was also *their* formula for coping with this onslaught of persecution.

In desperation, many Jews threatened by pogroms of the Crusades now embraced the story of Hanna and her seven sons and accepted the mother's claim that their martyrdom was inspired by the Akedah and even surpassed the Akedah as an expression of homage to God. Now their rabbis interpreted the Akedah as a glorification of martyrdom, though in the opinion of Haym Soloveitchik the glorification of martyrdom was an enormous breach of *halakha*.[14]

Spiegel refers to the *Book of Disasters of 1096*, which describes the mass martyrdom of an entire Jewish community

---

one" (Mintz, p. 88). They were in no mood to cooperate or even to pretend to cooperate with their converters.

14. Writes Soloveitchik: "Jewish law has very stringent regulations regarding rules of martyrdom. In a few extreme instances martyrdom is absolutely mandatory. In those cases in which it is not mandatory, it is forbidden, and most probably one who suffers voluntary martyrdom should be viewed as having committed suicide. Life is not optional in Judaism. And one knows of no allowance for committing suicide to avoid forced conversion. Yet from numerous crusade chronicles, both Jewish and Christian, it is perfectly clear that the Ashkenazic community, men, women, and children, did not all abide by these regulations. Scholars and simple folk, they committed suicide rather than have baptism forced upon them. . . . And let it be noted that we are not dealing with instances of mass hysteria, but with a pattern of conduct persisting over the course of centuries. . . . Parents slaughtered their own children to prevent them from falling into Christian hands and being raised as Christians, and even recited a blessing on the murder of themselves and of their own children. . . . One of the most tragic documents which has come down to us from the Jewish Middle Ages is an inquiry sent to the great Rabbi Maier of Rothenburg (d. 1293) as to what penance a man must do who slaughtered his children as a pogrom was in progress, in order to prevent them from falling into Christian hands, and then failed in his own attempt at suicide. Rabbi Maier was hard put to find a reply.

"The magnitude of this halakhic breach is enormous" (pp. 207–208).

when the Jews of Eller, Germany, learned of plans to capture their elders and force their defilement.

> [The Jews of Eller assembled in one hall,] recited their confessionals before their Creator. Then the saints volunteered to slaughter them all . . . three hundred souls. . . . With the doors shut, the saints took hold of their swords and slaughtered them all." (Spiegel, p. 134)

Faced with the threat of forced conversion or torture and persecution, Jewish fathers would slaughter their wives, their children, and themselves, "to emulate Abraham's willingness to sacrifice Isaac, and to follow the example set by Hannah and her seven sons." Jewish prayer books of that time contained prayers to be recited before slaughtering children and suicide (EJ, col. 984).[15] According to Zunz (1855), during those times there were no fewer than thirty Akedah prayers, many composed in stirring poetic language.

The practice of martyrdom is supported by a firm belief in resurrection; a father will slaughter his son if the father is sure his son's death is only temporary. This conviction was fostered by a rich output of rabbinical legends that Isaac was indeed slaughtered, perhaps reduced to ashes, perhaps immediately resurrected, perhaps ascended to heaven and returned to earth after three years.

> According to one legend, Isaac's "soul flew away" the moment Abraham's sword touched Isaac's neck, but when the angel's voice commanded Abraham not to harm the lad, "his soul returned to his body and he stood on his feet." He knew that in this way the dead are destined to live and he opened his mouth

---

15. Baron has noted "that there was no substantial discontinuity in Franco-German Jewish society as a result of the First Crusade. The towns were quickly resettled, commerce and trade were reconstructed, [and] some of the academies went on to produce scholars of great distinction" (Mintz, pp. 98–99).

and said, "Blessed is He who resurrects the dead." (Midrash
ha-Gadol on Genesis 22:12)[16]

[Spiegel recalls a midrash in which Abraham asks:] Perhaps the
lad is not fit to be a sacrificial gift. May I strangle him, may I
burn him, shall I cut him up in pieces before Thee? . . . Let me
bruise him, let me extract some blood from him, let me remove
from him one drop of blood. (pp. 46–47)

[Another midrash cited by Spiegel recalls that Isaac bled] from
the incision as the father began to slaughter him. . . .
[Abraham left one-quarter of Isaac's blood on the altar, while
Isaac lay on the altar bound and groaning until God] revived
him with dew for resurrecting the dead. (p. 47)

[That Isaac was slaughtered is also argued by the talmudic
statement:] There is no atonement without blood (Yoma 5a,
Zevahim 6a, Menahot 93b). [It is believed] the blood of the
Akedah made an offering on high where it might serve as a
protection and guardian of Israel until the end comes nigh.
(Spiegel, p. 58)

MeAm Lo'ez records the midrash, "That Abraham did begin
to slit Isaac's throat and actually perforated his windpipe.
When Abraham looked up and saw the ram, the angels
swooped Isaac away, brought him to the Garden of Eden, and
left him there until he was completely healed" (p. 344).[17]

In the twelfth century, Rabbi Ephraim ben Jacob of Bonn
wrote a poem on the Akedah in which he elaborated on this
radical modification of the Akedah story. His poem graphically

---

16. So persistent is the death-and-resurrection Akedah in Jewish
folklore, that there are those who argue the original, prebiblical
Akedah story was a death-and-resurrection story. This speculation is
examined in chapter 20, "In Search of the Ur-Akedah."

17. The following sources are given in *MeAm Lo'ez* (n. 149, p. 311)
for this midrash: Yalkut Shimoni 109, Tikkun Yesachar, Yalkut Re-
uveni, Sifthey Cohen, and Yafeh Toar.

describes the actual slaughter of Isaac, and his immediate revival by "the resurrecting dew."[18]

---

18. Rabbi Ephraim also wrote dirges on the suffering of the Jews during the Second Crusade. He lived at a time when Jews faced not only capricious and arbitrary death, but the cruelest of tortures, perhaps making suicide a reasonable alternative to unavoidable capture and persecution. Here are a few lines of his Akedah poem:

[Begged Isaac] bind for me my hands and my feet
    Lest I be found wanting and profane the sacrifice.
I am afraid of panic, I am concerned to honor you,
    My will is to honor you greatly.
. . . .
Then did the father and the son embrace,
    Mercy and Truth met and kissed each other.
Oh, my father, fill your mouth with praise,
    For He doth bless the sacrifice.
. . . .
He made haste, he pinned him down with his knees,
    He made his two arms strong.
With steady hands he slaughtered him according to the rite,
    Full right was the slaughter.

Down upon him fell the resurrecting dew, and he revived.
    [The father] seized him to slaughter him once more.
Scripture, bear witness! Well-grounded is the fact:
    And the Lord called Abraham, even a second time from
        heaven.
. . . .

In a nearby thicket did the Lord prepare
    A ram, meant for this mitzvah even from Creation.
The proxy caught its leg in the skirts of his coat,
    And behold, he stood by his burnt offering.

So he offered the ram, as he desired to do,
    Rather than his son, as a burnt offering.
. . . .
Thus prayed the binder and the bound
    That when their descendants commit a wrong

The popularity of martyrdom did not go unchallenged. Around the seventeenth century, Rabbi Isaiah ha-Levi Horowitz was "reluctant to sanction a blessing over the mitzvah of martyrdom because one should not seek out a situation which would require him to surrender his life." (EJ, col. 979)

Reexamining the history of the Jews of Medieval Europe, scholars are haunted by the questions: Did the wave of Jewish martyrdom, formalized in prayerbooks and piyyutim, truly express the theme of the Akedah story? Was this practice halakhically justified? Haym Soloveitchik thinks not.[19]

On the surface, it looks very much like the Jews of the Crusades unwittingly adopted the mind-set of their oppressors, but this is a conclusion Jewish scholars, understandably, are reluctant to accept. Was the death-and-resurrection Akedah borrowed from the religion of their Christian oppressors, or

---

This act be recalled to save them from disaster,
    From all their transgressions and sins.

O Righteous One, do us this grace!
    You promised our fathers mercy to Abraham.
Let then their merit stand as our witness
    And pardon our iniquity and our sin, and take us
        For Thine inheritance.

The entire poem is reprinted in The Last Trial, *by Shalom Spiegel, pp. 143–152.*

19. [Writes Soloveitchik:] "The Franco-German community was permeated by a profound sense of its own religiosity, of the rightness of its traditions, and could not imagine any sharp difference between its practices and the law which its members studied and observed with such devotion" (Soloveitchik, pp. 211–12).

The Franco-German community in its state of intense religiosity saw the word of God as being, as it were, incarnated in two forms: first, in the canonized literature . . . second, in the life of its people. . . . [Contradictions between the written law] and the practice of a God-fearing community . . . [resulted in] a radical reinterpretation of the Halakhah. (Soloveitchik, p. 212)

might it stem from Jewish or even pagan roots? This question is the central problem of Spiegel's densely documented monograph *The Last Trial*.[20]

---

20. The Middle Ages saw the zenith of Christianity: the Roman Catholic Church then dominated Europe, and the Jews of Medieval Europe lived in a very Christian world. To what extent did Jews assimilate, however inadvertently, Christian religious symbols and values? In what ways have Jewish interpretations of the Akedah, for example, been influenced by the dominance of Christian glory, Christian power, and Christian thought over the Jews of Europe? These are questions Spiegel wrestles with in *The Last Trial*.

Since ancient times, the study of Christianity was necessary for rabbinical scholars to answer the important question: Should laws concerning contact with idolators be applied to Christians? Besides, writes Werblowsky in *Encyclopedia Judaica*, "there always was—as is inevitable where cultures coexist—a certain amount of mutual interest. . . . Christian presence is noticeable not only in the direct and obvious influences on Jewish thinkers, but also in the more subtle and indirect ways resulting from what might be called *cultural osmosis*. . . . [For example, Yitzhak Baer has pointed to] specific Christian influences on certain aspects of the thought and devotional practice in the Zohar and in German Hasidism" ("Christianity," *Encyclopedia Judaica*, v. 5, co. 514, emphasis added).

To suggest the Jewish understanding of the Akedah story has been influenced by Christian thought, is an uncomfortable thesis and full of irony. The persecution of the Jews during the Middle Ages was an integral part of the Crusades, which was financed to a certain extent by the pillaging of Jewish property. Thus, Christian persecution of the Jews helped finance the Crusades, while a Christian influence on the Akedah story would predispose the victims to accepting their concept of martyrdom.

Spiegel argues that "the historical reality of the second century persecutions under the Roman Empire" diminished "the splendor and awe of the biblical Akedah story." The story of one aborted sacrifice, its object spared from the least harm, loses its dramatic impact in contrast with the sheer horror of fathers and sons *en masse* publicly butchered and burned for their faith (Spiegel 15). Spiegel seems to argue that a significant factor in transforming the Akedah story into one of actual sacrifice and resurrection was the actual persecution of the Jews by the Romans. The transformed Akedah

According to Spiegel, parallels between Moriah and Golgotha are based on a "common heritage of pagan beliefs." There is evidence "that as early as the eighth century before the Christian era . . . pagan conceptions of gods dying and returning to life in countless cycles of death and life were widely known among the people" (p. 113). Did Christianity's emphasis on death and resurrection lead the rabbis to revive ancient Hebrew legends of the death and resurrection of Isaac?[21]

Spiegel answers, Why not? Judaism was influenced by all the religions and civilizations of the ancient Near East. "Wittingly and unwittingly it borrowed from [Christianity] too" (p. 103). "Beliefs and opinions float from place to place and pass over from one religion to another. . . . [Sometimes] traditions get lost, and the loss is recovered through contact with an alien culture" (p. 118).

> In the [Christian-generated] atmosphere of holy war many Jews believed that the glory of the Lord and the honor of their law would be debased if they did not bear witness for them by open and public proclamation of their abiding truth in a chivalrous manner. Thus through *the curious workings of historic irony* the Christian crusading venture and Jewish martyrdom . . . each became in its own particular way expressions of a holy war waged for the glory of God. (EJ, Christianity, p. 983, emphasis added)

In the twelfth century, when Spain and Morocco were invaded by fundamentalist Muslims, the Jews of those lands

---

legend was not so much a copy of the crucifixion as it was a response to Roman brutality.

Spiegel cites evidence that the rabbinical belief in the sacrifice and resurrection of Isaac did in fact originate in ancient times, though it became a favorite idea in the Middle Ages (p. 50).

21. C. T. R. Hayward examines the evidence for the belief that the midrashim of the death and resurrection of Isaac might be "Jewish responses to Christianity and its doctrine of atonement." After examining Jewish texts of the second to fifth centuries c.e., Hayward concludes: "it makes perfect sense [that these midrashim arose] within a purely Jewish religious and theological context" (p. 299).

similarly faced a policy of forced conversion. Some Jews refused and suffered martyrdom. Some publicly embraced Islam and continued to practice Judaism secretly. The issue flared into public debate when a Jew who had submitted to a forced conversion asked a rabbi—"a distinguished talmudist"—to endorse his secret practice of Judaism. "The rabbi gave a halachic ruling that any Jew who made a profession of Islam would thereafter commit an additional sin with each commandment of Judaism that he performed" (Hartman, p. 13).

The great Maimonides (known in Hebrew writings as Rambam) was horrified by this ruling,[22] and in his *Epistle on Martyrdom* refuted this halachic ruling and defended the decision of those who preferred to publicly feign conversion rather than submit to martyrdom.

The Talmud often says: "The Torah rules that the forced individual is not culpable . . . and frequently the ruling is repeated; a forced individual is excused by the Torah" (p. 29).

The prophets have spelled out that a person who resides among nonbelievers is one of them. . . . [One must] separate himself from the heretics when they do not coerce him to do as they do;

---

22. Did Maimonides believe martyrdom was not the best Jewish response to forced conversion, or did he believe the Jewish community must tolerate weakness of will as well as heroism? Maimonides himself, when confronted with the likelihood he would face forced conversion, fled Spain and eventually settled in Egypt, where the practice of Judaism was tolerated.

According to Hartman, Maimonides believed the Jewish community must accommodate those of limited courage and weakness of will, as well as those who were capable of great heroism. Hartman argues that the law of the captive woman (Deuteronomy 21:10–14) "may have guided Maimonides in trying to salvage some form of dignified Jewish life for a community that was not prepared to make the heroic choice of martyrdom." States Hartman, "The Torah is not a law for ideal people living in idyllic conditions, but rather a normative system that guides people in imperfect situations and through personal crises of the will and spirit. . . . Compromise was preferable to total demoralization" (p. 10).

he should leave them . . . He must leave everything he has, travel day and night until he finds a spot where he can practice his religion. The world is sufficiently large and extensive. (p. 32)

Anyone who cannot leave [a place of persecution] because of his attachments, or because of the dangers of a sea voyage, and stays where he is, must look upon himself as one who profanes God's name, not exactly willingly, but almost so. At the same time, he must bear in mind that if he fulfills a precept, *God will reward him doubly*, because he acted so for God only, and not to show off or be accepted as an observant individual. The reward is much greater for a person who fulfills the Law and knows that if he is caught, he and all he has will perish. (p. 33, emphasis added)

So furious was Maimonides at this "halachic sage" for condemning feigned conversion and demanding martyrdom, that he condemned the halachic reply as "weak and senseless . . . of foul content and form . . . weak, tedious, and confused" (p. 15). The responsum was "long-winded foolish babbling and nonsense. . . . His talk begins as silliness and ends as disastrous nonsense" (pp. 16–17). Such advice, says Maimonides, brings "darkness into the hearts of men" (p. 17). Of course we must recognize the difference "between one who does not observe the Sabbath out of the fear of the sword and one who does not observe it because he does not wish to" (p. 16).

Whenever Jews face persecution and the victims cry out Why is this happening? What shall I do? the Akedah story, with all its ambiguity and force, looms in sight. "All the pogroms, the crusades, the persecutions, the slaughters, the catastrophes, the massacres by sword and the liquidations by fire—each time it was Abraham leading his son to the altar, to the holocaust all over again" (Wiesel, p. 95). The reflections of psychoanalyst Silvano Arieti on the Akedah and the Holocaust are summarized at the end of Chapter 19.

Perhaps no other Jewish writer of our time has so glorified martyrdom as a religious experience as Aharon Agus. He sees the Akedah as a martyrdom story. Isaac, bearing a heavy load of wood, is "a symbol of Jewish suffering" (p. 39). Likewise, "the ram that Abraham sacrifices in place of Isaac represents *the future martyrdoms of Israel.* Unlike Isaac, the ram is not spared from death, because martyrdom is the real Akedah, the actual holocaust" (p. 39, emphasis added). Agus writes of the deep and mysterious appeal of martyrdom, which makes it more than a response to persecution.

> Martyrdom is not always a result of the cruelty of history alone—something deep in the nature of religious man drives toward the heroic, the final, and the complete; martyrdom is Akedah. . . . The Law can be at once redemptive and oppressive. The beauty of the notion imbedded in our texts is that Israel finds its true deliverance in precariously hesitating between the absolute embrace of the Law and the daring yet freeing heroism of martyrdom. (p. 61)

Against Agus's glorification of martyrdom are the protests of Elie Wiesel and others who insist that martyrdom does *not* express the Jewish spirit, which is a spirit of survival. Emil Fackenheim makes the case for the spirit of survival by citing from the memoir of an Auschwitz inmate, the Polish noblewoman Pelagia Lewinska.

> At the outset the living places, the ditches, the mud, the piles of excrement behind the blocks, had appalled me with their horrible filth. . . . And then I saw the light! I saw that it was not a question of disorder or lack of organization but that, on the contrary, a very thoroughly conscious idea was in back of the camp's existence. They had condemned us to die in our own filth. . . . They wished to abase us, to destroy our human dignity, . . . to fill us with contempt for ourselves and our fellows. But from the instant I grasped the motivating principle . . . it was as if I had awakened from a dream. I felt under orders to live. . . . And if I died at Auschwitz it would be as a human being. I was not going to become the contemptible, disgusting brute my enemy wished me to be. (Fackenheim 1982, p. 25)

Fackenheim's view has been well summarized by Richard L. Rubenstein: "Lewinska's testimony represents a new kind of sanctification. In previous eras, the ultimate testimony of Jewish fidelity was *kiddush ha-shem,* the sanctification of

God's holy name. Such fidelity was expressed when a Jew voluntarily accepted martyrdom rather than betray his or her religion. According to Fackenheim," Rubenstein continues, "such martyrdom no longer made sense during or after the Holocaust. . . . Resistance embodied a new kind of sanctification, *kiddush ha-hayyim,* the sanctification of life. Any refusal to die, and thus to outlive the infernal process became holy, not only for individual survivors but for the religious tradition National Socialism sought to destroy" (1992 Rubenstein, p. 187).

In a mortal crisis where martyrdom is one alternative, what are the other alternatives?—resistance, combat, escape, feint, camouflage; explore whatever tactics favor survival. In a hostile environment, every survival tactic carries a risk. In Nazi Germany, a Jew hiding in the attic of a protective gentile faced the risk that he may be turned in by a hostile neighbor, to the peril of both himself and his gentile host. Resistance may end sadly in what might be called "risk martyrdom." The partisan fighter faced an enemy far superior in number and firepower. The ghetto uprisings likewise claimed their toll of martyrs. Those fighters who survived were already well-trained for their roles in the Haganah, which would fight for the establishment of the state of Israel, and for the right of Holocaust survivors to rebuild their lives.

Witness martyrdom, by contrast, is firmly rooted in the Christian tradition. The act of martyrdom imitates Jesus, for in the words of I Corinthians 15:3, "Christ died for our sins." The glorification of suffering is a distinctly Christian theme: "Resist not evil, but whosoever shall smite thee on thy right cheek, turn to him the other also. And if any man will sue thee at the law, and take away thy coat, let him have thy cloak also" (Matthew 5:38–39). In the language of the New Testament, self-mutilation becomes a metaphor for righteousness: "If thy right eye offend thee, pluck it out, and cast it from thee. . . . And if thy right hand offend thee, cut it off, and cast it from thee; for it is profitable for thee that one of thy members should perish, and not that thy whole body should be cast into hell" (Matthew 5:29–30).

Christian martyrs did not ordinarily kill themselves, but

allowed themselves to be killed as a public demonstration of
allegiance or faith. Witness martyrdom is also closely bound to
a firm belief in an afterlife or in bodily resurrection. In our
time, we have seen the secularization of witness martyrdom—
Vietnam War protesters who set themselves afire in public
places as a political statement.

The topic of witness martyrdom came into the news in 1946
when Mahatma Gandhi commented on the Holocaust: "The Jews
should have offered themselves to the butcher's knife. They
should have thrown themselves into the sea from cliffs. . . . It
would have roused the world and the people of Germany"
(Koestler, p. 106). A 1969 editorial in *The Reconstructionist* implied that this point of view had nothing to do with Jewish
tradition and questioned the *sekhel* of such an utterance (p. 3).

It is important to distinguish between martyrdom as a
statement and death as a risk. A person who volunteers for a
high-risk mission may face likely or sure death as the price to
pay for performing this service for the people. For dying in the
line of duty, that person deserves to be remembered as a
martyr. In a hostile world, this kind of martyrdom deserves a
place of honor in the memory of a people who give the highest
priority to the preservation of life.

This chapter raised questions of life and death, and for many
of them there are no answers. Perhaps one question can be
answered: Does the Akedah, in its biblical form, sanction or
perhaps promote martyrdom? Or rather does verse 12 under-
score the sanctity of human life: "Do not raise your hand
against the boy, or do anything to him." Writing on the Akedah,
Elie Wiesel answers the question thus: "In the Jewish tradition
man cannot use death as a means of glorifying God. Every man
is an end unto himself, a living eternity" (p. 76).

14

THE DEGLORIFICATION
INTERPRETATION

The glorification of the New Testament necessarily reduces the status of the Hebrew Bible to an Old Testament.[1] The Hebrew Bible becomes a piece of ancient history, where scholars can dig for clues about the coming of the Messiah, and dismantle old stories to see what they are made of. Traditionally, Christian scholars have found in the Akedah exactly what they were looking for: a prophecy, a forecast, a prefiguration (as they call it) of the Crucifixion.[2] The Church fathers elaborate many analogies between the Akedah and the Crucifixion. Both events

---

1. What is clearly valid in the portrayal of traditional Christian attitudes does not hold true, however, for all contemporary Christian scholars. See note 1 chapter 21, for a list of recent Christian articles on the Akedah.

2. The Old Testament is a Christian label for a corpus of writings known to Jewish scholars as the Bible, or more specifically, the Hebrew Bible. When Jewish scholars refer to their sacred writings, they are likely to refer not to the Bible as a whole, but to some portion of the Bible: the Torah (the Five Books of Moses), the Prophets (Nevi'im), or to the later books of the Bible (Ketubim). The word

happened on the same hill top. Both Isaac and Jesus carried wood for their sacrifice up to the mountain, Isaac carrying the firewood and Jesus the wooden cross. In Christian art, Isaac's load of wood may be arranged in the form of a cross. (See page 139) The ram caught in the thicket anticipates Jesus' crown of thorns. Ambrose described Isaac as "the prototype of the suffering Christ."[3]

Traditionally, the Akedah has been interpreted by Christian scholars to illustrate the primitive morality of people of the Old Testament, to dramatize the world's need for a spiritual renaissance that would raise humanity to a higher moral level. This use of the Akedah is well-illustrated in *The Interpreter's Bible (1952)*. Walter Russell Bowie opens his discussion of the Akedah by agreeing that today any man who harbored Abraham's thoughts that God wanted him to sacrifice his son, "if his thoughts were detected, [he] would be put in a mental hospital. Any man who actually carried it out would be convicted of murder and executed" (p. 642).

Similarly, a 1973 article by Reverend George W. Coats, describes God's commandment to Abraham as "slightly insane." "What kind of a God would be asking such a horrifying confirmation of obedience and loyalty?" Coats asked his Christian reader.

In 1954, the eminent Bible scholar[4] S. R. Driver wrote:

[Abraham regarded] a command to sacrifice his son, as Divine. [Christians] could not so regard such a command: an alleged command of God to sacrifice a child could not be accepted as

---

Torah often refers to all Jewish sacred texts, including the Talmud and rabbinical commentaries as well as the Bible.

3. "Isaac ergo Christi passuri est typus."—Ambrose, *De Abraham*, chapter 8. Church Fathers Irenaeus, Tertulliam, Ephraim, Isidor of Seville, and numerous others enlarged upon this parallel (Smith, p. 159).

4. To demonstrate Driver's reputation as a biblical scholar, E. A. Speiser, editor of the Anchor edition of Genesis, praises Driver's "rare combination of learning, lucidity, and plain common sense" (Speiser, lxii).

such; and if it were acted upon, the action would be condemned by the whole Christian Church; there had been, it
would be said, some hallucination or delusion. The reason is
that we live in an age, and under a moral light, in which we
could not regard as Divine a command to violate not only our
sense of what was morally right, but even our natural instincts
of love and affection. It was possible for Abraham so to regard
it, because he lived under the mental and moral conditions of
an age very different from ours. He lived not only in an age
when such sacrifice was common, but also in an age . . . when
a father's power over his son was far more absolute than it is
now. The command would not therefore shock the moral
standard to which Abraham was accustomed, as it would shock
ours. It would not be out of harmony with what he might
suppose could be reasonably demanded by God. (pp. 221–22)

Note Driver's statement that Abraham lived "in an age when
such sacrifice was common." The belief that child sacrifice was
a common practice in the time of Abraham is frequently found
in the writings of Christian scholars, and goes back to the
German theologian August Dillman. *Die Genesis Erklärt* was
one of his many Old Testament studies, first appearing in 1860,
and was translated into English in 1897. This belief that child
sacrifice was common in the time of Abraham is likewise
expressed by Otto Eissfeldt, whose 1965 *The Old Testament: An
Introduction*, according to Robert Alter, is "widely regarded as
the most authoritative general reference in the field" (1981, p.
14).[5]

The belief that child sacrifice was a common practice in the
time of Abraham has suggested to Christian scholars that the
message of the Akedah was simply to abolish child sacrifice
and to adopt animal sacrifice as a substitute for it.[6]

------

5. Eissfeldt wrote: "The idea of giving up the most precious and
dear possession, the first-born son, was always one that lay near at
hand in Israelite religion, which not only knew of human sacrifice
from the practices of related neighboring peoples . . . but always
had examples to hand in the record of its own past, whether these
were legendary or historical" (p. 411).

6. Claus Westerman writes: "From the time of Wellhausen there

> From the time of Wellhausen there has been widespread agreement that the narrative was concerned with the abolition of human sacrifice by substituting an animal. . . . Some exegetes have gone so far as to understand the chapter as a polemic against human sacrifice. But this thesis has been rejected and not taken up again. (Westerman, 1985, p. 354)

This pervasive Christian attitude is expressed at the popular level in the retelling of the sacrifice of Isaac story by Norman Vincent Peale.

> Human sacrifice was common enough in those days, eighteen or nineteen centuries before Christ, but to the gentle Abraham this command must have come like a thunderbolt, incomprehensible, terrifying, appalling in its injustice and inhumanity. It meant—or seemed to mean—that the God he had served and loved for so long was as ferocious and bloodthirsty as the pagan gods he had always despised. It meant that God, who had promised to make his descendants as numerous as the stars of heaven, was a liar, because if Isaac was killed there would be no such descendants. (p. 47)

Jewish scholars have tended to reject this popular Christian interpretation of the Akedah. It seems clear that well before the time of Abraham, animal sacrifice was well-established as a

---

has been widespread agreement that the [Akedah] narrative was concerned with the abolition of human sacrifice by substituting an animal." (*Genesis 12–36: A Commentary*, first published in German, 1981.) Julius Wellhausen was a leading Old Testament scholar of the nineteenth century.

Skinner likewise regards the Akedah as "a legend . . . explaining the substitution of animal for human sacrifices in some type of ancient worship. This view is worked out with remarkable skill by Gunkel," who speculated that the story alludes to a sanctuary where "the custom of child sacrifice . . . [was eventually] modified by the substitution of a ram for a human being" (Skinner, p. 332). Skinner refers to Hermann Gunkel's 1895 study, *Schöpfung und Chaos in Urzeit und Endzeit.*

Moskowitz documents the conclusion of scholars that child sacrifice was not a common practice in ancient Israel (p. 289).

mode of worship.[7] At the time of Abraham and afterwards, child sacrifice was largely a Canaanite practice that had infiltrated the religious life of the Hebrews to some extent, as indicated by the many biblical warnings against "passing infants through the fire."[8]

Christian scholarship[9] of the Old Testament has been guided by the hypothesis that the Bible is not the work of a single author, but a rewriting of pagan myths and a stitching together of several documents, edited by priestly redactors hundreds of years after the stories were first recorded. This scholarly activity, known as the Higher Criticism, tends to lose sight of the question, What is the ethical message of the Bible? Perhaps an implied message of the Higher Criticism is that such a corpus, being a patchwork of different authors and editors of various times and places, is not likely to present a coherent or unified theme. Martin Buber may have had scholars of the Higher Criticism in mind when he wrote of those who are more interested in "what is behind the biblical story . . . [than in] what is in it" (1968, p. 22). On the multiple authorship theory, Buber writes, "My ear, too, distinguishes a variety of voices in the chorus" (1968, p. 24). However, the various compilers shared "a common spiritual atmosphere" and a common vision (1968, p. 22).

To summarize, Christian scholarship has used the Akedah to argue that human sacrifice was common during the time of the ancient Hebrews, a time when concepts of morality were quite

---

7. References to animal sacrifice before the time of Abraham are not hard to find in the Bible. Abel sacrificed a lamb from his flock, Noah performed an animal sacrifice when the flood came to an end.

8. "Let no one be found among you who consigns his son or daughter to the fire" (Deuteronomy 18:10). This is one of over twenty prohibitions and denunciations of child sacrifice which can be found in the Bible. (For the complete list of prohibitions, see pages 45–48.)

9. Biblical criticism is a predominantly Christian field of study, but not an exclusively Christian field, and probably not Christian in origin. According to Irving Zeitlin, "Biblical criticism began as early as the second century c.e. and continued with the Jewish commentator Ebn Ezra (twelfth century c.e.) and with Baruch Spinoza (p. 284).

different from our own. Similarly, the Higher Criticism, while not an exclusively Christian enterprise, has shifted attention from the moral message of the Bible, to its "true" origins, its multiple authorship, its anachronisms, and its inconsistencies. To this summary, we may note the most recent tactic for belittling the stories of the Bible, including the Akedah: Christian feminism. In the name of feminism, Abraham is denounced as a wife-abuser, and Sarah as "an abused woman . . . a wholly tragic character" (Dennis, p. 61). Christian feminist deglorification of the Hebrew Bible is detailed in chapter 10 of this book.[10]

The Christian world is burdened, alas, by many centuries of anti-Semitism. Today, there are voices inside Christendom that are asking whether this disparagement of the Jews and Judaism is a necessary part of Christian theology, or whether the Church can survive without an anti-Semitic bias.[11] The deglorification of the Akedah is one small example of how, over the centuries, Christian scholars have looked at Judaism from a negative point of view.

---

10. Chapter 10 also documents the argument of a Jewish feminist that the main purpose of the Akedah was to demonstrate Abraham could do exactly what he pleased with Isaac, regardless of what Sarah might have said.

11. Rosemary Reuther, *Faith and Fratricide: The Theological Roots of Anti-Semitism* (New York: Seabury, 1974). See also Alan T. Davis, *Anti-Semitism and the Christian Mind: the Crisis of Conscience After Auschwitz* (New York: Herder and Herder, 1969); and Franklin H. Littell, *The Crucifixion of the Jews* (New York: Harper and Row, 1975).

15

The Akedah as a Test of Obedience and as the Triumph of Love over Duty

Gerhard von Rad advised that the Akedah is so rich in meanings no one interpretation can be named the primary one (1971, p. 238). Jacob Licht is among those who disagree. He argues that "the deeply significant theme of the story is that Abraham withstood the cruel last test of obedience by carrying out without murmur God's command to sacrifice Isaac" (pp. 115–116). Licht points to several details of the story supporting his thesis that the major theme of the story is Abraham's obedience.

> First, the story opens by telling the reader that this is a story of how God *tested* Abraham; i.e., tested his obedience. Certainly, he must have passed the test, or he would not have become the patriarch of Israel. As the story unfolds, the reader can learn *how* Abraham passed the test, not *if* he passed the test. Likewise, the reader can set aside his anxiety about any danger to Isaac's life.
>
> Secondly, a repeated phrase of the story is "Here I am," which really means "I am at your service; tell me what you want me to do and I will do it." Abraham utters the phrase when God first

calls him (verse 1). When the angel of the Lord calls out to Abraham, he again answers, Here I am (verse 11).

Historian Norman F. Cantor likewise asserts the Akedah is a testimony to Abraham's obedience.[1] There is a Christian tradition that makes the Akedah into a test of Abraham's faith. In what sense might the Akedah have been a test of Abraham's faith? Not in the sense that it proved Abraham believed in God. Abraham had already heard the voice of God and had even argued with God. "The existence of God is regarded in the Bible as being a self-evident proposition, not requiring affirmation" (Sarna, pp. 162–163).

In biblical Hebrew, the word *emunah* is sometimes translated as faith, but more specifically it means faithfulness, loyalty, and trust, expressed not so much in belief as in action. *Emunah* cannot mean faith in the sense of a belief in the existence of God, since the word *emunah* is used to describe God: *El Emunah*—a faithful God, a dependable God, a God you can put your trust in. In the Song of Moses (Deuteronomy 32:4) *El Emunah* is variously translated as:

"A God of faithfulness and without iniquity, Just and right is He" (JPS 1917).

"A faithful God, never false, True and upright is He" (JPS 1962).

---

1. A leading historian of medieval Europe, Cantor is unfortunately not a careful reader of the Bible. He refers to the Akedah as "God's command" (p. 20) or "dictate" (p. 43). The wording of verse 2 makes it clear that God is asking (not commanding, not dictating) Abraham to offer Isaac as a sacrifice. Whether Abraham was responding to a request or to a command, he obeyed. Writes Cantor: "The story of the sacrifice of Isaac had a profound message for the Hebrew mind down through the centuries" (p. 20).

Obedience is a key Jewish concept, as *faith* is a key Christian concept. Jonathan Magonet puts it thus: "what God seems to demand of man is neither belief nor disbelief but the right actions that would follow if he *did* believe" (p. 169).

"A God of truth and without iniquity, just and right is He" (Harkavy).

"A faithful God who does no wrong, righteous and true is He" (Oxford).

Significantly, the Akedah story does not contain the word *faith*. Abraham's obedience to God's command is recognized in the statement of the angel of the Lord: "Do not raise your hand against the boy, or do anything to him. For now I know that you fear God, since you have not withheld your son, your favored one, from Me" (22:12).

Søren Kierkegaard, the father of modern religious Existentialism, wrote *Fear and Trembling*[2] in the form of a commentary on the Akedah, in which he describes Abraham as the perfect knight of faith. Abraham demonstrates the highest level of faith, which is the surrender of one's ordinary sense of right and wrong to do God's will.

Faith is not merely a difference between presence or absence, stronger or weaker; there are, says Kierkegaard, different levels of faith. For example, suppose Abraham took Isaac to Moriah, prepared the altar, and then declared, "God, I cannot sacrifice my son. Let me give you my own life as an act of faith." Then, he plunged the knife into his own breast and died as a witness to his faith. Had Abraham done such a thing, "he

---

2. Maybaum traces the title of Kierkegaard's book to the eleventh line of Psalm 2: "Serve the Lord with fear, and rejoice with trembling." Maybaum's twenty-four-page essay attempts to differentiate between a Jewish interpretation of the Akedah and Kierkegaard's Christian interpretation. Writes Maybaum, a Jewish writer might name his commentary on the Akedah, not Fear and Trembling, but Trust and Peace (p. 5).

Maybaum is not on solid ground in asserting Kierkegaard necessarily got his book title from Psalm 2. The words "fear and trembling" also appear in Psalm 55:5, and in five lines of the New Testament (Mark 5:33, I Corinthians 2:3, II Corinthians 7:15, Ephesians 6:5, and Philippians 2:12). While Kierkegaard's title is out of spirit with Psalm 2:11, the title does express the spirit of Philippians 2:12— "Work out your own salvation with fear and trembling."

would have been admired in the world," says Kierkegaard (p. 35). He would have demonstrated a kind of faith, but not the level of faith Abraham showed at Moriah.

Abraham's faith was a surrender of his own judgment of right and wrong in favor of unconditional acceptance to God's will.[3] This separation of religious faith from moral judgment is,

---

3. Christianity stresses belief, and so Kierkegaard describes Abraham as "a man of perfect faith." Judaism stresses action and would describe Abraham as a man of monumental obedience.

Is the lesson of the Akedah that everyone should be ready to obey some extraordinary request from God, even if it violates the ordinary rules of morality? Martin Buber warned against this interpretation, as has already been noted in chapter 8. "Molech imitates the voice of God," warned Buber (1952, p. 73). Keep in mind God speaks in "a still small voice" (I Kings 19:12), and fundamentally God "asks nothing but justice and mercy" (1952, p. 73).

The Akedah is clearly a eulogy to obedience, notes Alan Miller, expressed by the obedience of Abraham to God, and the obedience of Isaac to Abraham. Miller sermonizes, obedience is good only when it is balanced with defiance, represented by Abraham's smashing his father's idols, and by Abraham's arguing with God over the people of Sodom and Gomorrah (p. 31).

Perhaps this lesson of obedience has been too strong, Miller argues. Perhaps obedience has been too dominant a rule in the history of the Jewish people. Perhaps it was a necessary adaptation mechanism for their survival through centuries of persecution. Opposition was expressed secretly and through subterfuge, like the escape of Yokhanan ben Zakkai from Jerusalem by hiding in a box.

In Israel today, Miller continues, children are taught about bolder, more aggressive national heroes: Jabotinsky, Trumpeldor, Dayan. Perhaps today submission is not so worthy a ruling virtue in the state of Israel, which may be seeing the flowering of Jewish *chutzpah* (Miller, pp. 31–32).

Jerome Gellman writes of "Daas Torah," a Hasidic movement which advocates an "ethic of submission" based on the Akedah. As Abraham gave blind obedience to the command of God, "the individual sacrifices his intellect on the altar of blind obedience to the words of the sages" (pp. 54–55). Please note that "Daas Torah" advocates blind obedience not to privately-conveyed Divine commandments, but "to the words of the sages."

according to Joseph H. Gumbiner, "part of a long line of Christian thought starting with Augustine," and articulated by a long line of Christian thinkers, both historical and recent (p. 146).

In Jewish thought, the ways of God may be obscure, hidden, mysterious. However, God continues "to dispense the Torah" to reveal his wisdom, and the ways of God become increasingly better known to man. Meanwhile, obedience to God's commandments, even in matters that are not understood, is an expression of faith that the conduct of a God-fearing person will express the highest ethical values, and eventually in God's own time, may know the reasons for each and every commandment. "God has told man what is good, what he requires of him: that he do justice," writes Gumbiner (p. 146). Further, in Judaism "no suspension, setting aside, or dethronement of the ethical is possible."[4]

What do man and God want of each other? Two concepts which define this relationship are *duty* and *love*. Covenant, law, requirements, obligation, obedience, justice, and commandment all are duty concepts. On the other hand, mercy, faith, and compassion are love concepts. The God of Abraham is a God of justice and mercy. Which takes priority? Which is the greater good? What do these questions have to do with the Akedah?

At the outset of the Akedah narrative, God describes Isaac as

---

4. Gumbiner concedes "*Fear and Trembling* is beautifully written, salted with great wit, provocative of much philosophical meditation," and the book is a worthy exposition of Kierkegaard's crisis theology. However, he asserts it has taught him nothing about Abraham, either as a historical character or as a mythological figure (p. 148).

Responses of Jewish scholars to *Fear and Trembling* are mixed and range from condemnation to admiration. For example, Milton Steinberg regards Kierkegaard's point of view as "unmitigated sacrilege" (*Anatomy of Faith*, New York: Harcourt, Brace, 1960, p. 147). For a discussion of Jewish responses more sympathetic to Kierkegaard's thought, see Jerome I. Gellman. A middle position is advanced by Ernest Simon, in *Conservative Judaism*, Spring 1958, vol. 12, pp. 15–19.

the "one whom you love," and in the same sentence he commands Abraham to fulfill an extraordinary duty that would consume this love-object. Therefore, an important theme of the Akedah is this tension between love and duty.

The sacrifice of Isaac is an extraordinary commandment, even in Abraham's times. Vauter observes that "so terrible is the thing Abraham feels he must do, even though it has been commanded by God, he cannot bring himself to reveal it to his companions. Thus he dissembles to his servants, taking refuge in circumlocutions: We will worship and then come back to you. The same dissimulation he makes to Isaac, when the latter innocently inquires about the sheep for the holocaust" (p. 254). Abraham cannot bring himself to talk about it, cannot argue about it (as he argued with God about the destruction of Sodom and Gomorrah), and—so far as the Akedah narrative tells us—does not tell Sarah what he is about to do.

Is this absence of detail concerning Abraham's feelings a literary style, as Auerbach and others have suggested, or does the sketchy, emotionally-flat Akedah narrative express Abraham's mute dumbstruck reaction to an unthinkable command?

At the end of the story, of course, love triumphs over duty; the demanding Elohim is revealed as the compassionate Adonai. Abraham's love for Isaac triumphs over his compulsion to obey a terrible command. Arieti and Zeligs who study the Akedah from a psychological perspective, both interpret the story as the triumph of love over duty; ego over superego. Abraham symbolizes the love of a father for his son and for descendants not yet born. According to Arieti, "To love anything and everything that God makes us love is to love God" (p. 156).

16

THE DISASTER INTERPRETATION

"After these things . . ."—the opening words of Genesis 22 have a haunting ambiguity. After Satan cast doubt on Abraham's devotion? After Abraham expelled Hagar and Ishmael? After what things? Maybe we're making a fuss about nothing; maybe "After these things" means nothing more than "Once upon a time . . ." Apparently, this was the thinking that guided the Jewish Publication Society's 1967 translation which begins Genesis 22 with the words, "Some time afterward, God put Abraham to the test."

It is not easy to ignore (or rewrite) the opening words, "After these things." In this chapter, we will share the intuition of David Polish, Marc Gellman, Martin Buber, and others that a clue to solving the Akedah puzzle might lie in correctly establishing just what is referred to by "After these things."

It is not the expulsion of Hagar and Ishmael. Abraham was not living in so barren and hostile a wasteland that setting Hagar and Ishmael free was tantamount to murdering them. Gellman is sure God's voice "drips with irony and sarcasm" when he supports Sarah's wishes; but who shares this odd interpretation?

Martin Buber likewise searches for a referent to "After these things" (1968, p. 41). He focuses on Abraham's expression of doubt that God would ever give him an heir of his "own issue" (15:4).*

If all three are wrong in linking "After these things" with the expulsion of Ishmael or with doubt about the fulfillment of God's promise, what else might "After these things" refer to? Consider this possibility: "After these things" refers to some extraordinary episode somehow deleted from the Bible.

Deleted? Most scholars concede the Bible is the work of many writers and redactor-editors, working at different periods of history. Editors rewrite, editors add, and editors also delete. If the Bible had editors, it had deletions. This speculation raises two questions—What did the editors delete? Why did they delete it?

What was deleted from the chapters that precede Genesis 22? Consider the story of a major disaster—famine;[1] a terrible

---

*The disaster Interpretation is also set forth in the form of a midrash in Appendix 1.

1. Famine is a recurrent hazard in the ancient world, and this disaster strikes twice in Genesis, in chapters 12 and 26. The Akedah has an interesting parallel to a Greek legend in which an averted human sacrifice is intended to put an end to a famine.

This is a fragment of the Argonaut legend, concerning King Athamas (Abraham?) and his two wives: Queen Nephele (Sarah?) and her son Prixus (Isaac?)—and the wife he later took: Ino (Hagar?) and her son Melicertes (Ishmael?). The two wives hate each other. Ino schemes to create a famine by roasting the seed grain before it is planted. She then persuades Athamas to sacrifice Prixus to bring the famine to an end. Athamas is ready to comply and already holds the sacrificial knife in his hand, when he hears the voice of Hercules (the angel?), the son of Zeus, cry out, "My father, Zeus, King of Heaven, loathes human sacrifices!" A golden-fleeced ram sent by Zeus then appears, and Prixus is carried on its back to the Land of Colchis where he prospers. To escape the anger of Athamas, Ino and Melicertes (Hagar and Ishmael?) flee and eventually are deified by Zeus. This sketch is adapted from Graves and Patai (pp. 176–177).

This Greek parallel suggests that in the original myth, Hagar's wrath led to a famine, which the sacrifice of Isaac was prescribed to

disease suffered by himself or by members of his family; repeated invasions by desert robbers who rob, rape, and murder; a pestilence that wipes out whole flocks, or claims men, women, and children. Something monumentally terrible happens making Abraham reexamine ways of reaching God and pleading for mercy or forgiveness. (Had he sinned against God? Had he stirred God's wrath?)

The disaster hasn't gone away yet. Will it get better or will it get worse? Children are suffering and dying. Perhaps the pestilence will take his beloved Sarah and Isaac too. Should Abraham offer Isaac on a holy altar and save his entire neighborhood from a loathsome death?[2]

How could such a thought have occurred to Abraham? He was living in a world where people coped with extreme disaster in this way. Abraham was seventy-five years old when God called him to leave Haran and journey "to a new land which I

---

terminate. This story of the rivalry of the two wives of King Athamas resonates both with the midrash that the averted sacrifice was connected with the rivalry between Sarah and Hagar, and also with the conjecture that the Akedah was intended to avert a disaster.

Which came first, the Akedah or the Argonaut legend? The legends of ancient Greece were believed to have been recorded around 1000 B.C.E. (But when did they originate?) Abraham is believed to have lived around 1700 B.C.E. (But did the Akedah originate during Abraham's actual lifetime or was it written, as some have argued, many generations afterward?) Irving Zeitlin writes that the Greek myths probably originated in the world of the Near East (p. 11). Perhaps both of these legends had a common origin in the dim past of the ancient world.

2. The only person known to have set forth this case is Dorothy B. Hill. She writes:

> Inconsistent though human sacrifice may seem to be with all Abraham's other relations with his son, it is still possible that, threatened by some dire calamity to his tribe or frantic because of the spread of some fatal epidemic, Abraham could not resist the pleadings of his people to do something that would assuage God's anger. Their prayers and sacrifice of the best of their herds and flocks had been of no avail: the scourge continued to take its awful daily toll of life. What else could be done? they asked, and looked to Abraham for the answer. (p. 176)

shall show you." Abraham had grown up and grown to late maturity in a world where animal sacrifice was the normal way to express homage, thanksgiving, or contrition to the gods. Human sacrifice was a rare and extraordinary ritual evoked by some major crisis: famine, drought, disease, pestilence, or war.

Abraham faced an agonizing crisis. Perhaps many human lives were at stake. In this context, offering one life to save many lives is an agonizing thought but not an impossible one. "I am so deeply convinced this is what I have to do," Abraham thought to himself, "it is as if I can hear God telling me, 'Yes, Abraham; go ahead and do it.'"

In other parts of the Bible, human sacrifice is the response to an extraordinary danger. The most detailed account of the circumstances that led up to a human sacrifice is told in Judges, the story of Jephtha's daughter.

> When Ammon made war against Israel, the elders of Gilead reluctantly (we suppose) called upon Jephtha, "a mighty man of valor," to lead Israel's fight against the Ammonites. A most unlikely leader of the Hebrews, Jephtha had been driven out of his father's house because he was the son of a harlot. After having been disowned, he rounded up a gang of roughnecks and now was probably the chief of a band of raiders.
>
> Jephtha bargained with the Gileadites saying if they wanted him to be their chief warrior, they would also have to name him their leader. The Gileadites must have been facing rather desperate circumstances to seek such a leader and to accept such terms. Jephtha also bargained with God—if he was victorious over the Ammonites, "whatever cometh forth of the doors of my house to meet me, when I return in peace from the children of Ammon, shall surely be the Lord's, and I will offer it up for a burnt offering" (Judges 11:31).
>
> Jephtha did subdue the children of Ammon, and when he returned to his house, his only child, "his daughter came out to meet him with timbrels and with dances." Jephtha agonized over his fate, and his daughter begged that the sacrifice be postponed for two months time. During this period, she and her companions went up and down the mountains and bewailed her virginity. When she returned to her father, Jephtha "did with her according to his vow which he had vowed" (Judges 11:34–39).

Other specific instances of human sacrifice are documented in the pages of the Bible. For example, when his capital was under siege, the King of Moab sacrificed his only son. So shocking was this event, it scattered his adversaries (II Kings 3:27). Another example, during the Syro-Ephraimite War, Achaz "made his son pass through the fire" (II Kings 16:3). And another, Kings II also records that Manasseh, the flagrantly idolatrous king of Judah, "made his son pass through the fire."

Human sacrifice was, of course, prohibited and punishable by death. "Any man among the Israelites . . . who gives any of his offspring to Molech, shall be put to death; the people of the land shall pelt him with stones (Leviticus 20:2. This prohibition is repeated in Leviticus 20:3 and 4). In addition to the above five citations, the Bible includes no less than fifteen more denunciations of human sacrifice (listed at the end of chapter 17). A practice is repeatedly denounced for a reason: it is known to be practiced. (Cannibalism was never denounced because it was virtually never practiced.)

Now, let us ask the second question: Why should a disaster chapter have been deleted? If this hypothetical chapter were left standing, it would have reduced the Akedah to a desperate attempt to cope with a natural or social disaster. By deleting this hypothetical chapter and altering a sentence here and there, the Akedah now stands as a monument to Abraham's obedience, as a testimony to God's mercy, and as an eternal mystery. Those Divinely-inspired writers of the Bible were not only poets, historians, law-givers, priests, and visionaries, they were also, as Alter argues, master storytellers.

Much that we have said about this "disaster chapter" is speculation. The rabbinical tradition encourages speculation; that is what midrashim are made of. It is a matter of speculation that a disaster chapter preceded the Akedah. However, scholars tend to agree on what has been added to the original Akedah narrative. It is widely believed that verses fifteen through eighteen are later additions to the story. These verses are hortatory, preachy insertions into a story that has a consistently sparse, narrative tone. Further, reference to "seizing the gates of foes" reflects the interests of later generations, not of Abraham's era.

There are so many midrashim on the Akedah—the reader may protest—do we need a midrash on a missing disaster chapter? In defense of this midrash, it may be said that unlike many midrashim which only embellish the Akedah story, this disaster midrash attempts to solve two mysteries of the Akedah: 1) What is referred to in "After these things"? and 2) What real-life circumstances[3] led Abraham to believe that God wanted him to make the incredible move to sacrifice Isaac?

The reader may hesitate to consider this speculation because while it would solve the puzzle of the Akedah, it would also rob the Akedah narrative of its aura of mystery. Like a beautiful pearl hidden in an oyster, the Akedah can be enjoyed for what it has evolved into. However, it is also legitimate to ask, How did it become what it is now? We know that the beautiful pearl is the oyster's response to an irritant, a tiny stone that lodges inside the oyster. What was the irritant that produced the Akedah? In everyday language, what were the real-life circumstances that led Abraham to think of sacrificing Isaac? (Other conjectures on the origin of the Akedah are surveyed in chapter 20.)

If the disaster chapter were never deleted, would it make the Akedah a better story? No, it would then lose much of its mystery and fascination. Perhaps that is why it was deleted.

---

3. One of the first principles taught in an undergraduate course in psychology is that behavior is always the result of an individual in an environment. This viewpoint was formalized and refined by Kurt Lewin in his Field Theory. It must be said that, to an extent, Lewin formalized the obvious. To make sense of a person's actions, one must always ask, What's going on around him? What are the social pressures? What are the circumstances?

17

THE HUMAN-LIFE-IS-SACRED INTERPRETATION

Jewish scholars understandably reject the traditional Christian notion that the biblical Hebrews were still a morally primitive people, and that the message of the Akedah was to substitute animal sacrifice for child sacrifice, asserted to be a common practice among them at that time.[1] In chapter 4 of Genesis, Abel sacrifices a lamb to God. Noah's first act, after the flood, was to make a sacrificial offering. In all likelihood, animal sacrifice was a widespread form of religious worship many centuries before the time of Abraham.

Infant sacrifice[2] did not need to be a common practice in

---

1. For a discussion of this point of view, see chapter 14, "The Deglorification Interpretation."

2. The modern reader may be so overwhelmed with disgust and revulsion over the very idea of infant sacrifice that it becomes difficult to understand how this was once an established practice among sensible human beings.

We can begin to "understand infant sacrifice" by noting that, in ancient times, social cohesion was a powerful and successful survival mechanism in a world of famine, plague, and other threats and

order to be condemned in the strongest terms, as indeed it is throughout the Bible. Why did infant sacrifice exist at all among the Hebrews? It does appear to have been a Canaanite practice,[3] which made infant sacrifice a Hebrew problem. At one time a significant portion of the Hebrew people were either neighbors of Canaanites, Canaanite converts to the Hebrew faith, or the children of converts.

How did the Hebrew tribes suddenly grow from "a mixed

---

disasters. In the beginning of the human drama, the clan was everything, and the individual was nothing. Infant sacrifice was practiced to ward off disaster and save the clan from extinction. The absolute authority of the patriarch symbolized the absolute priority of the tribe over the individual.

Gradually, society would move from the rule that the community is everything, to a respect for the rights of the individual. First, every adult male might be recognized as an individual "created in the image of God." Then, a ban against infant sacrifice proclaimed that even an infant, however weak and defenseless, must be respected as an individual. (The liberation of women would come later.)

Note that in the Book of Job, all his children die ("they were sacrificed" one might say) to test Job's faith. After he passes his test, Job fathers more children. What does the Book of Job say about the regard for children as individuals?

True, the Akedah story does not deal with infant sacrifice literally, but it can be argued that for tactical reasons, the Akedah addresses the topic of infant sacrifice indirectly or obliquely.

3. Writes Vauter: "One of the sadder aspects of Canaanite archaeology is the constant recurrence of infant skeletons buried beneath the thresholds of city gates and houses, evidence of the tiny lives that had been sacrificed to ward away evil and ensure divine protection. Both in Israel's laws and in the works of its prophets and historians human sacrifice is excoriated as a heathen abomination, but the same sources leave us no doubt that it was often practiced by Israelites all the same, and that it was sometimes regarded by them as compatible with the worship of Yahweh" (p. 255).

Says Gottwald: "A much-debated issue concerns the incidence and obligatoriness of human sacrifice in ancient Canaan and within Israel itself" (1985, p. 215).

multitude"[4] to a mighty nation? There are scholars who propose a "peasant revolution" theory.[5] According to this theory, the Canaanites had lived a life of bitter subjugation[6] in city-states ruled by god-kings, who claimed a divine right to oppress their subjects.

When the Hebrews settled in the land of Canaan, they told the indigenous population their oppressive god-kings were imposters, so to speak, that no rulers are gods. There is in truth but one God of all the universe—hidden and invisible—a God of justice and mercy.

This revolutionary message undercut the claims of the god-kings and became a "liberation theology" to the Canaanite peasants. Many joined the Hebrews in fighting the professional armies of the god-kings. When the Land of Canaan was won by the Hebrews, not only did individuals and families join the Israelites, but many populations of Canaanite cities and towns remained on the land.[7]

The Canaanites were useful for more than forced labor; they

---

4. In these two places in the Bible, the Hebrews are referred to as a mixed multitude:

"And a mixed multitude went up also with them" (Exodus 12:38).

"And the mixed multitude that was among them fell to lusting, and the children of Israel also wept again and said, Who shall give us flesh to eat?" (Numbers 11:4).

5. George E. Mendenhall "The Hebrew Conquest," *The Tenth Generation*, 107.

6. Archaeologists study the size and quality of family living quarters to estimate living standards and judge the ancient Canaanites as being an oppressed people.

7. At first the Canaanites worked as a subject people, or became forced laborers, but undoubtedly many were gradually assimilated into the Israelite population. Judges 1:27–36 makes it clear the Israelites conquered the land, but much of the indigenous population remained.

Neither did Manasseh drive out the inhabitants of Bethshean and her towns, nor Taanach and her towns, nor the inhabitants of Dor and her

were members of an agricultural civilization and were able to
teach their semi-nomadic conquerors the arts of agriculture,
architecture, and other aspects of Canaanite civilization. Even
the language of the Israelites eventually bore the stamp of the
Canaanites; scholars of the ancient Semitic languages regard
Hebrew as a Canaanite dialect.[8]

Canaanite farming methods were intertwined with fertility
rites. Thus, Israelite farmers were brought into contact with
Canaanite religious ceremonies which were part of their formula for agricultural success. Infant sacrifice, however rare,
was a Canaanite practice[9] and, to some degree, took hold

---

towns, nor the inhabitants of Ibleam and her towns, nor inhabitants of
Megiddo and her towns: but the Canaanites would dwell in that land.
And it came to pass, when Israel was strong that they put the
Canaanites to tribute, and did not utterly drive them out.

Neither did Ephraim drive out the Canaanites that dwelt in Gezer,
but the Canaanites dwelt in Gezer among them. Neither did Zebulum
drive out the inhabitants of Kitron, nor the inhabitants of Nahalol; but
the Canaanites dwelt among them and became tributary. Neither did
Asher drive out the inhabitants of Accho, nor the inhabitants of Zidon,
nor of Ahlab, nor of Achzib, nor of Helbah, nor of Aphik, nor of Rehob;
but the Asherites dwelt among the Canaanites, the inhabitants of the
land; for they did not drive them out.

Neither did Naphtali drive out the inhabitants of Beth-shemesh, nor
the inhabitants of Beth-anath; but he dwelt among the Canaanites, the
inhabitants of the land: nevertheless the inhabitants of Beth-shemesh
and of Beth-anath became tributary to them. And the Amorites forced
the children of Dan into the mountain . . . yet the hand of the house
of Joseph prevailed, so that [the Amorites] became tributary. (Judges
1:27–35)

8. Among students of the ancient Semitic languages, it is a
generally accepted hypothesis that the Hebrew language is a Canaanite dialect. According to the *New Encyclopedia Britannica*, 15th
Edition, the Hebrew language "is closely related to Phoenician and
Moabite, with which it is often placed by scholars in a Canaanite
subgroup" ("Hebrew Language," *Micropedia*).

9. A turn-of-the-century archeologist reports that in Gezer he
found "a cemetery of infants, deposited in large earthenware jars. The
infants were all newly born, probably not more than a week old. A
cemetery containing some twenty infants, buried also in jars, about

among the Israelites. Hence, there are denunciations of infant sacrifice again and again throughout the Bible.

Taken from this perspective, the Akedah may be seen as one more strategy to eliminate human sacrifice entirely from the Hebrew people. The prophets denounced human sacrifice, and Deuteronomy legislates against human sacrifice. Fifteen such warnings appear throughout the Bible.[10] Addressed to those who could not be reached by direct denunciations and legis-

---

a rock-altar, was found afterwards in Taanach." The report is accompanied by photographs and drawings (1909 Driver, p. 68).

10. Fifteen denunciations of infant sacrifice that occur in the Bible:

1. "When the Lord thy God shall cut off the nations from before thee . . . and thou succeedest them, and dwellest in their land, take heed to thyself that thou be not snared by following them . . . [in their ways of serving their gods, for their ways are an] abomination to the Lord. . . .Even their sons and daughters they have burned in the fire to their gods" (Deuteronomy 12:29–31).
2. "Let no one be found among you who consigns his son or daughter to the fire" (Deuteronomy 18:10).
3. "For it came to pass, when Solomon was old, that his wives turned away his heart after other gods . . . Then did Solomon build an high place for . . . Molech . . . and likewise did he for all his foreign wives, who burned incense and sacrificed unto their gods" (I Kings 11:4, 7, 8).
4. "And the children of Israel did secretly those things that were not right against the Lord their God . . . and wrought wicked things to provoke the Lord to anger" [Another allusion to Molech worship?] (II Kings 17:9-11).
5. "And they left all the commandments of the Lord their God . . . and served Baal . . . and they caused their sons and daughters to pass through the fire" (II Kings 17:16–17).
6. [King Josiah orders the destruction of idols and pagan altars in Judah] "that no man might make his son or his daughter to pass through the fire to Molech" (II Kings 23:10). "We have sinned with our fathers, we have committed iniquity, we have done wickedly. . . . Our fathers . . . mingled among the nations, and learned their works, and they served their idols. . . .

lation, the Akedah adopts the more subtle tone of story telling. The Akedah speaks gently but firmly to "Hebrews by choice,"

Yea, they sacrificed their sons and their daughters . . . shed innocent blood . . . unto the idols of Canaan; and the land was polluted with blood" (Psalms 106:6, 7, 35–38).

7. "Are ye not children of transgression, a seed of falsehood, inflaming yourselves with idols under every green tree [perhaps referring to a fertility rite which involved sexual arousal], slaying children in the valleys under the clefts of the rocks?" (Isaiah 57:4–6).

8. "Go forth unto the valley of Hinnom . . . and proclaim there the words that I shall tell thee, and say, Hear the word of the Lord . . . Thus saith the Lord of hosts, the God of Israel, Behold, I will bring evil upon this place, concerning which whosoever heareth, his ears shall tingle. Because they have forsaken me, and have desecrated this place, and have burned incense in it unto other gods, whom neither they nor their fathers have known . . . and have filled this place with the blood of innocents. They have built also the high places of Baal, to burn their sons with fire for burnt offerings unto Baal, which I commanded not, nor spoke of it, neither came it into my mind. Therefore, behold, the days come, saith the Lord, that this place shall no more be called Topheth, nor The Valley of the Son of Hinnom, but The Valley of Slaughter" (Jeremiah 19:2–6).

9. "Thus saith the Lord of hosts, the God of Israel, Amend your ways and your doings. . . . Will ye steal, murder, and commit adultery, and swear falsely, and burn incense unto Baal, and walk after other gods whom ye know not? . . . But this thing I commanded them, saying, Obey my voice, and I will be your God. . . . But they hearkened not, nor inclined their ear, but walked in the counsels and in the imagination of their evil heart, and went backward and not forward. . . . And they have built the high places of Topheth . . . to burn their sons and their daughters in the fire, which I commanded them not" (Jeremiah 7:3, 9, 23, 24, 31).

10. "For the children of Israel and the children of Judah have only done evil before me . . . saith the Lord. . . . They built the high places of Baal . . . to cause their sons and their daugh-

to the Hebrew people's converts of Canaanite origin, and to those Hebrews who had fallen under the sway of their Canaanite neighbors: Listen, my dear kinfolk, even our Father Abraham believed with all his heart that God wanted him to sacrifice his son.[11] However, at the last moment he was commanded, "Do not raise your hand against the boy, or do anything to him." Thus God made it clear to Abraham and to

---

ters to pass through the fire unto Molech . . . this abomination . . . [this] sin" (Jeremiah 32:30, 35).

11. "Thou hast taken thy sons and thy daughters . . . and these hast thou sacrificed unto them to be devoured. . . . Thou hast slain my children, and delivered them to cause them to pass through the fire for them" (Ezekiel 16:20–21).

12. "The children rebelled against me; they walked not in my statutes. . . . Their eyes were after their fathers' idols. . . . They caused to pass through the fire all their first-born" (Ezekiel 20:21, 24, 26).

13. "For thus saith the Lord God: Behold, I will deliver thee into the hand of those who thou hatest . . . because thou art polluted with . . . idols . . . and have also caused their sons, whom they bore unto me, to pass for them through the fire, to devour them. . . . When they had slain their children to their idols, then they came the same day into my sanctuary to profane it" (Ezekiel 23:28, 30, 37, 39).

14. "O Israel, thou hast sinned. . . . And now they sin more and more, and have made them molten images of their silver. . . . Let them that sacrifice men kiss the [molten images of] calves (Hosea 10:9, 13:2).

15. "Shall I give my first-born for my transgression?" (Micah 6:7).

11.Michael Brown questions whether Abraham "believed with all his heart that God Wanted him to sacrifice his son." Perhaps Abraham responded with doubt, skepticism, and disappointment that God should ask for the sacrifice of Isaac. Abraham could not plead for Isaac, Brown reasons, because being granted a special favor would not tell Abraham the true nature of God. "Abraham had to know whether God respected human life in general, whether He protected children, all children, or devoured them. To find out, he had to test God, tempting Him by complying with His command (Brown 1982b, p. 21)."

Israel for all time, that God does not want children to be
sacrificed. That is not the Hebrew way to worship God—
animals yes,[12] but children no.

Modern commentators object that such an interpretation
reduces the Akedah to a historical footnote,[13] making it a story
of anthropological interest rather than a message of enduring
spiritual value. Maybe there is an enduring message even to
this interpretation of the Akedah—every child deserves to be
respected as a person.[14]

"Who is the real hero of the Akedah?" asks Moshe Moskowitz

---

12. When the Akedah was written, according to Gottwald, it was
an accepted idea that homage to God may at some time require the
sacrifice of one's dearest possession. The Akedah changes this
profoundly-held idea, and "gives a most emphatic rejection of child
sacrifice while it respects and retains the intention of sacrifice: the
giving of everything to God. Elohim accepts the intention in place of
the act" (Gottwald, p. 253).

13. Gottwald calls the Akedah "a polemic against widely accepted
human sacrifice" (1985, p. 215). The Akedah is not polemic in tone! It
appeals to the reader's love of a good story and conveys its message
without denunciation.

Arieti acknowledges that many interpretations "see in the story of
the Akedah only Judaism's opposition to child sacrifice—a practice
quite common in ancient times" (p. 136). However, this does not
explain the "great spiritual value" of the story today and reduces the
story to "at most only anthropological interest" (p. 137).

14. Respect for a young person's individuality is a plea that is often
heard from rabbis of our time—sometimes in connection with
Genesis 22 and sometimes not.

In his commentaries on the Akedah, Gunther Plaut discusses the
relevance of the Akedah to father-son relationships in our time:

Even as God is the dominant Father and Abraham a trusting and
obedient son, so in the purely human realm Abraham appears as the
dominant father and Isaac as the archetype of the submissive son. . . .

The story may thus be read as a paradigm of a father-and-son
relationship. In a way every parent seeks to dominate his child and is
in danger of seeking to sacrifice him to his parental plans or hopes. In
the biblical story, God is present and can therefore stay the father's
hand. In all too many repetitions of the scene God is absent and the

(pp. 288–89). "Is it God, who demands an outrageous act . . .?
Is it Isaac, being led like a proverbial sheep to the slaughter?

---

knife falls. Thus is the Akedah repeated forever, with its test and its
terror (pp. 150–151).

Sheldon Zimmerman states the case even more bluntly for protecting
the interests of Isaac:

> I do not think that it was such a great thing for Abraham to be willing
> to sacrifice Isaac. We've done it, you and I, throughout history. How
> many times have parents sent our children off to war for the sake of
> some ideal? We have been like Abraham . . . too quiet. . . . too
> willing. . . . I do not think that Abraham is necessarily a great hero in
> this story. . . . We remember the Vietnam War, when we/Abraham
> sent off our Isaacs. . . . How often do we sacrifice our children? Some
> ideals . . . we ought to sacrifice our children for, but I do not think
> every ideal is worthy of such a sacrifice (Miller, p. 11).

Again, Zimmerman observes: "There are many cases in which we do
sacrifice our children, in the simplest way, not allowing them
properly to develop for themselves" (Miller, p. 16).

Without reference to the Akedah, Harold Schulweis pleads with
parents to respect each child as an individual, rather than rating
them by how well they satisfy their parents' standard of academic
achievement:

> From infancy the child is trained to repay his parents for their sacrifice
> and love in one and only one way: the report card. . . . A grade of C
> or D is a mark of betrayal, a sign of ingratitude. . . . The complaint of
> indolence sounds as if the failing marks were deliberately intended by
> the child, more evidence of the child's moral failure than his academic
> limitations. . . . It is difficult for parents who place such an inordinate
> stress on grades to convince the child to feel other than a failure.
> . . . Responsible Jewish educators must [clearly distinguish between
> the moral values of] . . . Judaism and middle-classism. They must
> provide in the Jewish environment of schools and synagogues . . . a
> culture relieved of the mindless compulsion to succeed, an ambience in
> which character, prosocial behavior, and idealism are exhalted, and
> where the spirit of the child and adult are acknowledged as praiseworthy
> (pp. 115–17).

A few years ago, a family reunion brought me to the Detroit area and
to a synagogue where I chanced to hear a sermon—not about the

Can it possibly be Abraham, who raises his voice to argue for the safety of the innocent in Sodom and Gomorrah, but who raises only a knife when it comes to his own son? Or, perhaps it is the ram, actually rendering its life to God, that is the real hero."

The answer is "None of the above," says Moskowitz; the real heroes of the story are the angels, according to a midrash, who

---

Akedah—in which the rabbi pleaded that parents respect each child's individuality.

> Every child is different, and if we are honest we will admit that we love our children in different ways. One child we may love proudly, another child we may love protectively; one child needs tenderness, another child may need discipline, another child may need a great deal of freedom to grow in independence. And please let us never try to mould them in our image (Syme).

Editorializing in *Tikkun*, Michael Lerner writes:

> The point of the story [of the Akedah] is that Abraham didn't kill him. . . . Abraham is about to do what parents in every generation have done—to send their children to their deaths in order to placate the wrathful gods who seem to rule the universe. Indeed, attributing the necessity of pain to some god is a way of protecting oneself from a more troubling recognition: that the cruelty is *not* built into the structure of necessity. Rather the pain, cruelty, and oppression that we face in daily life is rooted in a vicious social order and . . . [we] have become the vehicles for passing on . . . the pain and suffering that keeps the larger order functioning. What makes Abraham the father of our people is that he is able to recognize that the voices of accumulated pain are *not* God, and that the real voice of God does *not* want him to sacrifice his child. (pp. 7–8)

To add an interfaith note, a Raleigh, North Carolina, minister C. Brand Jr. sermonizes on the underlying theme of the Akedah: "Our gods of today are still being honored by the sacrifice of children. . . . The god of nation, the state and national interest, national security . . . my country wrong or right. . . . We offer up our children to the god of economics, greed, capitalism; the god of work, property, value and money. Or there are children offered at the shrine of the god of fame and honor" (Brand, p. 20).

pleaded with God to spare Isaac simply because he is a human being. As Isaac was about to be slaughtered, the angels wept and pleaded: "Sovereign of all the world! Thou art called merciful and compassionate, whose mercy is upon all His works; have mercy upon Isaac, for he is a human being, and the son of a human being, and is bound before Thee like an animal."[15]

Whether responding to the pleas of angels, or expressing a Divine compassion that was ready to manifest itself, the angel of God calls out, "Do not raise your hand against the boy or do anything to him." With these words, God's love for human life rules out the practice of human sacrifice, even as an appeal to God under the most desperate of circumstances.

Even today, our courts have not quite reconciled the principle of parental rights with the principle of the best interests of the child. Does an infant or young child belong to his father in the sense that his father can do with him anything he considers proper, including using him to express his homage to God?

"Do not raise your hand against the boy" expresses God's love for the weak and defenseless and gives the child's own interests priority over the wishes of his elders.

The triumph of mercy over homage is a valid theme of the Akedah—mercy for the individual, young or old. If we see in the prohibition of child sacrifice a moral rule that a child's welfare comes first and deserves priority over the wishes or interests of parents, church, or state, then the Akedah is indeed relevant to our time.

Today, this is not a settled principle; do parents have the right to decide what is best for the child until the child is old enough to take responsibility for his own decisions? Or does the child have his own rights from birth? Do parents have the right to use their children to fulfill their own ambitions, or must children be free to live their own lives? Do governments

---

15. Moskowitz (p. 293, fn. 27) cites as a source for this midrash, *Pirke De Rabbi Eliezer,* translated by Gerald Friedhandler (London: 1916) 227–228.

have the right to draft young men, putting their lives at risk simply to advance the national interest? Is a human life something that can be sacrificed on a sacred altar, or is each human life sacred in its own right?[16]

---

16. Alan Miller makes an interesting observation: In the Akedah story, Abraham is referred to eighteen times, always by name. Only once is Isaac referred to simply by his name alone; almost always, Isaac is called "thy son" or "the lad." Says Rabbi Miller: "I do not believe this kind of thing can be accidental. I do not know what it means" (Miller, p. 20). One possible meaning is that referring to Isaac as "the lad" or "thy son" symbolizes a child is regarded as less than a full person in his own right.

Certainly in Abraham's time (as today) "the father possessed absolute right over the life and death of his children." writes Wellisch. The Akedah, Wellisch argues, transforms the meaning of fatherhood from absolute ruler to the all-loving parent who obeys God's command, "Do not touch the lad." That is to say, the biblical ethic says a man may not exercise his aggressive impulses against his son. Exercise them elsewhere, but not against your son. In the Akedah story, God himself changes from Elohim (as he is called in the beginning of the story), the vengeful and demanding God, to Adonai (as he is called at the end of the story), a God of mercy.

ILLUSTRATIONS

The Akedah is the only Bible story illustrated on this sixth-century synagogue mosaic floor at Bet-Alpha, Israel. *Left*: Entire floor design, dominated by zodiac; the Akedah is depicted at the entrance (right end). Work is signed by mosaicists Marianos and his son Hanina. *Right*: Akedah detail, rendered in naive style.

Above: Wall above Torah niche in third-century c.e. syna-
gogue at Dura-Europos, Roman outpost on the Euphrates.
Shown here are four symbols of Judaism (*left to right*): the
menorah, lulav and etrog, the Temple, and the Akedah.
Artist's sketch from photograph. Below: Plan of west wall at
Dura-Europos synagogue. Torah niche is 19, space with
Akedah scene is 16. Wall is covered with 17 biblical and
ceremonial scenes.
Reference for artist's sketch and wall plan: "Akedah," in
Encyclopedia Judaica.

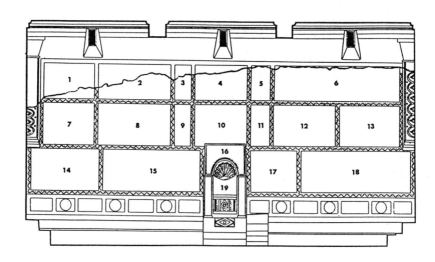

Right: Fresco mural of Sacrifice of Isaac in ancient Christian catacomb on Via Latina, Rome.
Artist's sketch from color photograph in Early Christian Art, *André Grabar, 1968. Below*: Christian image of Sacrifice of Isaac as prefiguration of the Crucifixion.
Artist's sketch of illustration in medieval Psalter of Queen Ingeborg. Psalter at Musée Condé, Chantilly, France.

A page from the Second Nürnberg Haggadah, 15th century, Germany, illustrating the midrash that Isaac had indeed been sacrificed and was now resurrected. Lettering below figure of Isaac descending from Heaven reads: חזר יצחק הדור מן הגן אשר נטע אל בעדינו מגן; Isaac returned glorified from the Garden [of Eden] that God planted for our protection.

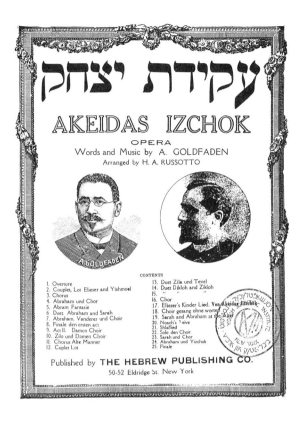

Above: Cover of libretto of the popular Yiddish opera, *Akeidas Izchok*, written by the father of the Yiddish theater, Abraham Goldfaden, and first performed in 1897. *Below*: Dutch tiles with Akedah themes. At left, circa 1675; at right, circa 1750. *Author's collection.*

Left: In 1635 and 1636 Rembrandt made two almost-identical paintings of the Akedah. The first is now at The Hermitage, in Petersburg. The second, shown here, is at die Alte Pinakothek in Munich, Germany. *Above:* Abraham speaking to Isaac; Rembrandt etching dated 1645, Staatliche Graphische Sammlung, Munich. Father and son pause on their journey. Bundle of wood, resting on ground, identifies this as an episode in Genesis 22.

Right: Rembrandt's "Abraham and Isaac" etching, produced 20 years after his oil painting. Rembrandt House, Amsterdam. Here angel embraces Abraham, and father holds son to his bosom. *Above:* Pen-and-ink sketch of the Akedah by Rembrandt; Staatlichen Kunstsammlungen, Dresden.

Above: Akedah folk art; multicolored wool embroidery on perforated cardboard. Palestine, 19th century. *Left*: Israeli postage stamp, 1978. *Right*: Minton tile, 1872, British; design by Moya Smith.

Above right: Moslem postcard (published in Ankara) of "Kurban." Ram is portrayed not caught in thicket but carried by angel, a typical Moslem detail. *Above left*: Traditional Jewish papercut. *Right*: Truck door with "Kurban" illustration, entitled: "God Tests Abram's [sic.] Faith." Photographed somewhere in Africa by Kenneth E. Schwartz of Dennville, N.J., while on safari in 1987.

Hz. İBRAHİMİN OĞLU İSMAİLİ
KURBAN ADAMA MISALİ

Above: Pastel drawing by Abel Pan. This pioneer Zionist artist produced several Akedah drawings. *Left*: Woodcut by Irwin Rosenhouse from *The Rabbi's Bible*, 1966. *Below*: Woodcut detail by Fritz Eichenberg from *What the Jews Believe*, Philip S. Bernstein, 1951.

Right: Woodcut by Hermann Feschenbach, dated 1926; author's collection. *Above:* Pen-and-ink drawing by W. Fletcher White, for *Old Testament Stories Retold for Children*, Lillie A. Faris, 1940. *Left:* Pen-and-ink drawing by E.M. Lilien, "the Jewish Beardsley," from *Die Bücher der Bibel*, Berlin-Vienna, 1923.

Right: Marc Chagall designed all the stained glass windows of St. Stephan's church in Mainz, Germany, including one that portrays the Akedah. At upper left, an angel is carrying a ram—a Moslem convention. At left background, Sarah is weeping. *Above:* Painting of the Akedah by Marc Chagall, in National Museum, Nice, France. In left background, Sarah sits weeping. According to Christian theologians, the Akedah prefigures the Crucifixion, which Chagall portrays in right background.

PART III

AKEDAH TOPICS

18

THE AKEDAH AND JEWISH PRAYER

Much of the talk that passes back and forth between strangers who want to get to know each other, between friends, between lovers, between husbands and wives, between parents and children, has nothing to do with the exchange of information. It has everything to do with an emotional need to hear each other's voices, to "touch each other," to express feelings toward each other.[1]

If God is part of a person's conceptual world, one wants not only to know God, but also to express his yearnings and feelings toward God. A person wants to thank God, to praise Him, perhaps to argue with Him (as Abraham did), to beg forgiveness for sin, and to plead with God for mercy, courage, guidance, understanding, protection, survival. As the psalmist advises: "Pour out your heart before him" (Psalm 62:8). This

---

1. *Phatic communication* is what rhetoricians call communication which serves emotional rather than intellectual purposes. Refusal to speak to another person expresses suspicion or even hostility. Man is a social animal. Solitary confinement (no one to talk to, no one to listen to) is a punishment of the greatest severity.

need to reach out to God is the function of prayer. It is an emotional need, just as we have an emotional need to talk to people.[2]

God may have the power to respond to prayer by granting all sorts of blessings and favors, but does one deserve them? A Jew deserves God's favor to the extent that he has fulfilled the commandments. However, who has lived a life so meritorious, so unblemished, as to have really earned God's favor? Either one must invoke God's mercy, or base his appeal, the rabbis advise, not on one's own merits, but on *Zekhut Avot*: the merits of the fathers.[3]

The principle of *Zekhut Avot*, it has been argued, is rooted in the Bible: When the Israelites worshipped the golden calf, a furious God said to Moses, "Let me alone, that my wrath may burn against them. . . . [Moses implored God:] Remember Abraham, Isaac, and Israel, thy servants. . . . And the Lord repented of the evil which he thought to do unto his people"

---

2. The custom of making a sacrificial offering may also be regarded as an expression of the wish to reach God by giving something back to God in return for all one has received from him.

3. The earliest use of the term *Zekhut Avot*, according to Birnbaum (p. 192) is the line in the Ethics of the Fathers, which goes: "Let all who work for the community do so from a spiritual motive, for then the merit of their fathers will sustain them, and their righteousness will endure forever" (Avoth 2:2). Here, the call is for performing acts of righteousness not for one's own sake, but for the sake of one's descendants. (This citation has little to do, it might be noted, with the liturgical principle of *Zekhut Avot*.)

The basic idea of *Zekhut Avot* overlaps the Christian concept of vicarious atonement. The early Church father Tertullian also credited Abraham with "the redemption of his posterity." "Abraham whom his faith made obey the command of God offered his only, beloved son as sacrifice to God so that God in His part bestowed on him the favor of the redemption of his posterity" (Tertlullian, *Adversus Judaeos*, 10).

The modern Lutheran theologian Gerhard von Rad reiterates Tertullian when Rad says that Abraham is not just the ancestor but the savior of his descendants. "From now on, every descendant of Abraham can say: . . . [From what he endured, *we*] *have the benefit* of the blessing that was given to him" (1971, p. 33, emphasis added).

(Exodus 32:10–14). "Therefore," said the rabbis, "whenever Israel comes into distress they call into remembrance the deeds of the Fathers." (Schechter, p. 175)

Accordingly, Jews at prayer ask for mercy not for the sake of their own merits, but for the merits which Abraham and Isaac displayed on Moriah. (Schechter says, see *Pesikta de-Rav Kahana 154a* and *b*, and *Pesikta Rabbati 171b*.)[4] This liturgical tactic is explicitly advocated by words in the Palestinian *Targum*, attributed to Abraham just after the sacrifice on Mount Moriah had been averted: "I pray for mercy before you, O Lord God, that, when the children of Isaac come to time of distress, you may remember for their sakes the Binding of Isaac

---

4. In opposition to the voices advocating *Zekhut Avot*, were those rabbis who claimed that *Zekhut Avot* was no longer true (Schechter, fn. 4, p. 175, 177). (Perhaps they felt that it was too close to the Christian doctrine of vicarious salvation.) These rabbis stressed that each person must earn his own salvation. The famous saying of Hillel was paraphrased to say, "If I have not acquired merit for myself, who will acquire merit for me, making me worthy of the world to come?" (Schechter, pp. 182–183). Again, "Let not a man say, my father was a pious man, I shall be saved for his sake" (Midrash Tehillim, 46:2).

Writes Marmorstein: "During centuries a fight of opinions wavered between the two schools which taught the doctrine of self-acquired and vicarious merits (p. 164). The latter remained victorious. . . . There must have been people who sinned and went astray, yet they relied on the virtues of their fathers. They thought, 'We can walk after the desire of our hearts, the "treasure" gathered by our fathers will always be good for us, will protect us, and grant us forgiveness.'" He then cites a number of voices that warned against reliance on the principle of *Zekhut Avot*. Here are just two: "The righteousness and deeds, merits and virtues of the fathers cannot redeem the unworthy offspring from the punishment they fully deserve. This was the view of Abtaljon and his followers" (p. 165). "In the sayings of the Amorim we detect traces of this opposition. . . . People who rely entirely on their own merits . . . as well as those who have no other merits than those of their fathers are rebuked. There must be a healthy proportion between one's own merits and those of his fathers" (p. 166).

their father, and loose and forgive their sins, and deliver them from all distress."[5]

Three times daily a Jew recites, in the opening benediction of the *Shemoneh Esreh* prayer: *Zokhrai hasdei avot*, "Remember the good deeds of the Patriarchs." The Akedah is a central theme in all penitential prayers (*selihot*). Rabbi Yaacov Culi writes: "All the merit of the Jewish people stems from this act. Whenever there is [a] time of trouble, we recite this chapter. We pray that God will have mercy on us and help us through the merit of the Akedah" (pp. 309–310).[6]

The redemptive value of the Akedah is an important theme in Jewish prayer, but it is not the only theme linked with the Akedah. The piyyutim composed during the Middle Ages linked two more ideas with the Akedah: the idealization of martyrdom, and a belief in Isaac's death and resurrection.[7]

These piyyutim are supported by midrashic references to "Isaac's ashes heaped upon the altar" (Leviticus Rabbah 36:5; Ta'anit 16a). This midrashic phrase has been interpreted to mean either Isaac died of fright on the altar and was quickly revived by a heavenly voice, or Isaac was actually sacrificed, rose to heaven, and was resurrected a few years later.

On the *selichot* of the day before New Year and before the Day of Atonement, the Ashkenazic ritual includes three Akedah piyyutim, and two Akedah piyyutim are scheduled for the *Minha* service of the Day of Atonement.

According to midrash Tanhuma, Genesis, God told Abraham that when the children of Isaac seek forgiveness of their sins, they should sound the ram's horn. This will recall the sacrifice of the ram that followed the Akedah, the deed by which Abraham earned the merit of his descendants.

---

5. Parallels in Jerusalem Talmud, Ta'anith 2:4 (65d), Genesis Rabbah 56:10, and Leviticus Rabbah 29:9.

6. *MeAm Lo'ez* (a Bible anthology) was written by Rabbi Yaacov Culi (1689–1732) and is regarded as an outstanding work of Judaeo–Spanish literature. Among Sephardic Jews it is considered a major classic.

7. See chapter 13, "The Martyrdom Interpretation," especially note 2.

In the words of Rabbi Abbahu, God asks Israel: "Sound before Me the ram's horn so that I may remember on your behalf the binding of Isaac, the son of Abraham, and account it to you as if you had bound yourself before Me."[8] Saadaih Gaon gave ten reasons for sounding the shofar on Rosh Hashana. In his list, he stressed that the shofar is sounded not only to remind God of the Jews' inherited merit, but "to teach us that we, too, must be ready at all times to offer our lives for the sanctification of God's name."[9]

In the Western tradition, New Year's Day is a day of noisy celebration. Rosh Hashanah, the Jewish New Year, by contrast, is observed with the greatest solemnity. By tradition, Rosh Hashanah is the day of Judgment and heralds the Day of Atonement that follows ten days later.

In the Remembrance Prayers, the *Zikhronot*, of Rosh Hashanah, there is an appeal to God to remember the Akedah, and on the second day of Rosh Hashanah, there is a reading of Genesis 22. The Remembrance Prayer goes:

> Remember in our favor, O Lord our God, the oath which Thou hast sworn to our father Abraham on Mount Moriah; consider the binding of his son Isaac upon the altar when he suppressed his love in order to do Thy will with a whole heart! Thus may Thy love suppress Thy wrath against us, and through Thy great goodness may the heat of Thine anger be turned away from Thy people, Thy city, and Thy heritage! . . . Remember today in mercy in favor of his seed the binding of Isaac" (Quoted from Landsberg).[10]

In the early rabbinic period, reference was made to Abraham's sacrifice in prayers of intercession. The Mishnah records

---

8. Babylonian Talmud, Rosh Hashana 16a.

9. Bodoff cites a nineteenth century German source. Bodoff p. 87, note 12.

10. This prayer, as cited by Landsberg, was inserted in the *musaf* arranged by Rab in the third century. Alan Miller conjectures that the Akedah was introduced into the Rosh Hashana liturgy during Christian times to remind Jews the God of Christianity carried out the Sacrifice, but the God of Israel did not (Miller, p. 9).

that the reader recited on public fast days: "May He that answered Abraham our father on Mount Moriah answer you and hearken this day to the voice of your pleading. Blessed art Thou, God, the Redeemer of Israel" (Ta'an 2:4).

The Mishnah also states that on fast days, ashes were placed on the Ark and on the heads of the nasi and the *av bet din* (Ta'anit 2:1); a later teacher explained this was a reminder of the 'ashes of Isaac' (Ta'anit 16a).

The observance of the first of the seventh month, *Tishri*, the reading of the Akedah is required, as it is the anniversary of Creation. It is also the anniversary of the binding of Isaac (Gray, p. 299).

In some places the Akedah is read daily during the morning service. Following this custom, this passage sometimes appears in prayer books as part of the early morning service:

> As Abraham our father overcame his compassion for his only son, and wanted to slaughter him in order to do Your will, in the same way may Your compassion overcome Your anger toward us, and may Your compassion overtake Your principles, and may You deal with us without recourse to the letter of Your Law, and may You deal with us, Lord our God, with the measure of beneficence and the measure of compassion, and in Your benevolence may Your wrath toward Your People and Your city, and Your country and Your portion be abated.

The liturgical significance of the Akedah is by no means limited to imploring God to remember the merit of Abraham. (Advises Rabbi Yaacov Culi: "When reading this chapter, one should shed tears, contemplating that he himself is ready to suffer martyrdom rather than disobey God" [p. 310]) The Akedah stirs all sorts of thoughts, memories, and feelings about faith, doubt, fear, suffering, martyrdom, survival, and forgiveness. Aharon Agus reflects:

> One may yet visit synagogues where, on the second day of *Rosh Hashannah*, the congregation trembles when the Binding of Isaac is chanted before the community. Its tune is a piercing one, an awaiting, a wondering, a weeping, a strength, a knowledge, a prayer, a demanding. This is a community whose

members survived, if survival is possible, the Holocaust. They know the ineluctibility of martyrdom for being Jewish, they know the command to *Akedah*; Abraham's vision comes as no surprise to them. They listen in hushed, sweating silence to the chanting. Their eyes fill with tears at the frightening truth of the myth. Their crying is the plea that the *Akedah* should no longer be demanded, that Abraham may draw back the knife, that history should be sufficient, that the Binding of Isaac they have seen and know should obviate the need for further martyrdom. For them Isaac's blood is truly shed, and they pray for it to be a vicarious deliverance, though it can be vicarious only in the sense that the survivors are spared, not in the mitigation of tragedy—for they have partaken of it. They will return home with a sense of relief, with a conviction that they have received a sanction for their quietism and passivity. (Agus, p. 252)

19

ISAAC AND OEDIPUS

The Akedah story has attracted the attention of several psychoanalytic writers, much as Sigmund Freud was attracted to the Oedipus drama of ancient Greece[1] for the light it seemed to throw on psychological development from infancy to maturity. In this chapter, we will study and compare what four psycho-

---

1. In the original Greek play by Sophocles, Oedipus murders Laius, king of Thebes, and marries Laius's widow, Jocasta. After many years of marriage, fathering two sons and two daughters, he learns to his horror that he murdered his own father and married his own mother. Horrified by the tragedy that has befallen their noble family, Jocasta kills herself, and Oedipus gouges out his eyes and exiles himself from his native city. To slay one's father and marry one's mother, Freud commented dryly, "is nothing more or less than a wish-fulfillment—the fulfillment of a wish of our childhood" (Freud, p. 308). The Oedipal story focuses on a mother's physical attraction toward her grown son, on the son's love for his mother and murderous hatred of his father. The Akedah describes a father's love for his son, a father's life-and-death power over his son, and the son's utter helplessness over the unlimited power of his father over him.

analytic writers, Erich Wellisch, Theodore Reik, Silvano Arieti, and Martin S. Bergmann, have written on the Akedah. First, let us compare the Akedah narrative and the Oedipus drama.

The Oedipus Complex

In their clinical practice, psychoanalysts (like all therapists) deal with people who, psychologically speaking, have never grown up. They are immature, perhaps even infantile. They cannot fight for themselves, or their aggressive impulses get out of control. They are excessively dependent on others, or they are so self-centered that other people do not seem to exist. If this is immaturity, what is psychological maturity? How is it normally attained? These are questions psychoanalysts and psychologists have asked, and the Oedipus complex has become a metaphor for describing the transition from psychological infancy to psychological maturity.[2]

An infant may be born into a civilization, but he is not born civilized. He is a wild, willful, selfish, destructive animal, and must learn to be kind, considerate of others, and a champion of all his society holds dear. How does it happen? It happens, said Freud, because the infant's willfullness[3] and selfishness bring him into direct conflict with the father and with the threat of terrible punishment.[4] The normal resolution of this

---

2. In her "Psychoanalytical Note on the Function of the Bible," Dorothy Zeligs writes, "The theme that runs like a unifying thread through the various books of the Bible is the story of man's struggle between the instinctual impulses and his wish and need for socialization. *This is indeed the kernel of the Oedipal conflict.*" (1957, p. 58, emphasis added.)

3. Underlying the infant's willfulness is his powerful need to love and be loved. Normally, parent and child are tied to each other in a powerful bond of love, when suddenly frustrated or denied, transforms into hatred.

4. In psychoanalytic theory, the boy's threat of punishment is felt as "castration anxiety." Not that boys have to be actually threatened; the knowledge that some children (girls) have no penis is sufficient "evidence" of the severity of punishment that may await a child who

dilemma is for the infant to identify with his father, and thus to introject all of the values and attitudes of his parents and of his culture.

The Biblical Psychology of Erich Wellisch

Wellisch opens his 1954 study, *Isaac and Oedipus,* with a statement that would seem to agree with Freud's formulation: "Psychology is based on the relationships of parents to children and children to parents. All other human relationships are modifications or extensions of the basic experiences within the family" (p. 3). Wellisch goes on to theorize that parent-child relationships advance through three stages, from a primitive to an intermediate to a morally advanced level.

Wellisch emphasizes there is a primitive level of parental behavior as well as infant behavior. At the most primitive level, parents regard the child as their possession and feel free to use it in any way they wish; even expressing their most intense aggression toward it or to performing religious rituals of child-sacrifice. (Wellisch offers a detailed review of the anthropology of child-sacrifice to demonstrate that it is a deeply rooted and widespread practice of mankind.) At this primitive stage, the child is at the total mercy of his parents and is rightly terrorized by their power over him.

Wellisch labels the "Oedipal complex stage," which to Freud defined psychological maturity, as only an intermediate stage of parent-child relationships. Now, a sense of guilt prevents parent and child from expressing their most aggressive impulses toward each other. Now, the child has introjected his parent's aggressive character. Now, the child has made his truce with his father and is ready to give his offspring the same harsh treatment he got from his own father! Is this maturity? Wellisch says No.

---

challenges the status quo. Our sketch of parent-child relationships disregards cultural differences. Kalman J. Kaplan argues that there are important differences between the biblical and Greek family life, and these differences strengthen Wellisch's thesis.

There is a morally-higher stage of development which cannot be found in the Oedipus drama because it was not a part of Greek culture from which the Oedipus drama was taken. This higher stage of development is expressed in the Akedah story, which Wellisch traces in considerable detail. The command, "Do not raise your hand against the boy, or do anything to him" (22:12) calls for the "abandonment of possessive, aggressive and especially infanticidal tendencies and their replacement by a covenant of love and affection between parent and child" (p. 4).

This conscious renunciation of force and control, and its replacement by a bond of love and affection, is the Akedah Motif. This "third stage of moral development of the parent-child relationships" goes beyond Freud's Oedipal resolution and describes a truer psychological maturity (pp. 4–5).

Wellisch was a deeply religious person. He believed the Oedipus complex is an essentially biological phenomenon,[5] but "the Akedah Motif is a religious phenomenon" that can raise human character to an even higher level than is possible by a resolution of the Oedipus complex alone. Resolution of the Oedipus complex results in a mature self-centeredness, but experience of the Akedah Motif endows the individual with "an altruistic aim" guided by an "image of man's divine calling. . . . The life instinct and desire for action are promoted, and the death instinct and contentment with meditation only are relegated" (p. 114).

Wellisch believed the therapist had an essentially religious task on his hands, and he could only perform it if he was a religious person himself. The best way to bring religious experience into one's life, he advises, is through prayer. "Few

---

5. Perhaps it would be more accurate to say the Oedipus complex is a bio-social phenomenon. The human infant's need for affection is rooted in the biological fact of infantile helplessness. He needs the love of a mothering person to survive. This survival need leads to powerful social attachments and sets the stage for the classic rivalry between father and son for mother's affection. For an anthropologist's discussion of human infantility, see Weston La Barre's *The Human Animal*, especially chapter 9.

people consciously pray but there is hardly a person who, unconsciously, has not prayer-like experiences. By this is meant experiencing as if a power outside and above man personally and morally influenced him" (pp. 97–98).

Wellisch was, like Freud, a Viennese Jew who fled to England to escape the Nazis. Wellisch arrived in England in 1938 and went to work at the Grayford Child Guidance Clinic in Kent, where he became Medical Director. His formulations grew out of his work as a child therapist there. Experience seemed to teach him he could not really help a troubled child until he had made a profound impact on the parent (p. 114) and the parent came to recognize "the external moral power of God" (p. 113). When the parent accepts an altruistic rather than a self-interest norm, only then can the child's emotional problems be resolved.

Apparently Wellisch dealt with children who had suffered from the severest kind of strict, self-righteous "child training"— boys who had been terrorized by their father and suffered from "Akedah dreams" of a threatening father holding a knife in his outstretched hand (p. 100). Wellisch apparently discovered the only way he could help the child was to impress the parent with the moral message of the Akedah: "Do not raise your hand against the boy, or do anything to him" (22:12) and the parent should regard this command not as the advice of "that psychiatrist," but as the word of God.[6] Wellisch could talk to his patients and to their parents about the word of God because he was a religious man, who in a therapy session would sometimes pray for his patient or ask his patient if he wanted to pray.[7] He believed biblical values could enrich one's under-

---

6. Wellisch apparently did not promote a sudden religious conversion experience, but gradually introduced the religious attitude into the therapy sessions. He writes, "The Akedah experiences of everyday life usually develop slowly, inconspicuously, and incompletely" (p. 108).

7. A child patient reported that his parents were fighting again and added, "I wish they would love each other." Wellisch responded, "Would you like to say a little prayer about this?" The boy folded his hands and said, "Dear God, I love Mummy and Daddy. I wish they

standing of modern psychological theories. He regarded therapy as a religious experience in which the patient acquires new spiritual values (p. 110). He felt self-centeredness, even the most enlightened self-interest, was not a high enough aim for the human spirit. "Ancient Greek philosophy has not the vision of salvation" (p. 115). Indian and Chinese religions similarly dwell on self-centeredness and self-realization. "There is a need for a Biblical psychology," he wrote; a psychology which would uphold the norm not of self-realization but of "messianic object-love" (pp. 115, 116).

Theodor Reik

Seven years after the publication of Wellisch's *Isaac and Oedipus*, Theodor Reik, a prolific psychoanalytic writer who had already written several books on Jewish topics, issued his book on the Akedah, *The Temptation*. In it he averred that the Wellisch book is open to "merciless criticism" (p. 70) though it also does contain "quite a few thoughtful remarks" (p. 71).

Reik mainly objects to Wellisch's claim that the ordinary resolution of a neurotic relationship between parent and child is incomplete, and that the Akedah Motif allows for a loving and affectionate relationship between parent and child with the virtual abandonment of aggressive and possessive emotions.

It is unimaginable that with the interruption of Isaac's sacrifice—"the Akedah experience"—a new and entirely different

---

would love each other as Uncle Tom and Auntie Bessie do" (pp. 106–107).

Elsewhere Wellisch writes, "In suitable cases the use of prayer [in therapy] may be advised" (p. 99). Wellisch understood that his way of combining psychiatry and religion was not widely accepted. He commented, "In a similar way in which sex used to be taboo, religious belief is now taboo amongst wide circles of psychiatrists in the lay world. The taboo against the serious admission of religious experiences is even more severe than the taboo against sexual matters used to be and is more difficult to overcome" (p. 97).

attitude in the relationship between father and son suddenly entered the world, as this psychoanalyst asserts. All historical and psychological indications contradict such a venturesome assumption.

Emotional changes of such a deep kind do not occur abruptly. The ambivalent attitude of fathers to sons and sons to fathers is a fateful and lasting one and can never be entirely obliterated. A "modification of instincts" such as Wellisch considers is a psychological impossibility. One can speak only of changes in the intensity of their mutual correlation. . . .

In reality only compromise solutions are possible between the opposing emotional tendencies in the relationship between fathers and sons. The fundamental conflict and contrast is not solvable. Needless to say, the Akedah experience presents only a partial and provisional adaptation. (pp. 225–226)

"The arrested sacrifice of Isaac . . . [has not] changed the fundamental facts of the human condition," furthers Reik (p. 234).

Having disposed of Wellisch, Reik then takes on Kierkegaard. In *Fear and Trembling,* Kierkegaard removed the ancient Hebrew spirit of the Akedah narrative and transformed it into a New Testament story (p. 62).

The prevailing difference between the world of the Old Testament and that of the New lies in the distinction between trust and faith. Kierkegaard regards faith as an "action." Trust is, in contrast to faith, an attitude and has no aim. Abraham, who trusts, does not need to make those "movements upward" nor "the leap" of which Kierkegaard speaks. The patriarch walks humbly before his God. (p. 63)

Kierkegaard unconsciously identified with a helpless and distraught Isaac, writes Reik, because the Danish philosopher had been subjected to "the 'crazy' educational devices of his father, who was doubtlessly an emotionally deeply disturbed man." Kierkegaard "morbidly pondered" the Akedah story, and his writings on the topic are charged with an "intensity of emotion," but his personal history disqualified him from making a clear-minded analysis of the Akedah (p. 61).

Reik also refers to the Akedah interpretation in *The Meaning of Sacrifice,* by the British psychoanalyst Roger E. Money-Kryle. Abraham is too remote, too heroic a figure to identify with, Money-Kryle suggests. It is easier to identify with Isaac. Since every son has the unconscious wish (according to the psychoanalysts) to kill and displace his father, the Akedah becomes an "inverted Oedipus fantasy, in which the killing is done, not by himself, but by his father, and in which he, not his father, is the victim." To identifiers with Isaac, the Akedah offers "some masochistic compensation," an expiation, a working off of some of the unconscious guilt generated by these universal parricidal feelings (Money-Kryle, pp. 234–235).

Reviewing psychoanalytic interpretations of the Akedah is only a small part of Reik's interest in this topic.[8] His real interest is in advancing the novel thesis that the Akedah narrative replaced the description of an ancient Hebrew initiation ceremony in which Isaac the boy becomes Isaac the man. Why was this ancient story replaced? Reik argues that the postexilic editors wanted to attribute an ancient and powerful argument against child sacrifice to Israel's remote past. In fact, writes Reik, contact with other cultures had made child sacrifice a problem in postexilic times; it had not been a problem in Abraham's time.[9] The Akedah therefore has "a fake antiquity," Reik argues (p. 81). (What a fake!) A more detailed description of "the original story" according to Reik belongs to chapter 20, "In Search of the Ur-Akedah."

---

8. Reik does not think there is much to be gained by treating the Akedah as a case history. This method "is today [1961] obsolete and outdated, if it was ever justified" (p. 71).

9. Reik argues that the Akedah "reflects the attitude of certain contemporaries of the prophets, who passionately attacked the recent introduction of child sacrifice which the Israelites had adopted from their [Canaanite] neighbors. In short, the sacrifice of children to Yahweh is not a rationalization of the patriarchal period, but an aberration of the time of the late Israelite Kings. The [Akedah] . . . is a counterfeit portrait of the patriarch. It is, so to speak, a very clever copy of an old master, but it is not the original" (p. 80).

Silvano Arieti

In "The Binding of Isaac," chapter 4 of his 1981 book, *Abraham and the Contemporary Mind,* psychoanalyst Silvano Arieti surveys what others have written on the topic as a prelude to presenting his own thoughts on the Akedah. (He does not mention one word about Theodor Reik.) Arieti devotes about five pages to reviewing the study of Erich Wellisch, "the best known psychoanalytic study of the Akedah" (p. 137). Arieti's comments make it plain he admires Wellisch more for his "sincerity and devotion to his work . . . [than for] telling us something new and convincing."

> Nobody can doubt Wellisch's sincerity and devotion to his work. He attempts a harmonious fusion of his psychiatric-psychoanalytic training and experience with his Jewish heritage. Whether he succeeds in telling us something new[10] and convincing is another question. (p. 140)

> Wellisch's interpretation is another version of the theory that the Akedah represents a revolt against the practice of infanticide. It is presented in psychoanalytic terminology and as a derivative of the Oedipus complex, but it offers nothing new. (p. 141)

Arieti rejects Wellisch's argument that the Akedah was written as a condemnation of child sacrifice. "Child sacrifice has after all been outlawed for a long time, and yet the Abraham-Isaac story maintains its great spiritual value today," Arieti reasons (p. 136).

If the Akedah continues to have a "great spiritual value

---

10. Arieti expresses surprise that in Wellisch's psychoanalytic formulations of father-son conflict, the major expression of hostility comes from the father. In classic psychoanalytic thought, the neurotic problem arises mainly from the son's rivalry and hatred of his father (p. 138). Perhaps this is because psychoanalytic theory developed mainly from the treatment of adults, and Wellisch's clinical experience was with the treatment of children.

today," Arieti seems to say, the narrative should tell us something about the Holocaust. To Arieti, this would demonstrate the great and enduring spiritual value of the Akedah. Did God command the Akedah to give Abraham a foretaste of "the terrible tasks that Abraham's descendants will have to sustain through the centuries"? (p. 148).

When God commanded him to sacrifice Isaac, Abraham must have remembered well that God had already promised him he would become "the father of a multitude of nations . . . exceedingly fruitful . . . kings shall come forth from you." Trusting in God's promise, Abraham obeyed God's command.[11] What did Abraham learn from the Akedah experience? He learned he could survive great risk and danger. He learned how all-enveloping was his love for God, his love for Isaac, and God's love for him. He learned that love and trust could sustain one through life's darkest hours.

To Arieti:

> Isaac symbolizes the many aspects of love: family love, for Isaac is his son; love for one's neighbor (or for the other), for Isaac is a fellow human being; self-love, for Isaac is his only son and one of the most meaningful parts of Abraham's life, not only because Isaac is a living human being but . . . the progenitor of a great people, chosen to give to the world Abraham's revelation of the One God, the God of Love who cannot be seen but is everywhere. (p. 155)

Arieti reminds his reader that the Holocaust has not been the only great evil of our century—"two major world wars, the massacre of two million Armenians, a conspicuous number of lesser wars, the use of the atomic bomb" (p. 163).

This has been the incredible price humanity has already

---

11. Abraham's trust in God was great, but it was not absolute. For if it were absolute, Arieti reasons, there would be no need for a test. "Great . . . must be Abraham's faith, and great must be his doubt— both originating from God. . . . We can also assume that along with faith Abraham experiences a sense of mystery . . . that is capable of being comprehended eventually" (pp. 152–153).

paid for its gift of free will, the power that gives man the choice of good or evil. Arieti asks: "Was the risk that God took well taken when He created free will as part of the advent of man in a predominantly deterministic world?" (p. 162).

> The greatest of all of Hitler's evil ended with the extermination of one-third of the Jewish people and demonstrated how truly enormous evil can be. The greatness of love for God, however, proved to be greater even than this greatest of evils. It is true that six million Jews, out of eighteen million, perished. *It is as if one-third of Isaac had been sacrificed.* The comparison of course, is faulty because one-third of a person cannot be sacrificed. Isaac does not perish, and the faith of Abraham does not perish. (p. 158, emphasis added)

As a practicing psychoanalyst and a person uprooted by the Nazis, Arieti had undoubtedly heard many of his patients ruminate tearfully over the Holocaust and ask if this could have been God's punishment for their sins or for the sins of their elders. Arieti acknowledges that historically, disasters befalling the Jews have been interpreted by their prophets and by their rabbis "as punishment for having strayed from the law of God. Their interpretation may once have been correct," says Arieti. "It is my personal opinion, however—which I know might be wrong—that . . . what happened to the Jews in this century was not a punishment for lack of faith, but something extremely grave which happened to them precisely because they, or their parents, or their grandparents *kept* the faith of Abraham, sustained by Abraham's love for God" (p. 158).

> If the disaster of our century has to be compared to a biblical event, it should be compared not to the other tragic events described by the prophets, but to the [averted] sacrifice of Isaac. The greatest of all of God's requests—that Abraham sacrifice Isaac—ends with a demonstration of how enormous and all-embracing our love for God should be. (p. 158)

To Arieti, the Akedah served as a message to Abraham of the perils that await a Holy People, and also served to demonstrate once more God's love of Abraham and Isaac. It seems fair to conclude that Arieti's main use of the Akedah was not to demonstrate the power of the psychoanalytic method, but to probe the problem of evil, to raise the question which cannot be answered and cannot go away: the meaning of the Holocaust.

Martin S. Bergmann

In 1992, psychoanalytic psychologist Martin S. Bergmann wrote *In the Shadow of Moloch: The Sacrifice of Children and Its Impact on Western Religions.* Scholarly and wide-ranging, this psychoanalytic interpretation of religions compares the mythology of the ancient world, Judaism, and Christianity. As Bergmann demonstrates, in Greek mythology the Oedipus story is hardly unique as a story of parent-child conflict. Again and again, parents sacrifice their children or devour their children's flesh. Bergmann concludes that "a wish to destroy one's children is among the ancient and most unacceptable wishes of fathers.[12] The Akedah signalled "a new morality . . . that prohibited such sacrifices" (p. 25).

Accordingly to Bergmann, the Akedah is the signal event around which Judaism can be understood, just as the Cruci-

---

12. Bergmann notes that child abuse, neglect, and abandonment is not the malaise of the contemporary world, but has been part of the human condition throughout the ages, motivated by both psychological and economic factors. "The poor despaired at having yet another mouth to feed. The rich feared that distribution of their property among too many heirs would endanger the privileged status of their children." One might regard child sacrifice as "a special, religiously-sanctioned form of abandonment" (p. 305).

This dark impulse to get rid of an infant conflicted, of course, with powerful nurturant and protective impulses. "When a wish is unacceptable there are two ways of dealing with it: it can be repressed or it can be projected. Such a projection lightens the burden of repression" (p. 25). The parent now can say, "I do not want to get rid of my infant, but the gods want me to sacrifice him." In Judaism, writes Bergmann, eventually "a new morality emerged that prohibited such sacrifices" (p. 25). This new morality was conveyed by the Akedah.

fixion is the key event in Christianity. The averted sacrifice and the completed sacrifice symbolize a critical difference between Judaism and Christianity.

The Akedah captures the imagination of every generation, writes Bergmann, because "unconscious murderous wishes of children directed at their parents and murderous wishes of parents directed at their children are, at this stage in the development of our species, interwoven as parts of the human condition" (p. 314). The Akedah addresses this perversity of human nature and conveys a new rule of human conduct: "Do not raise your hand against the boy, or do anything to him" (22:12).

20

IN SEARCH OF THE UR-AKEDAH

Both Jewish and Christian scholars believe the Akedah narrative, like many other Bible stories, has its origin in an ancient folktale. There is no solid evidence to support this hunch; standard books on prebiblical parallels cite parallels to many Bible stories, but they give no parallels to Genesis 22. Nor do the Dead Sea Scrolls give a parallel to Genesis 22.[1] Neverthe-

---

1. The following sources of prebiblical legends, list nothing for Genesis 22.

Ancient Near Eastern Texts Relating to the Old Testament, edited by James E. Pritchard, 1950; lists parallels to Genesis chapters 2, 3, 4, 5, 6, 7, 8, 10, 12, 14, 16, 17, 18, 27, 31, 37, 39, 40, 41, 45, 46, 47, 49, 50.

Old Testament Parallels, by Victor H. Matthews and Don C. Benjamin, 1991; list parallels to Genesis chapters 1, 2, 4, 6, 7, 8, 9, 10, 14, 15, 16, 17, 18, 19, 21, 25, 27, 28, 30, 31, 34, 38, 39, 41.

Genesis Apochrophon, by Joseph A. Fitzmyer (one of the Dead Sea Scrolls); index refers to the following chapters of Genesis: 1, 2, 4, 5, 6, 8, 9, 10, 11, 12, 13, 14, 15, 16, 17, 18, 19, 20, 21, 23, 24, 25, 26, 28, 30, 31, 34, 35, 36, 41, 42, 48, 49, 50.

Striking similarities to the Akedah story are apparent in the Greek

less, both Jewish and Christian scholars insist the Akedah springs from prebiblical sources.

THE TWO AKEDAHS OF MICHA JOSEF BIN-GORION[2]

Critic, narrator, folklore collector, and scholar, Micha Bin-Gorion (Micha Joseph Berdyczewski, 1865–1921) studied the Higher Criticism and, guided by its principles, separated Genesis 22 into two distinct stories. In what Bin-Gorion believed to be the earlier story, Isaac is sacrificed; in the later story, Isaac is spared. Bin-Gorion's first story simply puts together verses 1 through 5, verse 9, and verses 15 through 19.

I. Isaac is Sacrificed: The Earlier Story

1] Some time afterward, God put Abraham to the test. He said to him, "Abraham," and he answered, "Here I am." 2] And He said, "Take your son, your favored one, Isaac, whom you love, and go to the land of Moriah, and offer him there as a burnt offering on one of the heights which I will point out to you." 3] So early next morning, Abraham saddled his ass, and took with him two servants and his son Isaac. He split the wood for the burnt offering, and he set out for the place of which God had told him. 4] On the third day Abraham looked up and saw the place from afar. 5] Then Abraham said to his servants, "You stay here with the ass. The boy and I will go up there; we will worship and we will return to you." . . . 9]They arrived at the place of which God had told him. Abraham built an altar there; he laid out the wood; he bound his son Isaac; he laid his son on the altar, on top of the wood. . . . 15] The angel of the Lord

---

legend of King Athamas and the averted sacrifice of his son Prixus. Perhaps this legend and the Akedah may share a common origin. See chapter 16, footnote 1.

2. On page 125, Spiegel summarizes Bin-Gorion's Two-Akedah theory.

called to Abraham[3] . . . from heaven. 16] and said, "By Myself I swear, the Lord declares: because you have done this and have not withheld your son, your favored one, 17] I will bestow My blessings upon your and make your descendants as numerous as the stars of heaven and the sands on the seashore; and your descendants shall seize the gates of their foes. 18] All the nations of the earth shall bless themselves by your descendants, because you have obeyed My command." 19] Abraham then returned to his servants, and they departed together for Beer-sheba; and Abraham stayed in Beer-sheba.

Comment: Bin-Gorion was responding to the popular legend that Isaac was indeed slaughtered and resurrected, either immediately or after a few years. Bin-Gorion was led to believe this theme harked back to a prebiblical legend. Midrashic and liturgical references speak of "the blood of Isaac" or "the ashes of Isaac." The popularity of this legend is indicated by the fact it was illustrated in a Haggadah of fifteenth century Germany (as shown on page 140). The death-and-resurrection legend also had its opponents. The renowned Jewish sage Abraham ibn Ezra (d. 1167) warned: "He who asserts that Abraham slew Isaac and . . . that afterwards Isaac came to life again, is speaking contrary to Writ" (Zuckerman, pp. 16–17).

In this "Isaac Is Sacrificed Story," the absence of Isaac in verse 19, otherwise puzzling,[4] is now understandable. In verse 17, God again promises to make Abraham's descendants "as

---

3. The phrase "a second time" is omitted from verse 15. (Presumably, this phrase did not appear in the original story.)

4. Note the difference between verse 6 and 19; verse 6 says "the two walked off together" to the height of Moriah. Verse 19 says that "Abraham returned to the lads and they continued on together. . . ." Where was Isaac? Spiegel notes this discrepancy, and Zuckerman agrees that Isaac's "unexpected absence from the story is striking; and . . . cannot be easily dismissed as an accidental oversight" (p. 19).

Zuckerman conjectures that "the writer(s) and/or editor(s) of Genesis 22 in some manner or form felt compelled to leave traces of the older story within the biblical text itself" (p. 20).

numerous as the stars of heaven." How God will arrange this is not made explicit.

The later story, according to Bin-Gorion's thinking, is made up of verses 6, 7, and 8; 10, 13, and 14. Here is how it would look:

II. Isaac Is Spared: The Later Story

6] Abraham took the wood for the burnt offering and put it on his son Isaac. He himself took the firestone and the knife; and the two walked off together. 7] Then Isaac said to his father Abraham, "Father!" and he answered, "Yes, my son." And he said, "Here are the firestone and the wood, but where is the sheep for the burnt offering?" 8] And Abraham said, "God will see to the sheep for His burnt offering, my son." And the two of them walked on together. . . . 10] And Abraham picked up the knife to slay his son. . . . 13] When Abraham looked up, his eye fell upon a ram, caught in the thicket by its horns. So Abraham went and took the ram and offered it up as a burnt offering in place of his son. 14] And Abraham named that site Adonai-yireh, whence the present saying, "On the mount of the Lord there is vision."

Comment: Without verses 11 and 12, the reader understands the sight of a ram caught in a thicket gave Abraham a sudden intuition that God wanted him to sacrifice the animal instead of his son. Verses 11 and 12 are a later interpolation, Bin-Gorion believed. Moreover, this interpolation ("an angel of the Lord called to him from heaven") makes the opening phrase in verse 13 inappropriate; if Abraham had just been called by an angel from heaven, why would he then have to look *up* to see a ram caught in the thicket?

HOW OUR PEOPLE ESCAPED DESTRUCTION

The contemporary German scholars Kilian and Reventlow also speculate that Genesis 22 stems from a prebiblical story. The theme of the original story, argue Kilian and Reventlow, was not the testing of Abraham, but "how our people escaped destruction." Reventlow attempted to reconstruct the original story, extracting from the biblical narrative those phrases which contain linguistic clues of greatest antiquity, and those phrases which best conform to the style of a folktale. Deleted from the story are what Reventlow and other scholars believe are later additions. (Reventlow claims to have followed the style of a folktale as defined in an unnamed 1909 writing of Alex Olrik, a Danish folklorist.) Translated from Reventlow's German-language monograph and sparingly adapted, here is Reventlow's *Ur-Akedah*: (Parenthesized numbers indicate the corresponding biblical verses.)

(1) Elohim spoke to Abraham: "Abraham!" The latter answered, "Yes!" (2) He spoke: "Take you son and go to a land which I will show you, and sacrifice him there as a burnt offering on one of the mountains, which I will show you." (3) Then Abraham departed early in the morning, saddled his ass, took his son and went to the holy place. (4) On the third day, Abraham lifted his eyes and saw the holy place in the distance. (6) Then Abraham took the sacrificial wood and loaded it upon his son; he himself took the fire and the knife in his hand. Thus the two walked together. (7) Then the son spoke to Abraham, his father, and said: "My father!" Abraham answered, "Yes, my son!" The son spoke: "Here is the fire and the wood—and where is the sheep for the sacrifice?" (8) Then Abraham spoke: "Elohim will provide a sheep for the sacrifice, my son." Thus the two walked together. (9) Now they came to the holy place. There Abraham built the altar, placed the wood upon it, bound his son, and placed him on the altar on top of the wood. (10) Then Abraham stretched out his hand and took the knife to slaughter his son. (11) Then the angel of Yahweh called to him and spoke: "Abraham, Abraham!" Abraham answered, "I hear!" (12) Said the angel: "Don't stretch forth your hand against the boy and don't harm him!" (13) Then Abraham raised his eyes and saw and behold! a ram in the background, its horns caught in the brushwood. Then Abraham took the ram as a burnt offering, instead of his son. (14) Now Abraham named this place

"Yahweh-provides," and he said, "Today, on this mountain, Yahweh has provided."

The Initiation Ceremony

Psychoanalyst Theodor Reik depicted himself as "an explorer of comparative religions" (1961, p. 206), took a special interest in the prehistory of Israel, and wrote books on that topic: *Myth and Guilt, Mystery on the Mountain,* and *The Creation of Woman.* In 1961, he wrote his fourth and last book on "the prehistory of Israel": *The Temptation,* which summarizes his thoughts about the Akedah.

When he was a young man in Vienna in 1915, a twenty-seven-year-old Theodor Reik gave a lecture at the Vienna Psychoanalytic Society: "The Puberty Rites of Savages, Some Parallels Between the Mental Life of Savages and of Neurotics."[5] Freud warmly commended the paper and bestowed upon it the first prize for applied psychoanalysis (1961. p. 237).

In *The Temptation,* Reik reflected that in 1915, "I could not then foresee that more than four decades later, I would return to the subject. I was not then aware that it had gotten hold of me and would not release me. The problem that had pre-occupied me as a young psychoanalyst re-emerged in old age" (1961, p. 237).

A close study of the initiation ceremonies of Australian and African tribes convinced Reik that the initiation ceremony served some very basic functions in human society: (a) it loosened the bond between the boy and his mother, and transformed him into a man among men;[6] (b) it taught him, through direct experience, that he could face and survive the worst imaginable dangers; (c) it taught him the tribe possessed

---

5. This paper was republished in Reik's 1946 book, *Ritual,* pp. 91–166.

6. "We recognize in all these rites the strong tendency to detach the youths from their mothers, to chain them more firmly to the community of men, and to seal more closely the union between father and son" (Reik, 1946, p. 145).

life-and-death power over the individual,[7] and the power of the tribe to castrate him—to take away his masculine power or even his life—was symbolized by its power to sever the foreskin of his penis; (d) it bonded him with other boys-become-men who shared the initiatory ordeal with him.

The initiation ceremony might include sessions in which the boys were taught the lore and codes of their tribe; exactly "what they would have to observe as adult members of their community" (1961, p. 236). After completing his initiation, a young man was free to marry.

Tribesmen feigned and dramatized life-threatening dangers that the initiates were forced to endure in death-and-resurrection ceremonies. (Occasionally, a boy was in fact accidentally killed.) The rule, "He must face and overcome great danger before the boy becomes a man" seems to underlie the "logic" of present-day fraternity initiations, of parents who expect the Army to "make a man" out of their son, and of adolescents who seem to go out of their way looking for dangerous ways to "prove their manhood."

Circumcision and a deliberately-sought, narrowly-averted danger—to Reik, these biblical episodes seemed like elements of an initiation rite. What other signs of an initiation rite might be detected in and around the Akedah narrative? Reik points to two such signs: (1) there is a midrash that after the Akedah, Isaac is sent to study at the house of Shem (initiation includes instruction in the lore of the tribe); and (2) following the Akedah narrative, Abraham sends his old servant to seek a wife for Isaac among the daughters of Mesopotamia. "It is as if the sacrifice scene were a prelude to this venture into marriage" (1961, p. 92).

These are the clues that convinced Reik that once upon a

---

7. This was a warning against any thought of rebellion against the rulers of the clan. This is the function of the brutal and cruel features of initiation ceremonies, its "bodily mutilations, punishments, curses and threats. . . . These stern educational measures for boys are [part of] the puberty rites found in all primitive societies" (Reik, 1961, p. 228).

time there was an initiation ceremony story in the ancient lore of the Hebrews. In this story an adolescent boy experienced: (1) circumcision;[8] (2) a narrowly-averted brush with death; (3) the study of the codes of the tribe; and (4) marriage. This initiation ceremony, not too different from those of the Australian and African aborigines, is Theodor Reik's *Ur-Akedah*. Why was this ancient tale eventually obliterated? For two reasons, says Reik. First, circumcision was eventually performed not at adolescence, but at the eighth day of life. Secondly, the postexilic editors needed a strong anti-infant-sacrifice story, to combat the postexilic tendency of Hebrews to adopt the infant-sacrifice ritual of their Canaanite neighbors. The Akedah is widely regarded as an argument against infant sacrifice. However, infant sacrifice was not a problem of the patriarchal period, Reik argues; it arose from close contact with the Canaanites at the time of the late Israelite Kings. As we have already noted, Reik believed the Akedah is "a counterfeit portrait of the patriarch. It is, so to speak, a very clever copy of an old master, but it is not the original" (1961, p. 80).

The initiation rite was part of an ancient tribal organization. As Hebrew society changed, the ancient puberty rites lost their function.[9] Circumcision was moved to the eighth day of birth, and the Jewish puberty rite was "later revived in the transformed and diluted form of the Bar Mitzvah" (1961, p. 172).

Reik had no illusions his conjecture[10] would be popular. He

---

8. At the time of the patriarchs, circumcision was performed on adolescents as it was for Ishmael. "The report that Isaac was circumcised when he was eight days old (Genesis 21:4) is certainly anachronistic" (Reik, 1961, p. 124).

9. "Several reasons why puberty rites moved into the background can be guessed. There were the migrations of the Hebrew clans, their struggle for place and pasture, their oppression by the Egyptians, their fights with the Canaanites, and finally their increasing assimilation with the more advanced civilizations around them" (Reik, 1961, p. 170).

10. "I arrived at the view that [the Akedah] cannot be an archaic account of a primitive custom of human sacrifice and its abolishment, but rather it is a relatively late story. It was perhaps composed

had become accustomed to "assault and abuse from Christian and Jewish theologians, believers and nonbelievers. . . . The results of my research were treated as though tracing the most valuable achievements of Jewish culture to crude and primitive beginnings amounted to their downgrading and degradation" (1961, p. 239). Reik admits that in his theorizing there are undoubtedly "shortcomings, gaps and inevitable mistakes." However, he believes that of his four books on the prehistory of Israel, "I am sure that the initiation rites will be recognized as the backbone of the religious and social culture of ancient Israel" (1961, p. 240).

---

at the time of the prophets who passionately attacked the contemporaneous practice of child sacrifice and its projection into the age of the patriarchs, and had the purpose of demonstrating that even in remote times the Lord considered human sacrifice an abomination" (Reik, 1961, p. 114).

21

THE AKEDAH AND
THE CHRISTIAN TRADITION

In Christian thought, Genesis 22 is known not as the Akedah (a rabbinical label) but as the Sacrifice of Isaac. Father Abraham stands out as something of an exception in the Hebrew Bible. As a whole, the Hebrew Bible emphasizes law and commandment, exactly what the New Testament rebels against. Genesis 22, on the other hand, can be read to emphasize the Christian virtues of faith and love. God sets aside Law (the prohibition of human sacrifice) to test Abraham. Father Abraham is seen as a Knight of Faith, and at the end of the episode, love triumphs over duty. In a sense, perhaps it is only a slight exaggeration to say, as seen through Christian eyes, the Sacrifice of Isaac appears to be a Christian story embedded in the Old Testament (as the Hebrew Bible is known).

The Sacrifice of Isaac glorifies Father Abraham as the Knight of Faith and God reveals himself as a God of love. In addition the story is traditionally believed to prophesy the crucifixion, which is the central theme of the Christian faith ("Christ died for our sins").

The church fathers elaborate many analogies between the Sacrifice of Isaac and the crucifixion. Both events are believed to have happened on the same hilltop. Both Isaac and Jesus carried wood for their self-sacrifice up to the mountain—Isaac carrying firewood and Jesus carrying a wooden cross. In Christian art, Isaac's load of wood is sometimes arranged in the form of a cross. (see page 139.) The ram caught in the thicket symbolizes Jesus' crown of thorns. Ambrose described Isaac as the prototype of the suffering Christ.[1]

As the Sacrifice of Isaac symbolizes the crucifixion, so Abraham represents the Christian ideal of a man of perfect faith, and Isaac is his miraculously-begotten only son (born to a 90-year-old mother). Abraham was clearly a believer in miracles; if he sacrificed Isaac, it would take a miracle for God to fulfill His promise that Abraham would directly father a Holy People. No wonder the Sacrifice of Isaac is an important story in the Christian tradition. It is explicitly referred to in the New Testament, often recounted in Christian liturgy, widely portrayed in many hundreds of early Christian icons and monuments of all kinds,[2] and often portrayed in the paintings and drawings of Renaissance Europe.

In Judaism, the dominant biblical figure is Moses, giver of the Law. In Christianity, the dominant Old Testament figure is Father Abraham, as he is referred to in Christian liturgy. In the Sacrifice of Isaac, the character of Father Abraham is delineated as a man of perfect faith, for his readiness to translate his faith into deeds, and for a demonstrated willingness to make the greatest of personal sacrifices as a testimony to his faith.

In Judaism, the emphasis is on practice: obedience to the Law and fulfillment of the commandments. In Christianity emphasis is on faith; "The letter killeth, but the spirit giveth life" (2 Corinthians 3:6), which seems to say: The letter of the

---

1. *Isaac ergo Christi passuri est typus* (Ambrose, *De Abraham*, ch. 8). Church Fathers Irenaeus, Tertullian, Ephraim, Isidor of Seville, and numerous others enlarged upon this parallel (Smith, p. 159).

2. Alison Moore Smith's 1922 article illustrates 9 early Christian Akedah monuments, and lists 123 monuments of that era. Isabel Speyart van Woerden's 1961 article lists no less than 371 early Christian and medieval Akedah images of various kinds, classified and located.

law killeth, but the spirit of love giveth life. Just as Moses is a symbol of commandment, Abraham is held as a symbol of faith—God promised him that an heir would yet come to this elderly patriarch out of his own loins. "Abraham believed in God, [and] it was accounted to him for righteousness" (Galatians 3:6).

In the Epistle to the Hebrews, the anonymous letter writer emphasises the faith of Father Abraham.

> By faith, Abraham, when he was tested, offered up Isaac; and he that had received the promises offered up his only begotten son, of whom it was said, In Isaac shall thy seed be called; accounting that God was able to raise him up, even from the dead, from which also he received him in a figure. (Hebrews 11:17–19)

In his Epistle to the Romans, Paul likewise celebrates Abraham's character as a model of Christian faith: "Abraham grew 'strong in faith, giving glory to God, and being fully persuaded that what he had promised, he was able also to perform, and therefore it was imputed to him for righteousness'" (Romans 4:20–22).

The Christian message shifts the emphasis from fear-of-God to faith-in-God. Fear of God demands action, but an emphasis on faith can lead to passivity. This seems to have been a problem in the mind of the writer of the Epistle of James. The Epistle exhorts Christians to action. ("Faith without works is dead" [James 2:20].) To dramatize this theme, Father Abraham is praised for being a man of faith and action, and thus an example of faith in action: "Was not Abraham, our father, justified by works, when he had offered Isaac, his son, upon the altar? Seest thou how faith wrought with his works, and by works was faith made perfect?" (James 2:21–22).

The Sacrifice of Isaac plays a prominent role in Christian liturgy. In the Roman Catholic Church when an altar is consecrated, the following Pontifical Mass is said: "May it have as much grace with Thee as that which Abraham, the father of faith, built when about to sacrifice his son as a figure of our redemption." In the ritual of the mass, the priest prays to God to accept the consecrated wafers "as Thou didst vouchsafe to accept . . . the Sacrifice of our Patriarch Abraham." Among the treasures of Church art is the pyx, a little box for the consecrated wafers, sometimes made of ivory and decorated with a picture of the Akedah.

On Holy Saturday, just before Easter, Genesis 22 is chanted as the third of twelve prophesies. Its chanting is followed by this prayer: "O God the Supreme Father of the faithful, who throughout the world didst multiply the children of thy promise . . . and by the paschal mystery dost make Abraham thy servant the father of all nations."

The First Lesson on Good Friday in the Church of England is a recital of the Akedah, which is followed by a reading of St. John XVIII reporting the beginning of the Golgotha events.

Like Jesus, Isaac was resurrected from the dead in many midrashim and piyyutim. Symbolically, Isaac was "as good as dead" when Abraham agreed to sacrifice him. The hope of resurrection, which is so central to Christian doctrine, has its roots, of course, in the Hebrew Bible:

> "Thy dead men shall live, together with my dead body, shall they arise. Awake and sing, ye that dwell in the dust: for thy dew is as the dew of herbs, and the earth shall cast out the dead" (Isaiah 27:19).

> "And after [worms] have thus destroyed my skin, yet from my flesh shall I see God" (Job 19:26).

> "And many of those who sleep in the dust of the earth shall awake, some to everlasting life, and some to shame and everlasting contempt" (Daniel 12:2).

A negative side of traditional Christian thought about the Sacrifice of Isaac is dealt with in chapter 14, "The Deglorification Interpretation." Chapter 20, "In Search of the Ur-Akedah," also deals with Christian scholarship in this area. (Christian scholarship has contributed to most chapters of this book.) Still, this book does not pretend to give a well-rounded presentation of the thinking of contemporary Christian scholars about the Sacrifice of Isaac.

In February 1995, the computerized *Religious Index* included Akedah as a keyword which retrieved 138 items (books, articles, and essays) from both Christian and Jewish publications. This supports the comment of a recent worker that the Akedah continues to be a popular subject among Christian scholars.[3]

---

3. *Vetus Testamentum,* a journal devoted to the study of the Old Testament, is an interfaith journal in the sense that both its editors and contributors include Jewish as well as Christian religious writers. In a 1988 article, R. W. L. Moberly writes, "Within recent years the regular appearance of articles and monographs devoted to the [Akedah] story attests its continuing fascination for the biblical commentator" (p. 303). He directs the reader to recent studies in this area (p. 303, fn. 2). The bibliography of this book also contains numerous articles from Christian journals and books.

22

THE AKEDAH IN ISLAM

The Prophet Muhammad did not intend to found a new religion but to continue the tradition of the faith of Abraham. Celebration of the Akedah in word and ritual is therefore of prime importance in Islam to assert this important tie. The Islamic version of the Akedah is found in the 37th Sura of the Qur'an, and reads as follows:

> And Ibrahim[1] said: '. . . O my Lord, grant me, I pray, an heir who will be numbered among the righteous.' So We gave him the good news of a gentle son. When the boy was old enough to share in things with his father, Ibrahim said: 'My son, in a dream I dreamt[2] that I should offer you in sacrifice. What can your thoughts be of that?' He said: 'Father, do what you are told:

---

1. Here Sura 37 is quoted from a modern translation by Kenneth Cragg, professor at Oxford University, an Arabic scholar and translator for almost half a century. Professor Cragg's translation uses the name Abraham, which we have chosen to change to Ibrahim.

2. A rabbinical midrash likewise claims that Abraham heard God's command in a dream. Verse 3 of Genesis 22, "Early next morning," it

189

God[3] willing, you will find me patient.' So together they submitted to God's will. Ibrahim laid his son down with his face to
the ground. Whereupon We called to him: 'Ibrahim, you have
kept faith with the vision. Yours is the reward We grant to those
whose deeds are worthy.' It was as clear a test as could be. We
redeemed his son with great sacrifice and through the generations that followed We left for him the benediction: 'Peace be
upon Ibrahim.'

In such ways are the righteous rewarded. He was one of Our
believing servants. We gave him the good news of Isaac, one of
the best of prophets whom We blessed along with Ibrahim.
Among their descendants there were some who did good deeds,
while others were blatant evil-doers[4] who sinned against themselves. (Cragg, p. 120)

Some comments on Islamic Akedah recorded above: The
command to sacrifice his son comes to Ibrahim in a dream,
and, by tradition, he dreams the same dream for three nights,
so he knows that it surely comes from God. Before carrying out
the command, Ibrahim asks his son, "What can your thoughts
be of that?" His son answers, "Father, do what you are told:
God willing, you will find me patient." Nothing in the biblical
Akedah matches the tenderness, candor, and devotion of this
father-son interchange.[5]

Note that in Sura 37, Ibrahim's son is not named, but in the

---

is argued, supports the inference that the command came to Abraham at night.

3. When the Hebrew Bible was translated into Arabic in the ninth
century for the benefit of Jews of the Arab world, the word *God* was
translated as *Allah*. Similarly, Arabic translations of the New Testament translate God as Allah. It is appropriate, therefore, when
translating the Qur'an into English to translate Allah back into the
word God.

4. This is a reference to those Jews who rejected Muhammad's
leadership.

5. In fact, this candid interchange between Ibrahim and his son
contrasts sharply with verse 7 of Genesis 22, in which Isaac asks,
"Where is the sheep?" and Abraham answers, somewhat evasively,
"God will see to the sheep."

final lines of Sura 37, God promises him the birth of Isaac, which makes it clear that the boy Ibrahim has brought to the altar was Ishmael.

In the Bible, God prevents the sacrifice of Isaac with a verbal command ("Touch not the lad"), but by Muslim tradition, the redemption of Ibrahim's son was symbolized by the appearance of an angel bringing Ibrahim a ram from Paradise.[6] (It is the very same animal which Abel had once sacrificed to God.) In the Bible, Abraham sees a ram caught in a thicket, but Muslims believe the ram was carried to Ibrahim from Paradise in the arms of an angel. This gives animal sacrifice a more powerful symbolic meaning.

Only Islam devotes a festival holiday to the Akedah, and it is, in fact, the subject of Islam's major festival called the Feast of the Sacrifice (*Id al-adha*, or *Id al-Qurban*) and takes place on the tenth *Dhu'l Hijjah*.

According to tradition, Ibrahim's dreams occurred on the eighth, ninth, and tenth days of *Dhu'l Hijjah*. Accordingly, the eighth, ninth, and tenth days of that month are known as the Day of Vision (for it was then the vision first appeared), the Day of Knowledge (for then it was known the order came from God), and the Day of Sacrifice (for it was then Ibrahim vowed to carry out the deed).

On the Day of the Sacrifice pilgrims journey to Mecca and assemble by the thousands in the nearby valley of the Mina for the ritual slaughtering of sheep, cattle, and camels. Mecca is the appropriate place for celebrating the Akedah because, according to Islamic tradition, the original sanctuary built at Mecca, the Ka'bah, was built by Ibrahim himself. Horns hanging on the spout of the Ka'bah were believed to have been from the very ram that Ibrahim had sacrificed.

---

6. In his 1943 article in *Ars Islamica*, Meyer Schapiro identifies several Akedah artworks created in medieval Spain, France, and Ireland, in which are depicted an angel carrying a ram. The author suggests this indicates the spread of Islamic teachings in medieval Europe and Ireland. The only Akedah artwork in the Western world which depicts an angel carrying a ram is the stained glass window, reproduced on page 148, created in 1977 by Marc Chagall for St. Stephan's Church in Mainz, Germany.

On this day of celebration, every Muslim, whether or not he makes a pilgrimage to Ka'bah in Mecca, is called upon to sponsor the ritual slaughter of a sheep if he can afford it (or be a one-tenth partner in the slaughter of a cow or camel). According to popular belief, the slaughtered animal will carry its owner across the *Sirat,* the bridge to Paradise.

Traditionally, the animal offered for sacrifice might have been raised by the person, or at least purchased a week ahead of time, fed and cared for so the person regards it as his own. The animal must be normal and healthy, not lame or partially blind.

The sacrifice is performed outdoors by binding the animal's forelegs and hindlegs, and laying it on its right side, facing Mecca. (If the ritual is performed inside the city of Mecca, the animal is faced toward the Ka'bah.) The sacrificer[7] slits the animal's throat with a sharp knife and makes sure he has severed its jugular vein. However he first proclaims the absolute greatness and goodness of God (the phrase, *Allah Akbar* is known as the *takbir*). Traditionally, the sacrificer recites paragraphs 161–163 of Sura 6.

> My Lord has guided me into a straight path, a right religion, the faith-community of Abraham who was a *hanif,* a man of pure faith. He was no idolator. . . .
>   . . . My prayer, my rite of sacrifice, my living and my dying belong to God, the Lord of the worlds.
>   Of His Lordship there is no partnering. Even so I was commanded: I am the first among those surrendering to Him. (Cragg, pp. 215–216, adapted)

By reenacting Ibrahim's Sacrifice, the sacrificer feels he, like Ibrahim, has submitted himself to God's will, just as a Jew eats matzoh on Pesach to reenact the flight from Egypt.

When the blood has drained from the animal's body, it is

---

7. Judaism assigns animal slaughter to the *shochet,* but in the Muslim world, any adult may perform this ritual if he follows the known rules of animal slaughter. This applies to animals that are slaughtered for food or in religious ceremony.

ready to be skinned and cut up. However, the limbs should remain intact; the carcass should not be mutilated. If the sacrifice accompanies a vow, the sacrificer may eat none of the animal and gives it all away for pious purposes. If the sacrifice is a free will offering, the sacrificer may enjoy one-third of the animal and donate the rest to the needy.

The Akedah is not the only averted sacrifice story in the Islamic tradition. Another sacrifice story tells of the father of Muhammad who was about to be sacrificed as thanksgiving for the discovery of the well at Zamzam. The sacrifice was redeemed by a vicarious sacrifice of a hundred camels.

The significance of the Akedah in the Islamic tradition, therefore, appears to be fivefold: (1) to proclaim Islam's continuity with the faith of Ibrahim; (2) to portray Ibrahim as a man of perfect faith; (3) to celebrate Ishmael, and portray him as obedient to the commitment of his father and to the will of God; and (4) to celebrate the goodness of God, who by accepting Ibrahim's sacrifice, made him a model for all humanity; and (5) to establish animal sacrifice as an important ritual in Islamic religious life. The Feast of the Sacrifice is the major religious holiday in Islam.

23

THE AKEDAH IN MUSIC AND LITERATURE

A Sampling

The Akedah has been described as a literary masterpiece. Deceptively simple and spare in style, at first glance the story seems almost artless, but its stirring ambiguity makes it, as Erich Auerbach has argued, a literary gem. The Rorschach ink blot of the Bible—each generation sees in it its own predicaments, all the paradoxes and dilemmas of its time. Every generation reaffirms the timelessness of the problems of faith and of the tensions between generations. Hence the appeal of the Akedah to authors and artists of all eras who rewrite the story as it appears to them and to their generation.

In Hebrew, *shir* means either *poem* or *song*[1] In this tradition, the ancient piyyutim were both artistic and musical, as well as liturgical. So familiar was one Judaeo-German Akedah piyyut, that when its melody was adopted for other songs, the notation was made, *be-niggun Akedah*, or *be-niggun Jüdischer Stamm*—to be sung to the Akedah tune mentioned by the fifteenth century

---

1. The Hebrew language does not differentiate between poem and song. (*Shir Ha'shirim* could be translated as *Poem of Poems* or *Song of Songs*.) Proponents of European opera believed they had brought together literature and music—created a "fusion of the arts." What they had done was not exactly new.

talmudist Jacob Moellin, and A.Z. Idelsohn. They "suggested that it was identical with the liturgical *Akedot* of the old west—Ashkenazi tradition" (EJ. "Akeda"). The Akeda *niggum* seems to be unknown, however, to cantors of the present day.

MUSICAL EXPRESSIONS OF THE AKEDAH[2]

In European music, there are at least fifty works on the Akedah, mostly oratorios and often linked with the Crucifixion. The oratorios of many eminent eighteenth century musicians were based on a libretto which was written for the Viennese court by the Italian poet Metastasio (1698–1782). In 1827, Chopin's teacher, Joseph Elsner wrote an Akedah opera.

In 1897, Abraham Goldfaden, the father of Yiddish theater, wrote the hugely successful opera, *Akedas Izchok*, arranged by H. A. Russotto (see p. 14). Goldfaden's operas were, in the words of his biographer, "touching, stirring, lyric, comical" (Sandrow, p. 45), and *Akedas Izchok* was no exception. Audiences were diverted by "devilish capers and byplay between angels and devils" (Sandrow, p. 63). An obstreporously vulgar Lot shows he had adopted the lifestyle of Sodom by singing a merry tune in which he "confesses slyly that though he's too old to enjoy his daughter's wedding, wine helps to heat his blood and put him in the mood for love" (Sandrow, p. 64). All of this contrasts with the spiritual heights to which the Akedah story reaches.[3]

In 1938, while Hugo Adler was cantor in Mannheim, Ger-

---

2. A more comprehensive statement on music of the Akedah is contained in the Akedah entry of *Enclyclopedia Judaica*.

3. Here is a bit of the lyrics from *Akedas Izchok*. As Abraham readies to slaughter his son, Isaac sings out:

Oi! futer (2), vart nur ein minut (2)
Veh mir (3); biter vus vet yezt tun mein areme miter.
Vus vet von ihr veren
As sie vet derheren
Vus du is geshehn

many, he scheduled the debut of an Akedah composition using the Buber-Rosenzweig translation of the Bible and *Akedot piyyutim*. The concert was cancelled because of Kristallnacht.

In 1964, Igor Stravinsky's *Akedat Yizhak* was first performed in Jerusalem. It was described as a sacred ballad for baritone and chamber orchestra, set to a Hebrew text.

In 1972, Judith K. Eisenstein composed *The Sacrifice of Isaac: A Liturgical Drama*. She uses an old poem, "Et Sha-arey Ratzon," interspersed with several penitential poems to produce a musical drama in the tradition of the Jews of medieval Spain and southern France.

Reviewing the composition, Eric Werner found it "full of grace and elegance. . . . The tunes are simple, but they are by no means plain or artless. . . . Their arrangement is eminently practical for the small synagogue of today: no instruments are required" (p. 39). In her introduction, however, the

---

As sie vet mir nit sehn
Ihr kind vus sie hot geboirn zu nainzig yur.

[Oh! father (2), wait for just a minute (2)
Woe is me (3); how bitterly it will affect my poor mother.
What will happen to her
When she hears
What has happened;
When she can no longer see me,
The child she bore at ninety years?]

Abraham answers:

No, main kind dus voile
Mach dich fertig zu der oile
Sei baharzt un mach sich grey
Zug far Got dein leztes frum gebet
Gots vilen (2) is dabai.

[No, my good child,
Get yourself ready to bear this burden;
Be brave and be prepared,
Say to God your last and holy prayer,
For this is God's will. (2)]

composer suggests the use of violin, cello, soprano recorder, small percussion, and guitar.

THE AKEDAH IN THE OLDER LITERATURE OF THE WORLD

A story as spare and connotative as the Akedah invites endless retelling and elaboration. An anthology of Akedah stories of all times, could fill a set of books. (For an encyclopedic statement on the Akedah in literature, see *Encyclopedia Judaica*, vol. 2, cols. 484–485.) Here we will present a sampling of Akedah writings.

THE AKEDAH AS A RELIGIOUS DRAMA OF MEDIEVAL CHRISTENDOM

In medieval times, religious dramas based on the Akedah story appeared in France, Italy, and England. An outstanding English play of the fifteenth century is called the *Brome Abraham and Isaac*, so-called because it was discovered in the library of the Brome Manor. It is a one-act play written with great poetic skill, focusing on the traits of Abraham and Isaac: the father's God-fearing piety in cruel conflict with his love for his son, and Isaac's childish sweetness and trust of his father.[4]

---

4. Here is a sampling from the Brome *Abraham and Isaac*, the anonymous fourteenth century English mystery play that dramatizes the Akedah story with great poetic skill. This excerpt appears on page 18 of the anthology, *The Development of English Drama*, (New York: Appleton-Century-Crofts, 1950) edited by Gerald Eades Bentley.

> The Angell: I am an angell, thow mayist se blythe,
>   That fro heyn to the ys senth.
> Owr Lord thanke the an C sythe.
>   For kepyng of hys commanawment
>
> He knowyt thi wyll, and also thy harte,
>   That thou dredyst hym above all thing;
> And sum of thy hevynes for to departe
>   A fayr ram yinder I gan brynge;

AN UNCOMPLETED AKEDAH PLAY
OF THE SEVENTEENTH CENTURY

Moses ben Mordecai Zacuto[5] (1620–1697), poet, rabbi, scholar of secular subjects, and editor, embarked on writing a play on

> He standyth teyed, loo! a-mong the breres.
> Now, Abraham, amend thy mood,
> For Ysaac, thy yowng son that her ys,
> Thys day schall not sched hys blood.

> Goo, make thy sacryfece with yon rame.
> Now forwyll, blyssyd Abraham,
> For unto heuyn I goo now hom;
> The way ys full gayne.
> Take vp thy son soo free.

A rendering of the play into modern English was done by Joseph Quincy Adams, and published in *Chief Pre-Shakespearean Dramas; a Selection of Plays Illustrating the History of the English Drama from Its Origin Down to Shakespeare* (Boston: Houghton Mifflin Co., 1924). Here is Adam's rendering of the excerpt given above:

> Angel: I am an angel, thou mayest see blithe,
> That from heaven to thee is sent.
> Our Lord thanketh thee a hundred times
> For the keeping of His commandment.

> He knoweth thy will, and also thy heart,
> That thou dreadest Him above all things;
> And some of thy heaviness for to depart
> A fair ram yonder I did bring.

> He standeth tied, lo, among the briars.
> Now, Abraham amend thy mood,
> For Isaac, thy young son that here is,
> This day shall not shed his blood.

> Go make thy sacrifice with yon ram.
> Now farewell, blessed Abraham,
> For unto heaven I go now home,
> The way is full straight.
> Take up thy son so free.

5. Born in Amsterdam of a Portuguese Marrano family, Zacuto's interest in kabbalah took him to Poland. He later settled in Italy, where he moved from Verona to Venice, and was rabbi in Mantua

the life of Abraham, which would certainly have included his interpretation of the Akedah, but he died when his play was perhaps one-third finished. Titled *Yesod Olam*, the play followed all the classical rules of dramatic theory and was composed almost entirely in sonnets, combining biblical Hebrew with talmudic idioms. The play opens with young Abraham, the idol-smasher. Lengthy monologues convey a rationalistic, humanistic philosophy, according to *Encyclopedia Judaica*. However, the author did not live to include the Akedah narrative.

THE AKEDAH IN AMERICAN AND BRITISH LITERATURE

The Willis Akedah

The Knickerbocker Group was a New York literary movement of the early nineteenth century. Nathaniel Parker Willis (1806–1867), one of its members, wrote a lengthy Akedah poem, one of the rare references to the Akedah in American literature. Here is a 20-percent sampling of the 111-line poem:

The Sacrifice of Abraham

It was noon—
And Abraham on Moriah bow'd himself,
And buried up his face, and pray'd for strength.
He could not look upon his son and pray;
But, with his hand upon the clustering curls
Of the fair, kneeling boy, he pray'd that God
Would nerve him for that hour. . . .

. . . He rose up and laid
The wood upon the altar. All was done.
He stood a moment and a deep, quick flush
Pass'd o'er his countenance; and then he nerved
His spirit with a bitter strength, and spoke—

---

from 1673 until his death. In Italy he was the foremost kabbalist of his time.

"Isaac! my only son!" The boy look'd up,
"Where is the lamb, my father?"—Oh, the tones,
The sweet, the thrilling music of a loved child!—
How it doth agonize at such an hour!—
It was the last deep struggle. Abraham held
His loved, his beautiful, his only son,
And lifted up his arm, and called on God—
And lo! God's angel stay'd him—and he fell
Upon his face and wept.

Billy Budd, *Herman Melville's Isaac*

Another rarity in American literature is the Akedah imagery in
Billy Budd, a story that takes place on the high seas during the
Napoleonic wars on a British fighting ship. This ship is commanded by a captain who is nervous about the Great Mutiny of
1797 and determined that nothing like it should happen to
him. To teach his crew a lesson that mutinous whisperings will
not be tolerated, an innocent young seaman is falsely charged,
convicted, and executed for mutiny. Billy Budd is this "martyr
to martial discipline" (p. 100).

Raised in an English orphanage, Billy Budd was probably the
offspring of a servant girl and her aristocratic employer. So
young, so handsome, so innocent; he contrasts sharply with
the gruff, rough-looking, and older crew. The handsome sailor,
twenty-one-year-old "Baby Budd" as he was known, "looked
even younger than he really was. This was owing to a lingering
adolescent expression in the as yet smooth face, all but
feminine in purity of natural complexion" (p. 14). It seems
events had allowed Captain Vere to choose the choicest of his
flock, the perfect lamb, to sacrifice at the altar of military
discipline.

When circumstances cast a shadow over the handsome
young sailor, at the court martial Captain Vere eloquently
persuades that in the interest of order, they have to convict and
sentence Billy Budd to death. Approaching the condemned lad
to announce the court's verdict, the captain who "was old
enough to have been Billy's father" must have inadvertently
felt as Abraham had about "young Isaac on the brink of

resolutely offering him up in obedience to the exacting behest"
(page 92). Billy Budd utters not a word of protest against his
fate but presents himself to the hangman with the words, "God
bless Captain Vere" (p. 102).

Wilfred Owen, a Poet of Protest

World War I produced a number of poetic protests against the
ugly mindlessness of war. Perhaps the most affecting was
written by Wilfred Owen, an English poet. Most of his works
were published after he was killed in action in France, November 4, 1918. Owen rewrote the Akedah in the following words:

> *The Parable of the Old Man and the Young*
>
> So Abram rose, and clave the wood, and went,
> And took the fire with him, and a knife.
> And as they sojourned both of them together,
> Isaac the first-born spake and said, My Father,
> Behold the preparations, fire and iron,
> But where the lamb for this burnt-offering?
> Then Abram bound the youth with belts and straps,
> And builded parapets and trenches there,
> And stretched forth the knife to slay his son.
> When lo! an Angel called him out of heaven,
> Saying, Lay not thy hand upon the lad,
> Neither do anything to him, thy son.
> Behold! Caught in the thicket by its horns,
> A ram. Offer the Ram of Pride instead.
>
> But the old man would not so, but slew his son,
> And half the seed of Europe, one by one.

THE AKEDA IN CONTEMPORARY LITERATURE

An in-depth study of the Akedah in Modern Jewish Literature—English, Yiddish, and Hebrew—is the subject of a recent
article by Michael Brown. In many cases, Brown observes, the
authors use the Akedah to symbolize "not faith beautiful, but
faith misguided and destructive. . . . Abraham and Isaac no

longer serve as role models to be emulated, as they did in premodern sources, but as object lessons to be avoided. . . . To be sure, some works, such as Wiesel's *Ani-Maamim* and Zeitlin's (Shir Ha-Akedah,) have remained within a generally traditional framework of understanding" (1982a, p. 111).

Howard Schwartz has edited an anthology of Jewish stories and (with Anthony Rudolf) an anthology of Jewish poetry. Both include a number of pieces with an Akedah motif. *Gates to the New City*, his prose anthology, contains four stories that touch on the Akedah[6] and *Voices Within the Ark* contains three Akedah poems.[7] In a variety of ways, each retells and interprets some aspect of Genesis 22.

THE AKEDAH IN TWO LULLABIES OF THE HOLOCAUST

In a 1976 collection of *Yiddish Lullabies*, collected by Katz-Kopstein, appear two Holocaust lullabies which contain allusions to the Akedah. Here are excerpts from both.

A Heavenly Father Cradle Song
H. Leivick

Sleep, God protect you, lying 'neath the flames,
And beneath the flaming swords.
Today we are huddled together
On this scorched and burnt-out earth.

Lie with us in this concentration camp cell,
In this world delirious with conquest.
Sleep, Lord of mercy, Holy One, Almighty,
Your head not far from the hangman's boot.

---

6. The Akedah theme is contained in "The Near Murder," by Jakov Lind (p. 147), "The Dream of Isaac," by Howard Schwartz (p. 149), "Isaac," by Michael Strassfield (p. 150), and "The Tale of the Ram," (p. 152) by Tsvi Blanchard.

7. See "The Sacrifice," by Chana Bloch (p. 425), "Isaac," by Stanley Burnshaw (p. 433), and "Story of Isaac," by Leonard Cohen (p. 750).

For a moment you can sit up
And not be seen, and not be heard.
On this stone floor perhaps you'll scratch out
Two tablets of the Law, Commandments Ten.

Rest yourself upon my shoulder
I see your lips, I see your teeth.
Dream, dear God, in heaven above us.
Below: a hard and cold stone floor.

You, the kin of Abraham
Bearing the Akedah-wood,
Our ancient and our honored name
Shines on this yellow badge we wear.

Though lightning, sunlight,
Flames surround us,
We now are together, and now you can sleep,
God of mercy, Halleluya!

Sleep, God of mercy, Lord of the Universe,
As side-by-side we sit in this cage.
We're not alone. Look! Here is Pishke, here is Tevya,
And here watching over you is Bontshe Shveig.

Cradle-Song of a Mother on a Wandering Ship
Benjamin Katz

Sleep, my child, it's early morning.
The heavy night's already past.
In the fog, so deeply hidden
Flickers a shoreline far away.

Soon the land will show itself,
Framed by sand and foamy waves.
Now you're with Mother, in her sturdy arms,
And drifting toward your land of dreams.

Wildly rocking and rolling waves
Now toss the ship back and forth.

I hold you closely in my arms,
Enveloping you as you know I am.

. . . .

You, my child, you are a member
Of a holy congregation,
Tender branch of a wandering tree.
While, like Isaac to the Akedah,
The ship carries us across the sea.

Sleep, my child; it's early morning.
Soon the waves will quiet down.
In the fog so deeply hidden
Lurks our people's abiding power.

BERNARD MALAMUD'S 1982 NOVEL: *GOD'S GRACE*

Imagine a postapocalyptic fantasy in which the only human survivor, Calvin Cohn, struggles vainly to teach a group of apes to live in harmony by following an explicitly Jewish ethic. As his frantic struggle ends in failure, his adopted "son" captures him and leads him toward a mountain.

Cohn's wrists were bound by leather thongs; he carried a bundle of split wood against his chest . . . as he plodded up the stone mountain.

"Buz," said Cohn, "you are my beloved son, tell me where we are going. I think I know but would like you to say so."

"Where's this ram in the thicket?" asked Cohn with a bleat . . . "Am I to be the burnt offering?"

"Untie my hands and I won't move, I promise you. I shan't blemish the sacrifice. If that's what I am, that's what I am."

Buz pulled his father's head back by his long hair, exposing his neck, aiming at his throat with a stone knife. / Blood, to their astonishment, spurted forth an instant before the knife touched Cohn's flesh.

Malamud's dark fable ends by noting that in the valley
below, "George the gorilla, wearing a mud-stained yarmulke he
had one day found in the woods . . . began a long Kaddish
for Calvin Cohn" (pp. 221–223).

In *God's Grace*, Malamud does with the Akedah what the
contemporary artists of Israel have done with the story: distort
it (an animal sacrifices a human), reverse it ("son" sacrifices
father), dismember it (no angel, no ram, no God). Robert Alter
sees the book as "an impassioned plea for kindness and pity
for all living creatures in the face of man's enormous capacity
for murderous destruction" (p. 40). Alan Lelchuk describes it as
"a fable by turns charming and foolish, topical and far-fetched,
provocative and innocent" (p. 1).

The Akedah in Modern Israeli Literature[8]

Writing in Hebrew, an author can allude to the Akedah with a
single word: *na-ar*, or *yehidi* (lad or only one). The briefest
phrase from Genesis 22 is more than enough. The Akedah is
often used to deal with the conflict between generations:
pioneer fathers and their soldier sons. According to Lawrence
Wineman's doctoral dissertation "The Akedah-Motif in the
Modern Hebrew Story," stories often parallel more closely
the midrashim in which Isaac is actually sacrificed, than they
follow the Genesis 22 story in which death is averted.

Abramson observes in modern Hebrew literature, the
Akedah story is loaded with all the dissonances of the father-
son relationship: the hostilities, the conflicts of interest, and
the failure of fathers (and God?) to fulfill their number-one
role, the protection of their children (pp. 104–105). Ruth
Kartun-Blum observes that to a secular writer, the Akedah
becomes a metaphor for all sorts of interpersonal, social, and

---

8. This section is based on Wineman's 1977 UCLA doctoral dissertation, "The Akedah-Motif in the Modern Hebrew Story," and also on
Abramson's 1990 article, "The Reinterpretation of the Akedah in
Modern Hebrew Poetry." Abramson's article covers novels and plays
as well as poetry.

political forces, but the central religious motifs of the Akedah are lost—"the love of God and his sanctification and the covenant" (p. 294).

The Akedah in Poetry

In a 1988 article, Ruth Kartun-Blum made a comprehensive and analytical study of the Akedah in modern Hebrew poetry. Before looking at the work of contemporary Hebrew poets, it is worth looking at a poem written almost eighty years ago by Haim Nahman Bialik. This "greatest of modern Hebrew poets used the Akedah as a metaphor for the relationship of God and Israel after the collapse of traditional faith under the weight of modernity's challenges" (Brown, p. 102). In a poem entitled "Alone" (*Levadi*) the Divine Presence is symbolized as a crippled bird that smothers its nestling. Writes Michael Brown: "In Bialik's poem there is no rewarding sacrifice of faith. Rather, faith itself has become a sacrifice on behalf of a God capable now only of stifling man, no longer of working with him" (pp. 102–103).

According to Abramson, this is the "most frequently anthologized" of Akedah poems. It expresses the impotence of the father, and was written by Amir Gilboa.

Isaac

Early in the morning the sun strolled in the forest
Together with me and my father.
My right hand was in his left.
Like lightning a knife flared between the trees
And I was afraid of the terror of my eyes
Seeing blood on the leaves.
Father, father, come quickly and save Isaac
So no one will be missing from the midday meal.

It is I who am slain, my son.
My blood is already on the leaves.
And my father's voice was stifled

And his face pale.
I wanted to cry out, struggling not to believe,
Tearing at my eyes.
And I awoke.
My right hand was bloodless.[9]

Abramson points to the poem's dreamlike quality, the depersonalization, and the father's confession of impotence: "It is I who am slain, my son. / My blood is already on the leaves."

Abramson quotes other poems that similarly express "the views of Israelis from the time of the War of Independence to the present day, in their protest at being forced into the sacrificial role of an eternal Isaac" (p. 108). Abramson quotes Gid'on Telpaz as having written: "I am not willing to be an eternal Isaac climbing onto the altar without asking why, or understanding."

After the 1982 war in Lebanon, Yehuda Amichai wrote this cynical commentary on the Akedah:

The True Hero of the Akedah

The true hero of the *Akedah* was the ram.
Unaware of the collusion of the others.
It seemingly volunteered to die in Isaac's place.
I want to sing a tribute to its memory,
It's curly wool and its human eyes
And its horns, so quiet on the living head,
Which were made into trumpets after its slaughter
For them to sound their peals of war
And to blare their vulgar joy.

. . . .
The angel went home
Isaac went home.
Abraham and God had long since gone.

---

9. "Yitzhak," in *Shirah tze'irah* Hannah Yaoz ed. (Elked Publishers, 1969), 166. The last line, writes Abramson, is an allusion to Deuteronomy 32:36, "For the Lord shall judge his people and repent himself for his servants when he seeth that their power is gone."

But the true hero of the *Akedah*
Is the ram.[10]

Israeli Theater

References to the Akedah in the Israeli theater have already
been made in note 1 of the Introduction. Glenda Abramson's
survey of the Akedah in modern Hebrew literature refers to a
1940 play (*Ha-adamah hazot*) by Aharon Aschman, in which
the death of a son evokes feelings of guilt over real or imagined
responsibility. "What if I had done things differently?" A
pioneer father loses his son to malaria and cries: "Abraham our
father burnt the ram and I burnt my son, my only son. . . . I
dragged you to the Akedah against your will."

Israeli Novels and Short Stories

The Akedah is a recurrent motif for modern Israeli storytellers,
and it is applied both to the Jewish past and to contemporary
Jewish experience. Among authors who use this symbol in-
clude S. Y. Agnon, Aharon Appelfeld, Amos Oz, Aharon Meged,
Moshe Shamir, S. Yizhar, Pinhas Sadah, and Avraham B.
Yehoshua.

Seven Israeli novels will be briefly described, to indicate how
the Akedah theme is applied to contemporary life.

In One Noose (Bekolar ehad) by Hayyim Hazaz

This 1963 novel is based on an event which occurred in British
Palestine: two Jewish terrorists were sentenced to death. In the
novel, one is an Ashkenazi (Menaham) and the other a
Sephardi (Eliyahu). Should they plead for clemency? This
might save their lives, but it would also recognize the authority
they deny. Instead, they plot to smuggle explosives into the
prison, and blow it up—sacrificing themselves on the altar of
principle.

---

10. Yehuda Amichai, *She'at hahesed* (New York: Schocken Books,
1982), 21.

The novel is replete with mentions of the Akedah. One of the prisoners muses, "Perhaps a miracle will occur" to save them from death. He adds, "No, martyrdom is the miracle."

The Agony of a Restitution (Lefi Hatsa'ar Hasakhar) by S. Y. Agnon

In this 1947 novel, Agnon is believed to be dealing allegorically with the Holocaust as he unfolds the story of a medieval piyyutist. Whenever he would write a poem, he would set it aside and wait until a beggar arrived at his door. From the appearance and traits of the beggar, he would judge the worth of his poem. If the beggar wore his rags neatly and was clean and well-mannered, the poet would take it as a sign from God that the poem was worthy, and he would recite the poem in his synagogue. If the beggar was foul, rude, and dirty, he would tear up his poem and burn it.

Once the piyyutist wrote a poem on the Akedah that seemed particularly precious, "holy and awesome." Soon he was visited by a most disgusting beggar—diseased, rude, incapable of being comforted.[11] The poet takes this as a condemnation not only of his poetry but of art in general. What right does one have to create a thing of beauty out of human suffering? Not only does he reduce the poem to ashes; he gives up writing poetry altogether.

Many years later on Yom Kippur, the words of that poem come back to him, like the resurrection of the ashes of Isaac rising from the altar. The poet tries to write down the words of the resurrected poem, but the words do not cling to the paper: "After the Akedah is accepted above, there is no longer any need for it below."

Agnon's story baffles human reason, as if to say that human reason cannot really comprehend this world, that the Holocaust cannot be understood with such familiar terms as faith and justice. Is Agnon saying, Wineman asks, that man must reach for some higher level of mental experience?

---

11. Kurzweil conjectures that this beggar symbolizes the Holocaust.

Isaac's Emendations (Tikkunei Yizhak) by Hanoch Bartov

This short story tells the plight of Reb Ishtele (Isaac) who has lived in Israel since the days of the pioneers but has never been accepted as a pioneer because he has lived "on the fringes of the literary-musical world." Living in an attic apartment (the mountain top?), he is shunned and mocked by his generation of "working pioneers." An outsider in his adopted land, he moves to Germany where he studies the Bible. In Sachsenhausen, site of a concentration camp, Reb Ishtele has an exploratory operation (the sacrifice?) and dies of cancer.

In Michael Brown's judgment, "the connection with the biblical story is formal and superficial, there being no sense that any of Bartov's characters are aware of the moral and theological concerns of the Bible. . . . Bartov does not take the biblical myth seriously" (p. 102).

Early in the summer (Be-tihilat kayitz) by A. B. Yehoshua

In this 1970 novella, author Yehoshua retraces the theme of the medieval midrash that Isaac was killed and resurrected.

> It tells of a father, significantly a Bible teacher, who hears that his son has been killed in the war and goes off to find the body. Through an absurd series of events, he discovers that the son is not dead at all, so in effect the son dies and lives again. In the story, the father experiences the death three times, on each occasion suffering Abraham's grief and guilt. The imagery of the Akedah in this novella, including repeated references to the only son, morning, a tangled thicket, knife, wood and fire, is specific. (Abramson, p. 113)

Observes Michael Brown: "In contemporary Israeli writing the Akedah often appears as an ugly metaphor for the unfeeling, self-aggrandizing sacrifice of children by their actual or communal fathers on the altars of purblind commitment to Zionism and to Israel's wars" (p. 100). Writes Abramson: "Immediately following the war of Independence, the image

settled on Isaac as the young *sabra* sacrificing himself on the
national altar, with the connivance of his father, Abraham" (p.
107).

The plains of the Negev (Ba-arot hanegev) by Yigal Mossinson

In Yigal Mossinson's popular 1949 novel, *Ba-arot hanegev*, "a
father, called Abraham, allows his son to sacrifice his life in an
act of military heroism."

The Days of Ziklag (Yeme ziklag) by S. Yizhar

In this 1958 novel, a character protests:

> Who created such a rotten world! We can't live without giving
> life or taking life. . . . I hate Abraham our forefather who goes
> off to sacrifice Isaac. What is his right over Isaac? Let him bind
> himself. I hate God who sent him to be bound, closed every
> avenue other than sacrifice. I hate the fact that Isaac is no more
> than the material for experimentation between Abraham and
> God. . . . Why must the sons die?

The Living on the Dead (Ha-Hay al ha-met) by Aharon Meged

Young Jonas, a thwarted writer, is dominated by two Abraham
figures: his father, who is no longer living, and Abrasha, a
fellow pioneer who is also a philanderer and wife-beater. Both
of them are "remembered for their heroic deeds in service of
the state-in-the-making." Abrasha "sacrifices his own son by
forcing the boy into the army, although he is so nearsighted
that death is inevitable" (Brown, p. 101). Writes Michael Brown
of Meged's novels: "[His] themes are the relationships of
fathers and sons, of past and present, of the weight of tradition
and the freedom to be one's self. Except in passing, however,
these questions are taken up in an entirely secular framework,

which reflects the biblical myth of Abraham and Isaac only dimly" (p. 101).

Observes Abramson, "Many Israeli critics claim that [the Akedah] has become a national symbol representing the tragedy of Israel in general and the sons in particular" (pp. 113–114).

24

THE AKEDAH IN ART

The Akedah is a popular theme in Jewish, Christian, and Moslem art.[1] A comprehensive survey of Akedah art, suitably illustrated, would require a set of volumes, not a single chapter. This chapter will suggest the scope of the subject, and discuss a few specific artworks in detail.

EARLY CHRISTIAN AKEDAH ART

Edwin Goodenough argues that early Christian art evolved out of both pagan art and Jewish art. For example, child sacrifice was a popular theme in the pagan art of the ancient Greeks and Romans, which gave early Christian artists plenty of examples after which to adapt illustrations of the Akedah. Hans-Jürgen Geischer shows twenty examples of human sacrifices in pagan art. His article also examines four early

---

1. A list of Akedah paintings and etchings in museum collections is given in Appendix 4.

Christian Akedahs that show a similarity to their pagan coun-
terparts.

There are well over a thousand representations of the
Akedah in early Christian art: monuments and icons of all
kinds (frescoes, sarcophagi, mosaics, glasses, gems, lamps,
amulets, and pyxes—sacramental wafer boxes). Princeton
University houses an index of biblical and New Testament art
up to the fifteenth century called the *Index of Christian Art,*
and it reportedly includes 1,430 depictions of the Akedah.[2] A
1922 article by Alison Moore Smith lists and locates 123 objects
illustrating the Akedah. A 1961 article by Isabel Speyart van
Woerden lists and locates 371 early Christian and medieval
Akedah icons.

Why so many early Christian Akedahs and virtually no
Crucifixions? To the early Christians, the Akedah symbolized
the Crucifixion as other Old Testament stories symbolized the
life of Jesus. For example, Jonah emerging from a fish's mouth
symbolized the Resurrection. The fact is early Christian art
typically illustrate stories from the Hebrew Bible.

Ernest Goodenough was impressed by this fact when he first
began to study early Christian art in the 1920s. He conjectured
that the early Christians were modelling their art after the
Jewish art of ancient synagogues, and perhaps from Jewish
illustrations in Septuagint manuscripts existing at that time.
What ancient synagogues?

No ancient synagogues were known to exist at the time
Goodenough first made his conjecture, but the archaeological
find of a third-century synagogue in Dura-Europos around
1930 (see below) confirmed Goodenough's hunch exactly! In
1955, his hunch was further confirmed by the discovery of the
Via Latina catacomb in Rome, an early Christian burial place
decorated with dozens of scenes from the Hebrew Bible
including two Akedah scenes, one of which is reproduced on
page 139. Not a single cross, not a single Crucifixion scene is to
be found there! That was to come later. Meanwhile, early

---

2. A duplicate of the *Index of Christian Art* is housed in the Art
Research Library of the University of California at Los Angeles.

Christian artists were content to copy designs they had probably seen in Roman synagogues, says Goodenough, "syna-
gogues now lost without a trace" (1962, p. 139).

THE AKEDAH MURAL AT DURA-EUROPOS

Perhaps the oldest Jewish portrayal of the Akedah was found in
a third-century synagogue at Dura-Europos, a Roman garrison
in ancient Babylon. The interior walls were richly covered with
murals illustrating stories of the Bible. When the synagogue at
Dura-Europos was excavated by a French and American archaeological team from 1928–32, the find was even more
spectacular, writes Goodenough, than the more recent discovery of the Dead Sea Scrolls. It was no surprise to scholars that
the Jews of ancient times were scribes and wrote different
variations of biblical themes. However, it was a major surprise
to discover an ancient synagogue whose interior walls were
richly covered with actual illustrations of Bible stories (1968, p.
179).

This ancient synagogue, built in a Roman outpost, was
preserved by an unusual historical circumstance. While the
murals at Dura-Europos were still new (about five years old),
the town was threatened by a Persian invasion. The defenders
of Dura, in a vain attempt to save their city, built a huge mound
of earth over their city wall, burying all of the buildings close to
it, including this newly-constructed synagogue. For almost two
thousand years, the synagogue walls remained as protected
from the elements[3] as Pompeii, until it was discovered quite
accidentally by a World War I British patrol. The excavation
took place about ten years after the war, and the findings are
documented in a 1956 Yale University publication by F. E.
Brown et al.

The interior walls of the Dura synagogue, as shown in the
Yale publication and in *Encyclopedia Judaica*, are lavishly

---

3. For example, when the synagogue was first uncovered, one
mural panel showed a sky of light blue. Within a few years, exposure
to the air faded it to white.

covered with murals of biblical stories, animals, plant life, as well as pagan figures. The Akedah is depicted at the front and center of the synagogue, above the Torah niche. This location, by itself, indicates the importance attached to the Akedah story.

Scholars, who have examined the synagogue directly, noted the panel above the Torah niche (see p. 138) was painted with different colors and a different kind of brush than the other mural panels. The panel above the Torah niche is rather crudely drawn, compared with the more sophisticated artistry of the other panels. Perhaps the Akedah artist was selected for qualities or qualifications other than artistic talent. The mural panels on all the walls are no doubt the work of several artists, since some are Persian in style and others Greek.

The panel directly above the Torah niche is divided into three sections of about equal size. At the center of the panel stands a representation of the Temple of Jerusalem, which is similar in design to the symbol on Jewish coins of the Second Revolt, issued in Palestine in the reign of Hadrian (F. E. Brown, p. 60). A picture of the Temple of Jerusalem probably says, in effect, "Although we dwell in Babylon, our hearts are in Jerusalem." The dominant, central location of this item indicates the importance attached to this theme. Undoubtedly, the symbols at either side of the Temple drawing also represent important themes in Jewish worship.

At the left side of the panel is depicted the great Menorah, symbol of Jewish antiquity and survival. Its origins go back to the portable sanctuary in the wilderness. (According to Numbers Rabbah 15:4, God made a menorah for Moses). When this menorah rendering is compared with the menorah that appears on another panel of the same wall, it is obvious that the panel above the Torah niche was rather crudely rendered.[4]

---

4. The Yale report (F. E. Brown et al.), by the team that examined the synagogue directly, admits that the space in which the Akedah is depicted is ill-adapted to a depiction of the Akedah, and that the figure of Isaac is crudely drawn (p. 56).

Tucked under the menorah are pictured a *lulav* and an *etrog,* which Leviticus Rabbah 30:2 associates with the forgiveness of sins. *Lulav* and *etrog* also symbolize male and female sexuality and thus represent fertility and love.

At the right of the Temple drawing, compressed into a limited and irregular vertical space, is the Akedah scene—the oldest known Jewish Akedah drawing. Into this restricted space are compressed five objects. Three figures are: (1) Abraham, brandishing a large knife; (2) Isaac, lying on a massive, high altar; and (3) a mysterious figure standing, back to viewer, at the doorway of a cone-shaped shelter (a building? a tent?). The remaining two objects in the composition are a ram, and the hand of God.

Who is the mysterious figure at the doorway of the cone-shaped tent? One conjecture is that this is the figure of Sarah, but Swetnam notes the figure is wearing a garment which, elsewhere on these murals, is worn only by males (p. 74). Perhaps it shows Isaac after the Akedah, at the school of Shem where, according to midrashim, he studied Torah. (At Dura-Europos, as elsewhere, it is customary for the artist to depict different scenes on the same panel.

Another puzzle: Why are all three figures facing away from the viewer? Other figures in the Dura-Europos have well-drawn faces, but perhaps the Akedah panel was drawn by an artist whose talents were so limited, he avoided drawing faces.

Why is the Akedah compressed into so small a space? Apparently, the artist was told to put three symbols just above the Torah niche, and he naïvely reserved equal spaces for each of the three symbols: the Menorah, the Temple, and the Akedah. The Akedah is therefore compressed into a smaller space than many of the Bible stories pictured elsewhere on the synagogue walls. That is less important, probably, than the fact that the Akedah is placed at the front and center of the synagogue, at the Torah niche, as one of three or four major symbols of Jewish worship. The Akedah deserved this special place adjoining the Torah niche at Dura-Europos. It was also the only biblical story on the floor at Bet-Alpha (discussed below), because it symbolized such a recurrent theme in the prayer service of the synagogue.

THE AKEDAH MOSAIC AT BET-ALPHA

In 1929 two Hebrew University archaeologists, Eliezer Sukenik and Nahman Avigad, discovered the remains of a sixth-century synagogue at Bet-Alpha, in the eastern Jezreel Valley at the foot of Mount Gilboa.

Nothing remained except the foundation, which was constructed of stones and cement and surfaced with a decorative floor of mosaic tiles. An Akedah illustration was the only Bible story represented in the mosaic floor (See p. 137), which was built tough enough to survive all the traffic of many generations and durable enough to survive the synagogue itself.

The synagogue floor has a simple geometric border; at the center is an area about nineteen by thirty-seven feet, decorated with three pictorial panels. First, nearest the bima is a composition of Jewish symbols—the Ark of the Synagogue, a menorah, *lulavim, etrogim,* a shofar, and incense burners. Second, in the center of the floor is a large zodiac wheel with a graphic symbol and the Hebrew name of each sign of the zodiac. Third, near the entrance is an illustration of the Akedah: Abraham pointing a knife at Isaac, who is bound near an altar. Behind Abraham a ram is tied to a tree. Abraham's two servants stand behind him, and the hand of God (or an angel?) is seen between the sun's rays above.

The Akedah design, like the others, is very clearly in naïve, folk art style, with simple and strong lines so typical of children's art work. Figures are shown in front view, with no concern for rules of perspective or realistic draftsmanship. Next to each figure, the Hebrew name is inscribed and there is a rendering of the Hebrew phrase "And behold a ram." The mosaicists signed their names in Greek: Marianos and his son Hanina.

The Bet-Alpha synagogue mosaic again attests to the popularity of the Akedah story in that ancient Palestinian community, for it is the only biblical story illustrated on the mosaic floor.

The remains of the Dura-Europos and Bet-Alpha syna-gogues also say something about the Jews of the Hellenistic world. History books tell us how much the Hellenists admired Greek culture, studied Greek literature, and participated in Greek sports. Here we see that the Hellenists also built syna-gogues! They were the Reform Jews of the ancient world.

A FIFTEENTH-CENTURY HAGGADAH ILLUMINATION: ISAAC DESCENDING FROM HEAVEN

This fifteenth-century illuminated Haggadah, known as the Second Nürnberg Haggadah, is now housed at the Schocken Institute for Jewish Research in Jerusalem. Its vellum pages are beautifully hand-lettered and richly illustrated with color drawings. On one page, the upper right-hand column shows Isaac descending from heaven head first (see p. 146). Below the floating figure is inscribed, in Hebrew, a sentence which may be translated, "Isaac returned glorified from the Garden of Eden, which God planted for our protection."

Here is a graphic indication of the popularity of the resur-rection midrash of the Akedah. In the fifteenth century, just before the invention of printing, the illuminated Haggadah was a family treasure, instructive as well as decorative in its function. Its illustrations "may have served as a means of holding the interest of the children through the long Passover eve ceremony." (*Encyclopedia Judaica,* Haggadah) Perhaps this is the first time this fifteenth-century illustration has appeared in print.

MUSLIM AKEDAH ART

A 1943 article by Meyer Schapiro is devoted to Moslem art on the Akedah. A unique feature of Moslem Akedah art is an angel is shown carrying the ram. Persian miniatures of the Akedah appear in "Abraham" and "Akedah" entries of *Encyclopedia Judaica.*

THE SACRIFICE OF ISAAC, A 16TH CENTURY TAPESTRY

At Hampton Court Palace in Surrey, England, seven tapestries on the History of Abraham are displayed. These tapestries were designed by the Flemish artist Bernard van Orley (1485–1542) and woven about 1540 by the famous Brussels weaver Wilhelm Pannemaker.[5]

One tapestry illustrates three scenes of the Akedah story. In the foreground, Abraham and Isaac walk up the mountain, while the two servants rest on a foothill. In the middle ground, Isaac sits on the altar, Abraham bares his knife, and an angel makes its nick-of-time appearance. In the background, father and son kneel at the altar where the sacrificed sheep is being immolated.

REMBRANDT VAN RIJN, CREATOR OF FIVE AKEDAHS

About fifteen of Rembrandt's works have been labelled portraits of rabbis (Landsberger, p. 59). Though there were probably never that many rabbis in Amsterdam during Rembrandt's time, it seems that Rembrandt had many Jewish friends and clients. He was a close friend of Rabbi Manasseh ben Israel, writes his biographer, and not only made a portrait and etching of the rabbi, but also produced a set of illustrations for one of the rabbi's books (Landsberger, p. 35). For whatever reasons, the rabbi chose not to use Rembrandt's illustrations, but Rembrandt was close enough to Rabbi Manasseh to be given the job in the first place. It is conjectured that Rembrandt also knew Baruch Spinoza and had studied Hebrew. It was fashionable in Rembrandt's time for educated Hollanders to read a bit of Hebrew.

Rembrandt lived in a district of Amsterdam that could be called a Jewish neighborhood not because it housed poor immigrants; it was a prosperous neighborhood near the great

---

5. The full set numbers ten tapestries. Seven now hang in the Great Hall, including the *Sacrifice of Isaac*. One hangs in the Second Presence Chamber, and two hang in the Chapel Royal, St. James's.

Portuguese Synagogue. Because it was within easy walking distance to that synagogue, it was a favored residential location for Amsterdam's well-established Jews. Whether Rembrandt was attracted to a Jewish neighborhood or settled there as other artists did, more or less by chance, the fact is that for many years, Rembrandt lived in an atmosphere of Jewish friendships and Jewish ideas. It seems altogether possible one by-product of this environment is that Rembrandt produced five Akedahs—two paintings, two etchings and a pen sketch (see pps. 142, 143).

In 1635, Rembrandt produced his first Akedah: a huge oil on canvas (76 x 52 ¼-inches) entitled *The Sacrifice of Isaac,* which now hangs in the Hermitage, Petersburg. This baroque zig-zag composition portrays a wildly-determined Abraham being physically prevented from carrying out his task. Abraham's left hand still grasps Isaac's face, while the angel grasps Abraham's right wrist and the knife falls from Abraham's fingers. This painting tells the Akedah story and also expresses the vigor and youth of its thirty-year-old artist.

Of special interest is that from Abraham's hand drops a small, rounded knife, rather than the menacing dagger, sword or large pointed knife Abraham very often brandishes in prints and paintings. If Rembrandt had sought the counsel of Rabbi Menasseh or another learned Jewish friend about this detail of his Akedah, it is quite possible his Jewish informant would have suggested something more like a *hallaf,* a ritual slaughtering knife, that most Akedah artwork shows.

One year later, one of Rembrandt's students produced a copy of the artist's *Sacrifice,* taking some liberties with the composition. Rembrandt completed this copy, which in its finished form differs from his 1635 painting in two interesting details. First, a ram appears in the background. Second, the angel approaches Abraham from a direction which heightens the element of surprise. This 1636 version now hangs in Munich at the Alte Pinakothek.

Nine years later, in 1645, Rembrandt produced a small etching of Abraham and Isaac, portraying them pausing on their journey, or perhaps they have already arrived at the mountain top. Abraham seems to be explaining what is about to happen; he holds his right hand over his heart, and with his other hand, he points to heaven. The boy Isaac stands expressionless, as if he doesn't quite understand. The Akedah narrative does not depict such a scene, but Rembrandt apparently felt Abraham must have made such a gesture.

About ten years later, around 1655, Rembrandt produced a quick impressionistic pen drawing of the crisis moment. (It is rarely reproduced, perhaps because it is so unfinished.) Isaac lies on the altar, baring his throat, while Abraham hovers over him as if ready to execute his horrible task. His knees are bent, as if trembling. The angel hovers over Abraham, touching his head.

Around the same time in 1655, Rembrandt produced a beautifully finished *Sacrifice of Isaac* etching, altogether different in mood from the wildly-determined Abraham portrayed in the two paintings he had completed about twenty years earlier. Now a more mature Rembrandt portrays a loving closeness between a distraught Abraham and a submissive Isaac, and also between Abraham and the angel. With one hand, Abraham holds the knife, with the other hand he presses Isaac's head against his chest as if to bare Isaac's throat, and at the same time to press the boy's head against his father's heart. The angel does not hover above Abraham, but shelters him, almost embraces him. Both the angel's hands grip Abraham's arms. By their physical closeness, the figures seem to express their love for each other; Abraham's love for Isaac, and the angel's love for Abraham.[6] Comparing the artist's painting done at age thirty, with the etching he completed twenty years later, Elie Wiesel commented, "Rembrandt's painting reflects the Christian idea of Abraham's Sacrifice; his etching is in the spirit of the Binding of Isaac; it shows a Jewish attitude" (1995 Lecture).

A notable detail of this etching is that Abraham holds the knife in his left hand. Why? When an etching is scratched into a copper plate, the drawing is a mirror image of what the paper

---

6. In a 1989 *Bible Review* article, Jack Riemer compares Rembrandt's earlier painting with his 1655 etching in a review of Jo Milgrom's Akedah book.

impressions will eventually show. The artist usually keeps this in mind, although if he loses himself in the creative process, the result may be a print where a word appears in reverse position, or where a left hand does the work of the right hand. Did Rembrandt lose himself when he produced this sublime interpretation of the Akedah?[7]

CHAGALL'S AKEDAH WINDOW AT ST. STEPHAN IN MAINZ

In 1973, Marc Chagall began the grand enterprise of designing a set of stained glass windows as part of the restoration of the thirteenth century St. Stephan's church in Mainz, Germany. In the four-section Akedah windows (shown on page 148), as in the others, a luminous royal blue fills the background, and the figures, boldly outlined and detailed in black, sparkle with white and color. The total effect combines the luminosity of traditional church windows with the Marc Chagall touch of simply-sketched, floating figures.

Two details make this Chagall rendering of the Akedah unusual. First, two angels, not one, hover above Abraham, who stands at the altar, holding a knife. At the upper right is the angel who brings the message not to touch the lad. Upper left is an angel carrying a ram. Here, a Jewish artist, designing an Akedah for a Christian church, has inserted a distinctly Islamic touch.

Schapiro's 1943 article focused on this distinctive feature in Moslem depictions of the Akedah: an angel carrying the ram. Probably Chagall saw this detail in a Persian miniature, or other Moslem depiction of the Akedah. Did Chagall incorporate this Islamic detail for artistic purposes (portraying a ram carried by a floating angel is so much more like Chagall than a ram caught in a thicket!), or as a gesture of interfaith good will?

The second detail making this Chagall Akedah remarkable is

---

7. In my description of the Akedah artwork of Rembrandt, I have drawn upon the comments of Gerhard von Rad's 1971 book. It should be noted that Rad thanks Dr. Christine Peter of Heidelberg, for critical background on Rembrandt.

the anguished Sarah, depicted in the background, opposite the figures of Abraham and Isaac. As noted at the beginning of this chapter, there are over one thousand known depictions of the Akedah; this is perhaps the only one which incorporates the figure of Isaac's mother.

The Akedah in Israeli Art—the Ramat-Gan Exhibit

In November 1987 the Museum of Israeli Art in Ramat-Gan, Israel, launched an exhibit of 253 items (paintings, drawings, prints, sculptures) of the Akedah, curated by Gideon Ofrat. The exhibit covered the widest spectrum of interpretations—from traditionalist, naïve, representational art to violent and twisted variants of the Akedah theme.

An example of a twisted Akedah theme: artworks where ram and angel are missing to symbolize that in the Akedah of our time, there is no substitute for the slaughter Isaac. Another example is there is no angel to stay Abraham's hand in some pieces. As if the absence of ram and angel is not enough to portray the savagery of our times, in the etching of Uri Lifshitz, Abraham is a beast, driving a sword through *ha na'ar.* In the crayon drawing of Menashe Kadishman there is no Abraham, and no angel; only a prostrate Isaac. Over Isaac hovers a ram, and next to him sits a wolf. Clearly, the exhibit expresses the nation's agony over the sacrifice of its youth, which has been the cost of the military power of the state of Israel. Wordlessly, the artists also seem to express horror and protest against the nation's military burden and its military excesses.

APPENDIX 1

GOD TESTS ABRAHAM, A MIDRASH

The conjecture advanced in chapter 16, "The Disaster Interpretation," is expressed here in the form of a midrash. As a matter of record, I wrote it in 1993, two years before I first learned about the Greek myth of Athamas and Prixus (see chapter 16, footnote 1).
—Louis A. Berman

Abraham and Sarah attended the wedding feast of the youngest daughter of Arak, one of the wealthiest herdsmen in his village. His host had already drunk far too many toasts and was speaking more freely than was his nature. Then, Abraham saw Arak's mood change from joy to dumb anxiety. "Arak, what can I do to relieve your sadness?" asked Abraham.

"Would that this tormenting thought did not prey upon my mind," answered Arak. "But tonight's celebration means that in a year or so my youngest daughter will be heavy with child. It grieves me to think how many of our wives and daughters have died at childbirth over the past year. What can it mean, that God shows His displeasure to the village by taking away so many of our wives and daughters at childbirth? What have we done to stir His wrath?

"Do we not obey all of our Lord's wishes? Indeed, do we not also pay homage to our Lord in ways our ancestors paid homage to the gods of ancient times? What else can we do, to put an end to this agony and punishment? Did I not offer up my firstborn son? Did not every man in this village offer up his firstborn to show our devotion to the God of Heavens and our willingness to give up what was indeed most precious to us?"

Arak's drunkenness had betrayed him, for he had confronted Abraham with the painful fact that of all the men of the village Abraham alone had not sacrificed his firstborn. "Forgive me for what I have just said, Abraham," begged Arak. "I have drunk too much wine. Everyone understands that Sarah was already an older woman when Isaac was born and his birth therefore was nothing less than a miracle. You could not have been expected to offer him up as young fathers did when their young wives gave birth to their firstborn. Forgive me, Abraham. Please forget what I said. Come, let us go sit by the music and singing, and watch the dancing and acrobatics."

For many days, Arak's unintended words preyed on Abraham's mind. It was true. Of all the villagers, only Abraham had not offered up his firstborn son, following the practice of their ancestors. It was also true that for a year now, nearly half the young mothers of their village were not surviving the ordeal of childbirth, leaving behind bereaved young widowers and half-orphans and grieving friends and kinsmen.

Could it be that God was displeased with Abraham's conduct? Could it be that God was angry that Abraham had never carried out the ancestral way of paying the highest homage to God? Isaac is dear to me, thought Abraham, but so is every son dear to his father; so is every wife dear to her young husband; and so is every mother dear to their children. Could my neighbors be blaming me for the untimely death of their young wives, sisters, and daughters? Could God be doubting my faith? O that the Lord of Heavens would lift this burden from my mind!

Did God not promise me that from my seed would come a great and holy nation? If not through Isaac, through whom? Having another son is unthinkable for someone of my years or of Sarah's age. Are my neighbors blaming me for their unnatural and untimely bereavements? Does God want me to put Isaac to the fire?

For many days, Sarah could see that Abraham was suffering from some private agony. She asked him whether he was ready to unburden himself but he only sighed and buried his head in his hands.

One evening, it seemed to Abraham that his agony was about to be resolved. It seemed to him that God was asking him to take Isaac to the land of Moriah, to offer him there as a burnt offering upon one of the mountains. Early next morning, Abraham rose, saddled his ass and took two of his young servants with him. Together with Isaac, they gathered and cut wood for a burnt offering, packed provisions for a week's journey and travelled toward Moriah.

On the third day of travel, they reached the mountain. Abraham asked his servants to wait at the foot of the mountain with the ass, while he and Isaac climbed up the mountain. Isaac bore the wood and Abraham carried the fire pot. As father and son climbed the mountain, Isaac asked: "I am carrying the wood and you are carrying the fire but where is the lamb for a burnt offering?" Abraham answered: "God will provide a lamb." They continued climbing up the mountain.

When they reached the top of the mountain, Abraham built an altar and laid out the wood upon it. Silently he proceeded to bind Isaac's legs and wrists and laid him on the altar. Then Abraham unsheathed his knife and called out, "Lord of Heavens, tell me what to do next." Then Abraham heard a voice, as if a messenger of God were imploring him: "Lay not your hand upon the lad, neither do anything to him. I know that you fear God, for you have not withheld your son, your only son, from me."

Abraham lifted up his eyes and saw behind him a ram caught in the thicket by his horns. Abraham took the ram, bound its legs and made of it a burnt offering at the altar. Together, Abraham and Isaac wept, embraced each other, praised God and returned to the foot of the mountain. With the two servants, and with their ass, they began their journey home.

As they made the silent journey together, Abraham spoke to God. "How will my neighbors know that I was ready to offer my son and you asked me not to touch him? How will my neighbors know I did not lose faith and selfishly refuse to give my son to the Lord?" God seemed to answer, "Arak's daughter will bear a healthy son and both will survive the ordeal of childbirth. The childbirth sickness will vanish from the village. You will tell your neighbors that through you, God sends the message that he wants no more human sacrifices. Ours is a God to whom every human life is precious."

APPENDIX 2

THE SEVEN BROTHERS

This is an English translation by Solomon Zeitlin (pp. 159–169) of the story of the seven brothers, as it appeared in Second Book of Maccabees. *It is the original document, in translation, from which stemmed the Jewish midrashim of Hanna (or Miriam) and her seven sons. Zeitlin's translation preserves the tone and texture of the Greek original.*

It happened also that seven brothers, with their mother, were arrested and tortured with whips and scorpions by the king to compel them to partake of swine meat forbidden by the Law. One of them made himself their spokesman, and said: "What do you intend to ask and to learn from us? It is certain that we are ready to die rather than transgress the laws of our fathers."

The king in his rage ordered that pans and caldrons be heated red hot. They were heated at once, and he ordered that the tongue of the spokesman should be cut out, that they should scalp him in the Scythian manner and cut off his extremities, while the rest of his brothers and his mother were looking on. When he had been reduced to a completely useless hulk, he ordered them to bring him, while he was still breathing, to the fire, and to fry him in the pan. As the vapor from the pan grew more dense, the children with their mother encouraged each other to die nobly, saying:

"The Lord God is watching, and in very truth will have compassion on us, just as Moses declared in his Song, which bears testimony against them to their very face, saying: 'And He will have compassion upon His servants.'"

When the first one had died in this way, they brought the second to be mocked. Then they tore off his scalp with the hair and asked him:

"Will you eat, or else have your body dismembered limb from limb?"

He replied in the mother tongue, and said: "Never."

For this reason he too underwent the same order of tortures. But with his last breath, he said:

"You accursed wretch, you may release us from our present existence, but the King of the Universe will raise us up to everlasting life because we have died for His laws."

After him the third one was brought to be mocked. When he was ordered to put out his tongue, he did so quickly. He courageously stretched out his hands, then nobly said:

"From heaven have I had these, yet because of God's laws I count them for nothing, for from Him I hope to have them back again."

The result of this was that the king himself and his men were struck with admiration by the spirit of the young man because he minimized his sufferings.

When he too had died, they mutilated and tortured the fourth one in the same manner. As he was dying, he said,

"Better it is for people to be done to death by men if they have the hopeful expectation that they will again be raised up by God, but as for you, there will be no resurrection to life."

Next they brought the fifth and treated him shamefully. As he looked at the king he said:

"Because you, a finite mortal, have authority among men, you may work your will; but do not think that God has abandoned our people. You will see how His overwhelming power will torment you and your offspring."

After him they brought on the sixth. As he was about to die, he said,

"Do not vainly deceive yourself. We suffer these things because of ourselves, because we sinned against our own God. That is why these astounding things have come upon us. But do not think that you will go free in thus daring to wage war against God."

Their mother was truly wonderful, and is worthy of blessed

memory. Though she saw her seven sons die in the space of a single day, she bore it bravely because of her faith in the Lord. She encouraged each one of them in their mother tongue, filled as she was with a noble spirit. She stirred up her womanly nature with manlike courage, and said to them,

"How you ever appeared in my womb, I do not know. It was not I who graced you with breath and life, nor was it I who arranged in order within each of you the combination of elements. It was the Creator of the World, who formed the generation of man and devised the origin of all things, and He will give life back to you in mercy, even as you now take no thought for yourselves on account of His laws."

Antiochus then thought that he was being treated contemptuously, and suspected the reproachful tone of her voice. As the youngest son was still alive he appealed to him not only by words but also by oaths that he would make him both rich and enviable if he would leave the ways of his fathers; that he would consider him as a friend, and would put him in an office of trust. When the young man paid no attention to him at all the king summoned the mother and urged her to advise the lad to save himself. After he had exhorted her for quite a while, she undertook to persuade her son. She leaned over to him, and jeering at the king, she spoke in the mother tongue as follows:

"My son, have pity on me, who carried you in my womb for nine months. For three years I nursed you, brought you to this stage of your life and sustained you. I beg of you, my child, to look up to heaven and earth and see all that is therein, and know that God did not make them out of things that were already in existence. In the same manner the human race came into being. Do not be afraid of this executioner, but show yourself worthy of your brothers. Accept death, that in God's mercy I may receive you back again along with your brothers."

While she was still speaking, the young man said, "What are you waiting for? I will obey the command of the Law that was given to our fathers through Moses. But you, who have shown yourself to be the contriver of every evil against the Hebrews, shall not escape the hands of God. We are really suffering for our own sins. Although our living God, in order to punish and discipline us, is angry at us for a little while, He will again be reconciled with His servants. You profane wretch, vilest of all men, be not vainly buoyed up by your insolent, uncertain hopes, raising your hand against His servants. You have not escaped the judgment of the Almighty, all-seeing God. Indeed, our brothers, after enduring brief trouble, are under God's covenant for everlasting life; while you under God's judgment will receive just punishment for your arrogance. I, like my brothers, surrender body and soul for our paternal laws, invoking God speedily to be merciful to our nation, and to make you acknowledge through affliction and torment that He alone is God, while it has devolved upon me and my brothers to stay the wrath of the Almighty which has justly been brought against the whole of our nation."

With this the king became furious, and dealt with him worse than with the others, bitterly resenting his sarcasm. He then died in purity, believing implicitly in God. Finally, after her sons, the mother also died.

Let this then be enough about eating of idolatrous sacrifices and inhuman tortures.

Appendix 3

Field Notes of
an Akedah Image Hunter

When travel takes me to museums, print shops, flea markets, antique shops, and art shops, I look for images of the Akedah and sometimes find them in the most surprising ways. In the city of Venice, better known for its outdoor beauty than for its museums, occurred my two most surprising encounters with paintings of Akedah.

The Scuola Grande of San Rocco is not exactly a museum, nor is it a church. The building does not have a typical Venetian facade, for it does not face a canal. When you enter this gloomy classical building, you find the grand and spacious interior of a clubhouse of the Renaissance elite. Its walls and ceilings are covered by paintings by Jacopo Tintoretto, expressing all of the color and high energy that is so typical of his work. On one of the enormously high ceilings, there is a painting of the Akedah, oval in shape. Using the perspective of a ceiling painting, Tintoretto gives the viewer the impression that the event is indeed happening on a mountaintop.

In the dim entrance of a Venice synagogue, I made the unexpected encounter with a large and beautiful Akedah painting. The entrance hall was too narrow for me to photograph the painting, except at an angle. I was told the painting was a gift to the synagogue from one of the city's churches.

I had seen many reproductions of the Rembrandt's 1665 etching of the Akedah, and I was eager to see an original print which hangs at the Rembrandt House in Amsterdam. Full-size copperplate etching (not halftone!) reproductions were on sale at the entrance. I bought one and ran upstairs to compare it with the original print. I was amazed at how closely the two prints matched. (The print I purchased is rubber-stamped on the back "Reproduction," to make sure it never gets on the market as a counterfeit.)

In Munich's Alte Pinakothek I saw what is perhaps the most famous Akedah painting: Rembrandt's second version of *The Sacrifice of Isaac*. Most travellers stop at the important museums in cities they visit. I, of course, always check a museum for its Akedahs. Appendix 4 lists paintings and prints in museum collections that I know of. Use this list to add interest to your museum going. If you can add to the list, let me hear from you (c/o Jason Aronson).

When I was in Los Angeles, I inspected the *Index of Christian Art*, a copy of the Princeton University index, located in the Art Research Library of the University of California at Los Angeles. After browsing through a rather "user-unfriendly" filing system, I wandered around the library and noticed a file drawer labelled, "Index of Jewish Art." It was ten minutes before closing time, so I riffled rapidly through the illustrated cards. In a few minutes, I found a print of the fifteenth century Nürnberg Haggadah page illustrating "Isaac descending from heaven head first." I had never seen such an illustration and asked the librarian for a photocopy of it. At first, she replied sternly, "We're closing," but then she relented and obliged me. The illustration, (reproduced in the pages of a book for the first time?) appears on page 140.

In an Arab stall in Jaffa's old flea market, I saw a small brass plaque of the Akedah and, after the customary haggling, purchased it. I admired the composition and congratulated the unknown craftsman for his artistic talent. Some time later, when I became acquainted with Julius Schnorr von Carolsfeld's beautiful wood engravings of the Bible, I could see where the brass-plaque craftsman had gotten his inspiration.

Speaking of "the customary haggling" reminds me of the time I found an original Persian watercolor of the Akedah in a Jerusalem antique shop. I asked the crucial question: "How much?" "Seventy-five dollars." "Wow! That's a lot of money." "It's a good price." "It's a good price for you." "It's a good price for you too," the dealer assured me, so I bought it.

The Akedah has for centuries been depicted on tiles. Among those in my collection is a new one, purchased for just a few dollars in the famous ceramic shop in the Armenian quarter of the Old City of Jerusalem. For about twenty-five dollars you may find a nineteenth century Minton tile (see p. 144) of the Akedah on London's Portobello Road, as I did a few years ago. If you're after something closer to a museum piece, visit Spiegelgasse, the street of beautiful antique shops near the Rijksmuseum, in Amsterdam. There, you will find a shop that stocks nothing but antique tiles, thousands of them—tiles of landscapes, flowers, people, animals, fruits, and, of course, Bible scenes. You may find an Akedah, as I did, that was once one of a series of Bible story tiles which adorned a seventeenth or eighteenth century fireplace somewhere in Holland (see p. 141). Such items are scarce and priced at about $100, depending upon beauty, age, and condition.

Steel or copper engravings of the Akedah from large nineteenth century Bibles are sometimes available for fifteen to fifty dollars. The biggest bargains in Akedah art, I believe, are to be found in new and old children's Bible story books, found wherever old books are sold and available for a few dollars or less. In older books, you may find a beautiful, multicolor stone lithograph. In newer books, you may find a woodcut or pen-and-ink illustration by a gifted book illustrator (see pp. 146, 147).

The Akedah has also appeared on such ephemera as postcards, postal stamps (see p. 144), and greeting cards. Postcards of the Akedah include two main sorts: reproductions of museum paintings, and illustrations distributed through Christian Sunday Schools. I have around twenty-five such cards, purchased at museums and from dealers in old postcards for fifty cents to five dollars. Yugoslavia and Israel have pictured the Akedah on postage stamps. The Akedah was an appropriate illustration on *Shana Tova* cards, since there are references to this   narrative in the High Holiday liturgy. One *Shana Tova* artist took his inspiration directly from del Sarto. My collection includes a modern card decorated with an Akedah illustration and headed "Mazel Tov on your Bar Mitzvah."

Perhaps my most unexpected encounter with an Akedah image happened a few years ago when I was having a reunion in Manhattan with a boyhood friend, Kenneth E. Schwartz. We grew up together in Detroit, Michigan. Kenneth handed me a batch of color photos which were lying on his desk and said, "Here are some pictures I took in Africa last year while I was on safari." Obligingly, I flipped through them: a giraffe nibbling the leaves on a tree, a lion sleeping, a lion walking . . . I couldn't believe it when I saw the close-up of a truck door with the Akedah pictured on it (showing, no doubt, the Sacrifice of Ishmael)! I asked, "Where did you see this?" My old friend Kenneth answered, "Somewhere in Africa. It looked unusual, so I took a picture of it (see p. 145)."

My interest in Akedah art stems partly from the fact that I was an art student many years ago and have always been interested in the visual arts. There is a bias against the visual arts in the Jewish culture, which hinges on how the Second Commandment is interpreted. Somewhere I read a statement by kinetic artist Yaacov Agam, claiming that abstract art was the only legitimate Jewish art because the Bible forbids naturalistic art!

Jewish artists have tried to escape from the more severe interpretations of this Commandment by such tactics as drawing human figures with animal heads, or making drawings out of lines of calligraphy, called micrography. Those who accepted a less restrictive interpretation of the Second Commandment have argued the actual intent of this Commandment was to outlaw the making of idols; graven images made for "bowing down to them or serving them" (Deuteronomy 4:19). The mosaics at Bet-Alpha and the frescoes at Dura-Europos are evidence there is a rich tradition of Jewish religious art. A scholarly article entitled "Demythologizing Ancient Judaic Iconoclasm" was written by my friend David Topper, Professor of the History of Art and Science at the University of Winnepeg, and was published in the Spring of 1991 issue of *Mad River: A Journal of Essays*, published by Wright State University.

APPENDIX 4

AKEDAH PAINTINGS AND PRINTS IN MUSEUM COLLECTIONS

Artist	Shown on page	Location of original
Allori, Allesandro	*	Uffizi Gallery, Florence
Allori, Cristofano	*	Pitti Gallery, Florence
Caravaggio	*	Uffizi Gallery, Florence
Carracci	*	The Louvre, Paris
Chagall, painting	148	National Museum, Nice
———, stained glass window	148	St. Stephan's Church, Mainz
Cranach	*	Fürstliche Lichtensteinische Gemäldegalerie, Vienna
Guardi	*	Cleveland Museum of Art
Mantegna	*	Kunsthistorisches Museum, Vienna
Metsu	*	Israel Museum, Jerusalem
Piazzetta	*	National Gallery, London
Reitern	*	Russian Museum of Alexandria III, Moscow
Rembrandt, etchings	143	Rembrandt House, Amsterdam Rijksmuseum, Amsterdam
	142	Staatliche Kunstsammlungen, Dresden

BIBLIOGRAPHY

"Abraham." *Encyclopedia Judaica*. Jerusalem: Keter, 1972.

Abramson, Glenda. "The Reinterpretation of the Akedah in Modern Hebrew Poetry." *Journal of Jewish Studies* 41 (1990): 101–14.

Adar, Zvi. *The Book of Genesis: An Introduction to the Biblical World*. Jerusalem: Magnes Press, 1990.

Adler, Morris. *The Voice Still Speaks*. New York: Bloch, 1969.

Agus, Aharon (Ronald E.). *The Binding of Isaac and Messiah: Law, Martyrdom and Deliverance in Early Rabbinic Religiosity*. Albany, N.Y.: State University of New York Press, 1988.

"Akedah." *Encyclopedia Judaica*. Jerusalem: Keter, 1972.

Allen, Woody. "The Sacrifice of Isaac." In *The Big Book of Jewish Humor*, edited by William Novak and Moshe Waldoks, p. 220. New York: Harper and Row, 1981.

Alter, Robert. *The Art of Biblical Narrative*. New York: Basic Books, 1981.

———. "God's Grace by Bernard Malamud." *The New Republic* 187 (Sept. 20/27, 1982): 38–40.

———. *The World of Biblical Literature*. New York: Basic Books, 1992.

Arieti, Silvano. *Abraham and the Contemporary Mind.* New York: Basic Books, 1981.

Bakan, David. *The Duality of Human Existence: An Essay on Psychology and Religion.* Chicago: Rand McNally, 1966.

Bamberger, Bernard J. "Fear and Love in the Old Testament." *Hebrew Union College Annual* 6 (1929): 39–53.

Barr, Wayne E. *A Comparison and Contrast of the Canaanite World View and the Old Testament World View.* Doctoral thesis, University of Chicago Divinity School, 1963.

Baumgardt, David. "Man's Morals and God's Will: The Meaning of Abraham's Sacrifice." In *Arguments and Doctrines,* edited by Arthur A. Cohen, 287–99. Philadelphia: Jewish Publication Society, 1970.

Bergmann, Martin S. *In the Shadow of Moloch: The Sacrifice of Children and Its Impact on Western Religions.* New York: Columbia University Press, 1992.

Berkovits, Eliezer. *Crisis and Faith.* New York: Sanhedrin Press, 1976.

Bernstein, Ignaz. *Jüdische Sprichwörter und Redensarten.* Warsaw, 1908.

Bin-Gorion, Micha. *Sinai und Garizim.* Berlin, Morgenland, 1926.

Birnbaum, Philip. *A Book of Jewish Concepts.* New York: Hebrew Publishing, 1964.

Bodoff, Lippman. "The Real Test of the Akedah." *Judaism* 42 (1993): 71–92.

Bowie, Walter. "Testing of Abraham (22:1–19)" in *The Interpreter's Bible,* edited by George A. Buttrick vol. 1, 642–646. New York: Abington Press, 1952.

Brand C., Jr., "The Story of Isaac." *Expository Times* (Edinburgh) 95 (1983): 20–21.

Brown, F. E., A. Perkins, and C. B. Welles. *The Excavations at Dura-Europos . . . Final Report VIII, Part I.* New Haven: Yale University Press, 1956.

Brown, Michael. "Biblical Myth and Contemporary Experience: The Akedah in Modern Jewish literature." *Judaism* 31 (1982a) 99–111.

———. "A Knight of Faith or Man of Doubt? A Contemporary Reading of the Akedah." *Conservative Judaism* 35 (1982b) 17–23.

Bruggemann, Walter. *Genesis: A Bible Commentary for Teaching and Preaching.* Atlanta: John Knox Press, 1982.

Buber, Martin. *On the Bible.* Edited by Nahum N. Glatzer. New York: Shocken, 1968.

———. "Le Sacrifice d'Isaac." *Dieu Vivant* 22 (1952): 69–76.

Buttrick, George A. "The Study of the Bible." In *The Interpreter's Bible,* edited by George A. Buttrick, 165–71. New York: Abington Press, 1952.

Cantor, Norman F. *The Sacred Chain: The History of the Jews.* New York: HarperCollins, 1994.

Coats, George W. "Abraham's Sacrifice of Faith: A form-critical Study of Genesis 22." *Interpretation* 27 (1973): 389–400.

Cragg, Kenneth, trans. *Readings in the Qur'an.* London: Collins Religious Publishing, 1988.

Davidson, Robert. *Genesis 12–50.* Cambridge: Cambridge University Press, 1979.

Delaney, Carol. "The Legacy of Abraham." In *Beyond Androcentrism: New Essays on Women and Religion,* edited by Rita Gross, 217–36. Missoula, Montana: Scholars Press, 1977.

Delaney, John. *Dictionary of Saints.* Garden City: Doubleday, 1980.

Dennis, Trevor. *Sarah Laughed: Women's Voices in the Old Testament.* Nashville: Abingdon Press, 1994.

Dreessen, Wulf-Otto. *Akedass Jizhak.* Hamburg: Leibniz-Verlag, 1971.

Driver, Samuel R. *Modern Research as Illustrating the Bible: The Schweich Lectures of 1908.* London: H. Frowde 1909.

———. *The Book of Genesis,* 8th rev. ed. London: Methuen & Co., 1911.

Eisenstein, Judith K. *The Sacrifice of Isaac: A Liturgical Drama.* New York: Reconstructionist Press, 1972.

Eissfeldt, Otto. *The Old Testament: An Introduction.* rev. ed. Translated by P. R. Ackroyd. New York: Harper and Row, 1965.

Fackenheim, Emil L. *What is Judaism? An Interpretation for the Present Age.* New York: Summit Books, 1987(a).

———. *The Jewish Thought of Emil Fackenheim: A Reader.* Edited by Michael L. Morgan. Detroit: Wayne State University Press, 1987(b).

Fitzmyer, Joseph A. *The Genesis Apochryphon of Qumran Cave I*. Rome: Biblical Institute Press, 1986.

Francisco, Clyde T. "Genesis." In *The Broadman Bible Commentary*, Clifton J. Allen, ed. 101–288. Nashville: Broadman Press, 1969.

Freud, Sigmund. "The Interpretation of Dreams." In *The Basic Writings of Sigmund Freud*, 181–549. New York: Modern Library, 1938.

Fromm, Erich. *You Shall Be As Gods: A Radical Interpretation of the Old Testament and Its Tradition*. New York: Holt, Rinehart and Winston, 1966.

Garber, Zev, and Bruce Zuckerman. "Why Do We Call the Holocaust 'the Holocaust'? an Inquiry Into the Psychology of Labels." In *Remembering the Future*, by Yehuda Bauer et al., 1879–92. New York: Pergamen Press, 1989.

Geischer, Hans-Jürgen. "Heidnische Parallelen zum Frühchristlichen Bild des Isaak-Opfers." *Jahrbuch für Antike und Christentum* 10 (1967): 127–44.

Gellman, Jerome I. *The Fear, the Trembling, and the Fire: Kierkegaard and the Hasidic Masters on the Binding of Isaac*. Lanham, Maryland: University Press of America, 1994.

Gellman, Marc. "Abraham and Isaac," *Moment*. vol. no. 1, 10 (1976): 39–41.

Ginzberg, Louis. *The Legends of the Jews*. 7 vols. Translated by Henrietta Szold. Philadelphia: Jewish Publication Society, 1912.

Goodenough, Erwin R. *Jewish Symbols in the Greco-Roman Period*, abr. ed. Princeton: Princeton University Press, 1968.

Gordis, Robert. *Judaic Ethics for a Lawless World*. New York: Jewish Theological Seminary, 1986.

Gottwald, Norman K. *A Light to the Nations: An Introduction to the Old Testament*. New York: Harper and Row, 1959.

———. *The Hebrew Bible—A Socio-Literary Introduction*. Philadelphia: Fortress Press, 1985.

Graves, Robert, and Raphael Patai. *Hebrew Myths: The Book of Genesis*. New York: McGraw-Hill, 1963.

Gray, George Buchanan. *Sacrifice in the Old Testament: Its Theory and Practice*. 1925. Reprint. New York: Ktav, 1971.

Gumbiner, Joseph H. "Existentialism and Father Abraham," vol. 5, no. 2 *Commentary*, (1948), pp. 143–148.

Gunkel, Hermann. *Schöpfung und Chaos in Urzeit und Endzeit.* 1895.

Hadas, Moses, ed. and trans. *The Third and Fourth Books of Maccabees.* New York: Harper, 1953.

Harkavy, Alexander, trans. *The Twenty-Four Books of the Holy Scriptures According to the Masoretic Text.* New York: Hebrew Publishing, 1916.

Hartman. *See* Maimonides.

Hartsoe, Colleen Ivey. *Dear Daughter: Letters from Eve and Other Women of the Bible.* Wilton, Conn.: Morehouse-Barlow, 1981.

Hayward, C. T. R., "The Sacrifice of Isaac and Jewish Polemic Against Christianity." *Catholic Biblical Quarterly* 52 (1990): 292–306.

Hertz, J. H., ed. *The Pentateuch and Haftorahs*, 2d ed. London: Soncino Press, 1965.

Hill, Dorothy B. *Abraham: His Heritage and Ours.* Boston: Beacon Press, 1957.

The Interpreter's Bible, vol. 1. New York: Abington-Cokesbury Press, 1952.

Jacob, Benno. *Das Erste Buch der Torah, Genesis.* Berlin: Schocken Verl., 1934.

Kaplan, Kalman J. "Isaac and Oedipus: A Re-examination of the Father-Son Relationship." *Judaism* 39 1 (1990): 73–81.

Kartun-Blum, Ruth. "The Binding of Isaac in Modern Hebrew Poetry." *Prooftexts* vol. 8 no. 3 (1988): 293–310.

"Kiddush Ha-Shem." *Encyclopedia Judaica.* Jerusalem: Keter, 1972.

Kierkegaard, Søren. *Fear and Trembling and The Sickness Unto Death.* Garden City: Doubleday, 1954.

Kilian, Rudolf. *Isaaks Opferung.* Stuttgarter Bibel-Studien #44. Verlag Katholisches Bibelwerk Stuttgart, 1970.

Kravitz, Leonard and Kerry M. Olitzky. *Pirke Avot: A Modern Commentary on Jewish Ethics.* New York: UAHC Press, 1993.

Koestler, Arthur. "Mahatma Gandhi: The Yogi and the Commissar," *New York Times Magazine*, Oct. 5, 1969.

Kurzweil, Baruch. *Massot al sipurei S. Y. Agnon*. Jerusalem: Shocken, 1966.

Lang, Berel, ed. *Writing and the Holocaust*. New York: Holmes and Meier, 1988.

La Barre, Weston. *The Human Animal*. Chicago: University of Chicago Press, 1955.

Landsberg, Max. "Akedah." In *The Jewish Encyclopedia*. New York: Funk and Wagnalls, 1901.

Landsberger, Franz. *Rembrandt, the Jews and the Bible*. Philadelphia: Jewish Publication Society, 1946.

Lelchuk, Alan. "God's Grace." *New York Times Book Review*, Aug. 14, 1982.

Lerner, Michael. "The Binding of Isaac." *Tikkun* 7:7 (Sept/Oct 1992): 7–8.

Liebowitz, Nehama. *Studies in Bereshit (Genesis)*. 3d rev. ed. Lewiston, N.Y.: Edwin Mellen Press, 1989.

Licht, Jacob. *Storytelling in the Bible*. Jerusalem: Magnes Press, 1978.

Lind, Jakov. "The Near Murder." In *Gates to the New City: A Treasury of Modern Jewish Tales*, edited by Howard Schwartz, 147–8. Northvale, N.J.: Jason Aronson Inc., 1991.

Maccoby, Hyam. *The Sacred Executioner: Human Sacrifice and the Legacy of Guilt*. New York: Thames and Hudson, 1982.

Magonet, Jonathan. "Abraham and God." *Judaism* vol. 33 no. 2 (Spring 1984): 160–170.

Maimonides, Moses. *Crisis and Leadership: Epistles of Maimonides*. Translated by Abraham Halkin. Discussions by David Hartman. Philadelphia: Jewish Publication Society, 1985.

Malamud, Bernard. *God's Grace*. New York: Farrar Straus Giroux, 1982.

Marmorstein, Arthur. *The Doctrine of Merits in Old Rabbinical Literature*. 1920. Reprint. New York: Ktav, 1968.

Matthews, Victor H. and Don C. Benjamin. *Old Testament Parallels: Laws and Stories from the Ancient Near East*. New York: Paulist Press, 1991.

Maybaum, Ignaz. *The Sacrifice of Isaac*. London: Valentine, Mitchell, 1959.

Melville, Herman. *Billy Budd and Other Prose Pieces.* New York: Russell and Russell, 1963.

Milch, Robert J. "An Encounter with the 'Akedah.' " *Judaism* vol. 22 no. 4 (1973): 397–99.

Milgrom, Jo. *Akedah, a Primary Symbol in Jewish Thought and Art.* Berkeley, California: Bibal Press, 1988.

———. *Handmade Midrash.* Philadelphia: Jewish Publication Society, 1992.

Miller, Alan W., Riskin, Shlomo, and Zimmerman, Sheldon. *Community Study: The Binding of Isaac.* Edited transcript of a forum held Sept. 16, 1981, New York, 1981.

Mintz, Alan. *Hurban: Responses to Catastrophe in Hebrew Literature.* New York: Columbia University Press, 1984.

Moberly, R. W. L. "The Earliest Commentary on the Akedah." *Vetus Testamentum,* vol. 38 no. 3 (1988): 302–323.

Moskowitz, Moshe. "Toward a Rehumanization of the Akedah and Other Sacrifices." *Judaism* 37 (Summer 1988): 288–94.

Neusner, Jacob. "Take Your Son, Your Favored One, Isaac." In *The Bible and Us,* by Andrew Greeley and Jacob Neusner, 103–15. New York: Warner Books, 1990.

Ofrat, Gideon. *Akedat Yizhak B'amanut Ha-Yisroalit* (The Akedah in the Art of Israel). Israel: Ramat-Gan, n.d.

Ostriker, Alicia Suskin. *Feminist Revision and the Bible.* Oxford: Blackwell, 1993.

Owen, Wilfred. *The Collected Poems of Wilfred Owen.* New York: New Directions, 1963.

Peale, Norman Vincent. *Bible Stories told by Norman Vincent Peale.* Carmel, New York: Guideposts Associates, n.d.

Plaut, W. Gunther, ed. *The Torah: A Modern Commentary.* New York: Union of American Hebrew Congregations, 1981.

Polish, David. "Akedat Yitzhak—The Binding of Isaac." *Judaism* vol. 6 no. 1 (1957): 17–21.

———. *Abraham's Gamble: Selected Sermons for Our Times.* Evanston: 1988.

Pritchard, James B. ed. *Ancient Near Eastern Texts Relating to the Old Testament.* Princeton: Princeton University Press, 1950.

Rad, Gerhard von. *Das Opfer des Abraham.* Munich: Chr. Kaiser Verlag, 1971.

———. *Genesis, a Commentary.* London: SCM Press, 1961. (Trans. *Das Erste Buch Mose,* 1956.)

"Rashi" (Solomon ben Isaac) *on the Pentateuch Genesis.* Translated by James H. Lowe. London: Hebrew Compendium, 1928.

Reik, Theodor. *Ritual; Psycho-analytic Studies.* New York: Farrar, Straus, 1946.

———. *The Temptation.* New York: George Braziller, 1961.

Reimer, Jack. "The Binding of Isaac: Rembrandt's Contrasting Portraits." *Bible Review* 5 (December 1989): 26–27.

Rendsburg, G. A. *The Redaction of Genesis.* Winona Lake, Ind.: Eisenbrauns, 1986.

Reuther, Rosemary. *Faith and Fratricide: The Theological Roots of Anti-Semitism.* New York: Seabury, 1974.

Reventlow, Henning Graf. "Opfere Deinen Sohn—Eine Auslegung von Genesis 22." *Biblische Studien* 53. Neukirchen, 1968.

Rubenstein, Richard L. *After Auschwitz: History, Theology, and Contemporary Judaism.* 2nd ed. Baltimore: Johns Hopkins Press, 1992.

———. *The Religious Imagination: A Study in Psychoanalysis and Jewish Theology.* Indianapolis: Bobbs-Merrill, 1968.

Sandrow, Nahama. *Vagabond Stars.* New York: Harper and Row, 1977.

Sarna, Nahum M. *Understanding Genesis.* New York: Jewish Theological Seminary and McGraw-Hill, 1966.

Schapiro, Meyer. "The Angel with the Ram in Abraham's Sacrifice: A Parallel in Western and Islamic Art." *Ars Islamica* 10 (1943): 134–47.

Schulweis, Harold M. *In God's Mirror.* Hoboken: Ktav Publishing House, 1990.

Schwartz, Howard and Anthony Rudolf, eds. *Voices Within the Ark: The Modern Jewish Poets.* New York: Avon, 1980.

Segal, A. *Other Judaisms of Late Antiquity.* Atlanta: Scholars, 1987.

Skinner, John. *Critical and Exegetical Commentary on Genesis.* New York: C. Scribner's Sons, 1910.

Smith, Alison Moore. "The Iconography of the Sacrifice of Isaac in Early Christian Art." *American Journal of Archaeology, Second Series* 26 2 (1922): 159–73.

Soncino Bible. *See* Hertz.

Speiser, E. A., trans. *Genesis, Anchor Bible.* Garden City: Doubleday, 1964.

Steinsaltz, Adin. *In the Beginning: Discourses on Chasidic Thought.* Northvale, N.J.: Jason Aronson, 1992.

Stemberger, Günter. "Die Patriarchenbilder der Katakombe in der Via Latina im Lichte der Jüdischen Tradition." *Kairos* N.S. 16 (1974): 19–78.

Stern, Chaim, ed. *Gates of Repentance; The New Union Prayerbook for the Days of Awe.* New York: Central Converence of American Rabbis, 1978.

Swetnam, J. *Jesus and Isaac: A Study of the Epistle to the Hebrews in the Light of the Akedah.* Rome: Pontifical Biblical Institute, 1981.

Syme, M. Robert. "When Parents Play Favorites." Unpublished sermon delivered at Temple Israel, West Bloomfield, Michigan, Nov. 12, 1993.

Topper, David. "Demythologizing Ancient Judaic Iconoclasm." *Mad River: A Journal of Essays* 2, (Spring, 1991).

Vaux, Roland de. *Ancient Israel, Its Life and Institutions.* New York: McGraw-Hill, 1961.

van Woerden, Isabel Speyart. "The Iconography of the Sacrifice of Isaac." *Vigiliae Christianae* 84 (1961): 214–55.

Vauter, Bruce. *On Genesis: A New Reading.* Garden City: Doubleday, 1977.

Visotzky, Burton L. *Reading the Book: Making the Bible a Timeless Text.* New York: Doubleday, 1991.

Wellisch, Erich. *Isaac and Oedipus: A Study in Biblical Psychology of the Sacrifice of Isaac.* London: Routledge & Kegan Paul, 1954.

Werner, Eric. "Review of Judith Eisenstein's *Sacrifice of Isaac.*" *Reconstructionist* 38 (May 19, 1972): 39.

Westerman, Claus. *Genesis 12–36: A Commentary* Translated by John J. Scullion, S.J. Minneapolis: Augsburg Publishing House, 1985.

———. *Genesis, a Practical Commentary.* Grand Rapids: William B. Eerdmans, 1987. Translated from the Dutch, 1986.

Wiesel, Elie. "The Sacrifice of Isaac: A Survivor's Story." In the author's *Messengers of God: Biblical Portraits and Legends,* pp. 69–97. New York: Random House, 1976.

————. "The Akedah Revisited." Lecture given at Moriah Congregation, Deerfield, Ill., Sunday, April 2, 1995.

Wineman, Lawrence. *The Akedah-Motif in the Modern Hebrew Story*. Dissertation, UCLA, 1977.

Woolley, Sir Leonard. *Abraham: Recent Discoveries and Hebrew Origins*. London: Faber and Faber, 1936.

Zeitlin, Solomon, ed. *The Second Book of Maccabees*. New York: Harper, 1954.

Zeitlin, Irving M. *Ancient Judaism*, Cambridge, England: Polity Press, 1984.

Zeligs, Dorothy F. *Psychoanalysis and the Bible*. New York: Bloch, 1974.

————. "A Psychoanalytic Note of the Function of the Bible," *American Imago* 14 (1957): 57–60.

Zuckerman, Bruce. *Job the Silent: A Study in Historical Counterpoint*. New York: Oxford University Press, 1991.

Picture Sources and Credits

Bet-Alpha: *Beth ha-knesseth ha-atik Be-beth Alfa*, by Eleazar Lipa Sukenik. Jerusalem, 1932. Dura-Europos: *Encyclopedia Judaica*. Via Latina Catacomb: *Early Christian Art*, by André Grabar, Odessey Press, 1968, p. 229. Queen Ingeborg Psalter: "The Iconography of the Sacrifice of Isaac," by Isabel Speyart van Woerden. *Vigiliae Christianae*, 1961, p. 224. *Second Nürnberg Haggadah*: Reproduced with permission of the Schocken Institute for Jewish Research of the Jewish Theological Seminary of America. *Akedes Yitskhok* libretto: Yivo Institute. "Sacrifice of Isaac" by Rembrandt, oil painting, Alte Pinakothek, Munich, Germany. "Abraham Speaking to Isaac," etching, Staatliche Graphisce Sammlung, Munich. Rembrandt's pen-and-ink sketch of "Abraham's Sacrifice," Kupferstich-Kabinett der Staatlichen Kunstsammlungen Dresden, Germany. Rembrandt's etching of "Abraham's Sacrifice," Rembrandt House, Amsterdam, Holland. Embroidered Akedah panel: Jewish Museum, New York/Art Resource. Akedah by Abel Pann: Ithiel Pann, Jerusalem, Israel. W. Fletcher White illustration reprinted with permission of The Putnam and Grosset Group, New York. Chagall "Sacrifice of Isaac" stained glass window and painting © 1997 Artists Rights Society (ARS), New York/ADAGP, Paris. Pen-and-ink renderings of Dura-Europos panel, Via Latina fresco, and Queen Ingeborg Psalter, by Jerry Warshaw. Digitalized mezzotints by Matthias Minde.

Index